GOOD WORDS

LITERATURE, RELIGION, AND
POSTSECULAR STUDIES
Lori Branch, Series Editor

GOOD WORDS

Evangelicalism and the Victorian Novel

MARK KNIGHT

THE OHIO STATE UNIVERSITY PRESS
COLUMBUS

Copyright © 2019 by The Ohio State University.
All rights reserved.

Library of Congress Cataloging-in-Publication Data
Names: Knight, Mark, 1972– author.
Title: Good words : evangelicalism and the Victorian novel / Mark Knight.
Other titles: Literature, religion, and postsecular studies.
Description: Columbus : The Ohio State University Press, [2019] | Series: Literature, religion, and postsecular studies | Includes bibliographical references and index.
Identifiers: LCCN 2018050373 | ISBN 9780814213933 (cloth ; alk. paper) | ISBN 0814213936 (cloth ; alk. paper)
Subjects: LCSH: Evangelicalism in literature. | Religion in literature. | English fiction—19th century—History and criticism.
Classification: LCC PR830.E85 K58 2019 | DDC 823/.8 09382—dc23
LC record available at https://lccn.loc.gov/2018050373

Cover design by Laurence J. Nozik
Text design by Juliet Williams
Type set in Adobe Minion Pro

♾ The paper used in this publication meets the minimum requirements of the American National Standard for Information Sciences—Permanence of Paper for Printed Library Materials. ANSI Z39.48-1992.

CONTENTS

Acknowledgments vii

INTRODUCTION Rethinking Our Stories of the Victorian Novel 1

CHAPTER 1 The Pilgrim's Progression to *Vanity Fair* 25

CHAPTER 2 Dickens's Tale of Conversion 53

CHAPTER 3 Good Words and the Great Commission 77

CHAPTER 4 Hermeneutics, Evangelical Common Sense, and *The Moonstone* 105

CHAPTER 5 Samuel Butler's *The Way of All Flesh* and Our Stories of Evangelicalism 137

Bibliography 167
Index 181

ACKNOWLEDGMENTS

I started this book when I worked at Roehampton University, continued it at the University of Toronto, and finished it when I took up my current post at Lancaster University. All three institutions offered considerable support, and I appreciate that they did so. I was fortunate, too, to be awarded a Marjorie G. Wynne Fellowship in 2010–11 by the Beinecke Rare Book and Manuscript Library at Yale. The staff there were amazing, and I thoroughly enjoyed and benefited from the month I spent with them.

It is difficult to convey how grateful I am to everyone who has helped bring this book to completion. I am particularly thankful to those who read parts or all of the manuscript: Lori Branch, Jo Carruthers, Louise Lee, Simon Marsden, Emma Mason, Laura Peters, Jan-Melissa Schramm, and the two peer reviewers chosen by The Ohio State University Press. The book is infinitely better as a result of their input.

I am also pleased to acknowledge the contribution made by those who heard some of the material and responded so generously. I think, here, of audiences at Baylor University, the Beyond 1611 conference in London, the British Evangelical Identities conference in London, Queen Mary University of London, the Midwest Victorian Studies Association conference in Ohio, various North American Victorian Studies Association conferences, Redeemer College, the University of Toronto, the Victorian Studies Association of Ontario,

Warwick University, and Wheaton College. And I am grateful, too, to all the individuals who have spoken with me about aspects of this book over the years and helped me work through ideas. This motley crowd of friends and colleagues include Ilana Blumberg, Christine Bolus-Reichert, Gavin Budge, Susan Colón, Christopher Ferguson, Josh Gang, Audrey Jaffe, Colin Jager, Andrew King, Joshua King, Charles LaPorte, Timothy Larsen, Graham Law, Gerard Loughlin, Deidre Lynch, Bill McKelvy, Terry Robinson, Russell Rook, John Schad, Lesa Scholl, Cannon Schmitt, Paul Stevens, Joseph Stubenrauch, Andrew Tate, Mark Turner, Nadia Valman, and Danny Wright. I'd also like to thank all my graduate students in Toronto for their wise input and pertinent questions, both in seminars and during individual conversations.

The book has benefitted from my involvement with other intellectual communities, too, beyond those I have been privileged to work with regularly. Back in 2003, I was honored to be part of a two-week summer faculty seminar, organized by the Erasmus Institute at Notre Dame University and led by Geoffrey Hartman. That seminar changed my thinking in so many ways and helped set this book in motion. It was one of the guest speakers at that seminar, Don Marshall, who first introduced me to Gadamer, and I will always be thankful that he did so. Inspired by my experience during those two weeks, I applied with Lori Branch to the National Endowment for the Humanities to codirect a four-week summer faculty seminar in 2016 on Postsecular Studies and the Rise of the English Novel. That proved to be another spectacular experience, and the wonderful participants and guest speakers did much to help me bring the various threads of this book to completion.

Lori Branch, the series editor for *Literature, Religion, and Postsecular Studies* has been terrific. In addition to calling me to articulate my ideas more boldly, she has become a good friend and regularly offers thoughtful counsel. The staff at The Ohio State University Press have also been a joy to work with. Lindsay Martin was an outstanding commissioning editor, and it was as a result of my memorable conversation with her at the NAVSA conference in Arizona that I decided on The Ohio State University Press as the publisher I wanted to work with. When Lindsay left the press, I started working with Kristen Elias Rowley and then Ana Maria Jimenez-Moreno, and they have been impressively helpful, encouraging, and professional. Thanks, too, to Rebecca Bostock for her speedy and cheerful assistance in resolving various queries, and the considerable expertise and assistance provided by the production staff.

I could not have written this book without the support of my family. My wife, Jo, is a constant reminder of the determination, wisdom, and integrity that all good intellectual work requires, and I thank God daily for her role in my life. And I am similarly thankful for my son, Samuel, whose inquisitiveness and zest for all that this world has to offer encourage me try and live accordingly.

I would like to finish these acknowledgments by dedicating the book to two people who never met each other and continue to strike me as an unlikely pairing. It was Phil Wall who encouraged me to think about what the gospel might look like when incarnated into everyday life, and I would never have been able to conceive of this project without his input throughout my early adult years. And my conversations with the late Geoffrey Hartman, beginning in our seminar in 2003, have made me so much more cognizant of what it means to be a literary critic. This book is for them.

INTRODUCTION

Rethinking Our Stories of the Victorian Novel

*D*oes evangelicalism have a meaningful role in the stories we tell about the Victorian novel? There are certainly those who think that it should. Elisabeth Jay describes the religious movement as "a powerful literary voice," and Jan-Melissa Schramm considers how some of evangelicalism's theological interests can be heard in the fiction of the period: "That the Victorian novel is so intensely interested in both the salvific and the fraudulent potential of substitution is perhaps a self-conscious attempt to reflect on its origins, as the 'heir' of Scriptural narrative."[1] Yet others are less convinced. George Levine famously insists that "despite the piety, the novel as a form . . . was intrinsically secular," and the absence of detailed references to evangelicalism in the majority of scholarship on Victorian literature suggests that his view has prevailed.[2] We begin, then, in contested territory, configured by the multiplicity of ways in which one thinks about the sacred and the secular. As a result, my exploration of the relationship between evangelicalism and the Victorian novel entails much more than a narrow exercise in ecclesial history. It is, rather, part of a larger and shared theoretical project about the place of religion in the modern world, one that is concerned with understanding the "interface between literary and religious discourses" and showing "the way

---

1. Jay, *The Religion of the Heart*, 7; Schramm, *Atonement and Self-Sacrifice in Nineteenth-Century Narrative*, 215.
2. Levine, *Realism, Ethics and Secularism*, 212.

people engage with such complex and multifaceted [religious] texts . . . [to be] a complicated business."³

One of the things that interests me about the lack of attention to evangelicalism in our studies of Victorian literary culture is that it occurs in spite of broad acknowledgement that evangelicalism was important to the sociopolitical life of Victorian Britain. Part of the explanation for this mismatch is the methodological difficulty caused by the movement's ecclesial elasticity. Evangelicals were a party within the Church of England *and* a pan-denominational Christian movement, and adherents could be Calvinist or Arminian, Tory or Whig, pro-imperialist or critical of the British Empire. While evangelicals in the nineteenth century found plenty of common ground, they were sometimes even less united than George Whitfield and John Wesley had been during the evangelical awakenings of the eighteenth century. The creation of the Evangelical Alliance in 1846 was meant to consolidate the movement by establishing an organizing body, but theological differences remained; only some evangelicals joined, and other settings continued to be required for bringing evangelicals together.⁴ One of the best known of these, Exeter Hall, was a venue in London that hosted separate meetings by different evangelical groups. But this arrangement only underlined the movement's lack of cohesion. Evangelicals may have commonly referred to themselves as "the religious world," but the boundaries of that world were less clear than the phrase suggested. The choice of title for J. C. Ryle's 1867 pamphlet, "Evangelical Religion: What It Is and What It Is Not," epitomized a desire among evangelical believers to demarcate the limits of belief. However, the perceived need for such a pamphlet in the first place suggests more ambiguity than its author cared to admit. Ryle's style of writing sought to convey certainty through a heavy reliance on declarative sentences, the extensive use of numbered points, and an explicit preference for simplicity over ornamental language. Yet his insistence that "there can be no unity without soundness in the faith" followed fellow evangelicals in using an ethereal and nonquantifiable metaphor to measure theological orthodoxy.⁵

Who were the evangelicals and what did they believe? The main response of religious historians to these questions has been to identify key priorities of

---

3. Burstein, *Victorian Reformations*, 7; Asad, *Formations of the Secular*, 10.

4. In their account of the 1846 meetings that led to the formation of the Evangelical Alliance, Ian Randall and David Hilborn note how various doctrinal and denominational differences proved less important than a major disagreement over slavery. Several prominent British evangelicals insisted that slaveholders should be explicitly excluded from the proposed organization, which is why the Evangelical Alliance ended up being a British organization rather than the worldwide body that some of those gathered had envisaged. See Randall and Hilborn, *One Body in Christ*, chapter 3.

5. Ryle, "Evangelical Religion: What It Is, and What It Is Not," 9.

the movement and use these to trace the work of evangelicals. Back in 1989, David Bebbington articulated a quadrilateral of evangelical priorities that he thought "emerge[d] clearly" from the history of the movement: "*conversionism*, the belief that lives need to be changed; *activism*, the expression of the gospel in effort; *biblicism*, a particular regard for the Bible; and what may be called *crucicentrism*, a stress on the sacrifice of Christ on the cross."[6] Taken singularly, these qualities are not unique to any part of the church, but, as Bebbington explains, their collective emphasis made evangelicalism distinctive. In a later book, Bebbington acknowledges how these qualities "faded in certain quarters and . . . underwent unconscious change and deliberate adaptation," yet he still insists that they "remained the defining features of evangelicalism down to the end of the century and beyond."[7] Much of the subsequent scholarship in religious history has agreed. Although Bebbington's quadrilateral has been subject to numerous modifications and revisions, his summary remains, according to the majority of those who work in this area, the "most effective" distillation of key evangelical "convictions and attitudes," and it is the starting point for my book.[8]

Bebbington's quadrilateral can seem an overly capacious definition. To take just one example, the Bible is important for the whole of the Christian church and only acquires significance in Bebbington's account by virtue of the stress evangelicals place on it as both the primary means of God's revelation

---

6. Bebbington, *Evangelicalism in Modern Britain*, 2–3.
7. Bebbington, *The Dominance of Evangelicalism*, 23.
8. Noll, *The Rise of Evangelicalism*, 16. Examples of scholars seeking a modification to Bebbington's quadrilateral include Joseph Stubenrauch, who adds a fifth distinguishing feature—"attention to the workings of the Holy Spirit"—in *The Evangelical Age of Ingenuity*, 7, and Timothy Larsen, who commends Bebbington's work but prefers to work with his own longer five-point definition. Larsen writes:

> An evangelical is:
> 1. an orthodox Protestant
> 2. who stands in the tradition of the global Christian networks rising from the eighteenth-century revival movements associated with John Wesley and George Whitefield;
> 3. who has a preeminent place for the Bible in her or his Christian life as the divinely inspired, final authority in matters of faith and practice;
> 4. who stresses reconciliation with God through the atoning work of Jesus Christ on the cross;
> 5. and who stresses the work of the Holy Spirit in the life of an individual to bring about conversion and an ongoing life of fellowship with God and service to God and others, including the duty of all believers to participate in the task of proclaiming the gospel to all people. Larsen, "Introduction," in Larsen and Treier, eds., *The Cambridge Companion to Evangelical Theology*, 1.

and a text that does not depend on the mediation of the church. Bebbington is well aware of similar limitations across all four of the priorities he assigns to the evangelicals, and we should remember that his oft-cited definition is augmented by a huge amount of clarifying detail over the course of his book. Although the quadrilateral makes most sense when one reads the fuller story that puts flesh on the bones, starting with a minimal definition of evangelicalism gives us the freedom to read with more nuance later on. John Wolffe is right, I think, to argue that "identifying evangelicals by their convictions and attitudes rather than by their affiliations is particularly helpful in facilitating an awareness of how evangelical impulses transcended and sometimes subverted the efforts of those who sought to direct them into closely defined channels."[9] And the theoretical looseness of Bebbington's initial definition is apposite for thinking about a religious movement that has always been more interested in practical Christianity, as William Wilberforce put it, than in theological minutia.[10] Joseph Stubenrauch makes a persuasive argument for the critical importance of "the evangelical attitude towards 'the use of means,'" and much of the unity across evangelical groups in the eighteenth and nineteenth centuries came from their shared techniques and goals for mission rather than the finer points of doctrinal detail.[11]

Yet the lack of hard and fast definition has proved an obstacle for many of the literary critics who already struggle to make sense of the complex map of Victorian Christian belief. This may seem a strange thing to say about a group of scholars who are acutely aware of the mutability and nuance of language, and typically suspicious of any definition that is too heavily determined. But religion in all its Victorian forms is a common stumbling block for literary critics who do not specialize in this area, and the lack of clarity about evangelicalism often compounds the problem. With notable exceptions, literary scholars often end up marginalizing the importance of religion, failing to see its complexity and/or translating theology into a critical language (gender, race, economics, etc.) with which they are more familiar. Although the resulting misreading of religion has a particular and involved history in twentieth- and twenty-first-century criticism, the predicament of knowing how to interpret evangelicalism is not unknown to earlier generations. In George Eliot's *Middlemarch* (1871–72), the narrator encapsulates the dilemma in an early scene when she introduces the character of Mr. Bulstrode, the evangelical banker whose pious story unravels over the course of the novel: "Some

---

9. Wolffe, *The Expansion of Evangelicalism*, 21.
10. Wilberforce, *A Practical View of the Prevailing Religious System of Professed Christians* (1797).
11. Stubenrauch, *The Evangelical Age of Ingenuity*, 251.

called him a Methodist, others a hypocrite, according to the resources of their vocabulary."[12] While I have some reservations about Eliot's vantage point here, to which I will return later in this introduction, her observation helps me highlight one of the purposes of my book: to improve the vocabulary that literary scholars bring to our reading of evangelicalism.

Improving our vocabulary is not the same as learning new terms via a short primer in theology, nor does it involve filling our minds with as much contextual detail as possible. I have chosen not to begin this book with a detailed survey of evangelicalism.[13] Since the publication of Bebbington's seminal work, religious historians have had a great deal to say about nineteenth-century evangelicalism, and readers whose primary concern is religious history in its wider sense should probably start with the work of scholars such as Bebbington, Wolff, Stubenrauch, Timothy Larsen, Mark Smith, Ian Bradley, and Boyd Hilton. I appreciate that deferring to religious historians so quickly runs counter to the interdisciplinary impulse of recent decades, and I continue to see myself as engaged in interdisciplinary research. In this book I draw extensively on the work of historians and theologians, and both disciplines are an important influence on my reading of literature. Yet I am not a religious historian by training. Historians, at least the ones with whom I am familiar, know more historical details and routinely read a greater range of sources than I. That does not make their work better or worse than that undertaken by literary specialists, but the differences are worth acknowledging.[14] Thinking historically is part of my work in *Good Words*, but my focus is firmly on the form of the novel, and when I talk about improving our vocabulary, I am thinking primarily about the critical language of literary critics, the group to which I belong.

There are several reasons why the vocabulary of literary scholars is currently impoverished when it comes to evangelical religion: awareness of the explicit distrust of many nineteenth-century evangelicals regarding the work of the novel; familiarity with the profusion of hypocritical and socially conservative evangelical characters penned by well-known Victorian authors; confusion over the movement's most important years, fed by novelists seeking to throw off the story with which they grew up; an on-going commitment in

---

12. Eliot, *Middlemarch*, 97.

13. For a single-chapter literary history of evangelicalism in the nineteenth century, see Knight and Mason, *Nineteenth-Century Religion and Literature*, chapter 4.

14. The methodological differences between literary specialists and religious historians are not always clear-cut. One thinks, for instance, of Isobel Rivers's important work on evangelicalism in the eighteenth century, *Vanity Fair and the Celestial City*, which, methodologically speaking, follows more of a middle ground.

some critical circles to uncovering the false ideology of religion rather than engaging with its diversity; a clumsy and ultimately misleading conflation of evangelicalism and modern American fundamentalism; and widespread ignorance of the "evangelical tonalities" referred to by Andrew Miller in his wonderfully suggestive *The Burdens of Perfection: On Ethics and Reading in Nineteenth-Century Britain* (2008).[15] Miller's evocative phrase, introduced as he seeks to acknowledge "the most broad and deep" influence on the moral perfectionism with which he is concerned, directs us to the difficulty of the task at hand.[16] We are not simply trying to define some unfamiliar theological terms for their own sake, but thinking about how Victorian novels contain a concatenation of religious sounds, voices, and reverberations. These tones can be heard across a wide range of novelists, many of whom did not identify personally as evangelical but were influenced by the movement nevertheless.

Once we have ears to hear and a more theologically sensitive critical language through which to interpret evangelical tones in fiction, it becomes easier to follow the prompt of Danièle Hervieu-Léger and, "instead of thinking of a dwindling religious domain . . . [to] look for covert signs of religion"—in this case evangelicalism—"in every sphere of human activity."[17] The ideas, networks, and practices of evangelicalism permeate the content of the Victorian novel, and identifying markers of the religious movement and connecting them to our existing critical discourse allows us to see the extent to which Victorian fiction is invested in repentance, convinced that words can affect readers, and preoccupied with questions of morality. As we will see, the form of the novel was molded by evangelicalism, through the conscious and unconscious decision-making of authors and the wider publishing industry that sustained them. I argue that it is at least in part due to the impact of the evangelical movement that Victorian novelists approached the fictional form in the way they did: insisting on its capacity to transform readers, emphasizing stories of personal transformation and conversion, and exploring novel means by which words of moral seriousness and sociopolitical consequence might be conveyed.

EVANGELICALS, NOVELISTS, CRITICS

The last major study of evangelicalism and the nineteenth-century novel was Elisabeth Jay's *Religion of the Heart: Anglican Evangelicalism and the Nineteenth-*

---

15. Miller, *The Burdens of Perfection*, 20.
16. Ibid., 20.
17. Hervieu-Léger, *Religion as a Chain of Memory*, 29.

Century Novel (1979). It remains essential reading and has been a formative influence on my own thought. A lot has happened over the four ensuing decades, however, including the emergence of a body of scholarship (some of it written by the religious historians already named) that lessens the need for me to follow Jay in giving over such a substantial initial portion of my monograph to "identify[ing] the Evangelicals, what they believed, the demands that their faith made upon their everyday life, and the impact that they made upon the non-Evangelical world around them."[18] Although references to Victorian novels can be found throughout the first three chapters (four if you include the introduction) of Jay's book, her focus on a spread of historical and theological detail gets in the way of lengthy close readings and an extended engagement with questions of literary form. In the chapters that follow, I opt for a different approach, privileging the forms that "are everywhere structuring and patterning experience" and preferring detailed readings of selected texts that open up the intersection between literature, theology, and history.[19] While this approach lacks the range of literary and cultural reference that we find in Jay, I hope that it will help readers see what an evangelically rich religious vocabulary might offer in practice. There are other differences, too, between our books. First, I employ a very different theoretical and critical lexicon, not because I am in particular dispute with Jay's literary methodology but because the critical landscape of the last forty years has changed considerably following the rise and subsequent assimilation of literary theory into the way we read. Second, I do not follow Jay in thinking about evangelicalism primarily as a party within the Church of England.[20] Larsen's account of evangelicalism makes a persuasive case for the limitations of giving too much weight to the Church of England when studying the movement, and my own work pays more attention to the presence of evangelicalism in dissenting churches than Jay does in her book.[21] Recognizing the contribution of dissent has the additional advantage of helping us to see how material that has frequently been read as evidence for secularization (e.g., the shift away from requiring university students to be part of the Church of England and assent to the Thirty-Nine Articles of faith) can be seen as demonstrating the vitality of Protestant dissent throughout the nineteenth century. My third point of departure from Jay concerns her description of evangelicalism as a religion of the heart. This

---

18. Jay, *The Religion of the Heart*, 2.
19. Levine, *Forms*, 16.
20. This is the reason I do not capitalize the term *evangelical* throughout this book.
21. Larsen writes: "Many stereotypes about Victorian Christians generally, and Victorian evangelicals in particular, break down when Nonconformists are brought into the foreground." Larsen, *Contested Christianity*, 2.

quality was clearly very important to evangelicalism and retains on-going relevance to the movement and our critical thought. As Misty G. Anderson observes: "The story about what Methodism, the most consolidated expression of modern evangelicalism, did to the modern self, and the question of whether its converts could be said to be modern selves, continues to put the historical narrative of secular modernity on the line."[22] But evangelicalism can also be thought about in other ways, from the more minor note of an intellectual tradition focused on particular forms of biblical commentary to the more significant concern with practical and outward expressions of faith.[23] This practical orientation led to the creation of numerous missionary and philanthropic organizations in the nineteenth century and evangelicalism had as much consequence for public life as it did for one's personal beliefs.

I share Jay's conviction that the form of the novel and the history of evangelicalism are entwined. To appreciate their close relation, we need to question the pervasive assumption that the novel is a secular form. The assumption has been with us a long time. By the early twentieth century, members of the Bloomsbury circle were able to find prominent textual precedents for their belief that religion was a barrier to serious artistic and intellectual thought and their efforts to plot a different route for the novel.[24] Other scholars followed in these critical footsteps. Georg Lukács famously described the novel as the "epic of a world that has been abandoned by God," and Ian Watt's influential account of the rise of the form gave a plausible explanation as to why the novel had left religion behind.[25] Identifying and privileging formal realism as crucial to the novel's rise, Watt argued that the emerging literary form shared empirical philosophy's concern with "the production of what purports to be an authentic account of the actual experience of individuals."[26] The concern with probable everyday life, consistently posited by Watt as the most reasonable way of engaging with the world we inhabit, was alleged to render religion redundant. Subsequent critics were quick to confirm the inevitable and unambiguous nature of this secular development. For Fredric Jameson, the recogni-

---

22. Anderson, *Imagining Methodism in Eighteenth-Century Britain*, 235.
23. For more on evangelical biblical hermeneutics, see chapter 4.
24. On hearing about T. S. Eliot's conversion, Virginia Woolf wrote to her sister in 1928: "I have had a most shameful and distressing interview with poor dear Tom Eliot, who may be called dead to us all from this day forward. He has become an Anglo-Catholic, believes in God and immortality, and goes to church. I was really shocked. A corpse would seem to me more credible than he is. I mean, there's something obscene in a living person sitting by the fire and believing in God." The quotation is cited and glossed by Pericles Lewis in *Religious Experience and the Modernist Novel*, 142.
25. Lukács, *The Theory of the Novel*, 88.
26. Watt, *The Rise of the Novel*, 27.

tion that "we are operating within a secular corpus" means that "we no longer have to do with religion or sacred texts."[27] And for George Levine, probably the most influential theorist of the Victorian realist novel over the last few decades, there is little doubt that "Victorian fiction . . . is a secular form if ever there was one."[28] While there are theological problems with such arguments, most notably the concept of extreme transcendence that is employed to explain why religion can be left behind, the bigger problem is the failure to acknowledge the myriad of secular assumptions mobilized to support these accounts of the novel.[29] Colin Jager makes a persuasive case for the "Humean echoes" of Levine's formulation of realism, and we might hear, too, the influence of twentieth-century contributors to a hermeneutics of suspicion when Levine declares that "the great resurgence of religious activity among the Victorians" suggests its opposite, namely a people embracing secularism as they struggle "to come to terms with that naturalistically described world that science was so successfully describing."[30] Though the affable and elegant nature of Levine's writing can lead us to think that he offers a relatively even-handed treatment of religion, we should heed those moments in which his opposition to religion becomes more marked, such as the tongue-in-cheek revision to a popular Christian slogan in his choice of title for the book *Darwin Loves You: Natural Selection and the Re-Enchantment of the World* (2006).[31]

Secular accounts of the novel have not gone unchallenged. Back in the 1970s, one of the most striking counterreadings came from Valentine Cunningham, whose book *Everywhere Spoken Against: Dissent in the Victorian Novel* (1975) dovetailed nicely with Jay's interest in Anglican Evangelicalism. Although Cunningham begins by insisting, not unreasonably, that evangelicalism should be distinguished from dissent, his subsequent chapters reveal various points of overlap and make a compelling case for the vitality of dissent (including its evangelical aspect) in the Victorian novel. One can still find stories of "the decline of orthodoxy, the explosion of secularism, [and] the

---

27. Fredric Jameson, "The Experiments of Time: Providence and Realism," in Moretti, ed., *The Novel*, 2:110.
28. Levine, *Realism, Ethics and Secularism*, 210.
29. For a more complex understanding of transcendence, in which contributors show how theological talk is never isolated from the concerns of the world, see Schwartz, *Transcendence*.
30. Levine, *Realism, Ethics and Secularism*, 10. My talk here of the hermeneutics of suspicion is influenced by the language used by Ricoeur in *Freud and Philosophy: An Essay on Interpretation*, chapter 2.
31. Colin Jager, "Literary Enchantment and Literary Opposition from Hume to Scott," in Lloyd and Ratzman, eds., *Secular Faith*, 192. For further discussion of the secularity of critical readings of the novel, see Branch and Knight, "Why the Postsecular Matters: Literary Studies and the Rise of the Novel."

falling population of church attenders" in Cunningham's readings, but we are simultaneously encouraged to consider the diversity of nonconformist religion in the novel and its capacity for reinvention.[32] Cunningham is not alone in drawing attention to the novel's theological dimension. More recent instances of a counterreading to the novel's supposed secularity can be found in work by Patrick O'Malley, William McKelvy, J. Russell Perkin, Susan Colón, Jan-Melissa Schramm, Norman Vance, Emily Walker Heady, and Miriam Burstein, to name just some of the scholars who have written important books in this area over the last decade or so.[33] The religious dimension of the novel is also brought to life by the work of other scholars—such as Kirstie Blair, Duc Dau, Richard Gibson, Ellis Hanson, Michael Hurley, Joshua King, Charles LaPorte, Lizzie Ludlow, Emma Mason, Stephen Prickett, Frederick Roden, and Michael Wheeler—who write about a variety of different literary forms and their relation to Victorian Christianity.

While the scholars mentioned above have helped make our studies of the Victorian novel more hospitable to religion, evangelicalism remains in the background. This might seem unremarkable given the enormous diversity of religious belief in the Victorian period and the need for individual scholars to concentrate their focus so that they can do justice to the intricacies of various theological traditions. But evangelicalism is left out so consistently that we would do well to consider some of the other factors at play. Even those whose area of study intersects most strongly with the concerns of evangelicalism—Heady's writing about conversion, Vance's interest in the Bible, and Schramm's work on atonement—do not speak about the movement at length. There are, I think, very different reasons for this. In the case of Heady, the motivation appears to be a desire to situate her readings within the framework of existing literary criticism on realism, and with the exception of her chapter on Wilde, the theological community in which she is personally invested is left on the margins. Vance's lack of attention to evangelicalism seems less strategic and driven more by a preference for liberal configurations of theology over instances of the strongly held belief that we find among evangelicals. Perhaps it is unsurprising, then, that the few references he does make to evangelicalism record instances of authors moving away from a tradition they found constraining. The rationale behind Schramm's approach is different again. Her

---

32. Cunningham, *Everywhere Spoken Against*, 284.

33. O'Malley, *Catholicism, Sexual Deviance, and Victorian Gothic Culture*; McKelvy, *The English Cult of Literature: Devoted Readers, 1774–1880*; Perkin, *Theology and the Victorian Novel*; Colón, *Victorian Parables*; Schramm, *Atonement and Self-Sacrifice in Nineteenth-Century Narrative*; Vance, *Bible and Novel: Narrative Authority and the Death of God*; Heady, *Victorian Conversion Narratives and Reading Communities*; and Burstein, *Victorian Reformations*.

engagement with nineteenth-century theology is deliberate and astute, and the desire for historical specificity leads her to concentrate on particular Anglican theologians and debates from the 1850s. Although her work maps closely onto evangelicalism and offers an important interlocutor for my own chapters here on Charles Dickens and Wilkie Collins, my sense is that she does not name the movement at length because she finds evangelicalism too amorphous a category to help with her line of argument.

There are multiple reasons why evangelicalism gets occluded from our modern histories of the novel, and it is not just an inevitable outcome of the eighteenth- and nineteenth-century clash between nonevangelical writers of fiction and their evangelical critics. Moreover, the history of this clash is less clear-cut than we might think. It is true, of course, that influential Victorian novelists penned characters such as Mr. Brocklehurst (*Jane Eyre*, 1847), Mr. and Mrs. Murdstone (*David Copperfield*, 1849–1850), Miss Clack (*The Moonstone*, 1868), and Mr. Slope (*Barchester Towers*, 1857), all memorable for their cruelty, hypocrisy, or stupidity. And it is also true that these characterizations were mirrored by hostility and suspicion from evangelical critics, such as the anonymous writer of an 1866 article in the *Evangelical Magazine*, "Character: How It Is Formed and What It Is Worth": "If a man would build up for himself, a strong and useful character, he must read very sparingly fiction of any kind."[34] But there were not clear dividing lines between evangelicals and novelists in the nineteenth century. For a start, evangelical figures in fiction are more complex than our memories often recollect, as I will show in subsequent chapters, and we would do well to consider why these creations feature so prominently in the novels of the period. And it is worth stopping to look more closely at evangelical criticism about the novel. R. W. Dale, writing in 1867, suggested that it was a hundred years since "devout people" had been "almost unanimous in excluding novels from their houses," and Jay is right to note how "even [nineteenth-century] reviews which deplored the specific treatment accorded to religion in various novels rarely questioned that, rightly understood, religion was native to the novel's sphere."[35] To illustrate Jay's point, we might return to the article on "Character" mentioned earlier in the paragraph, where the invectives against the work of particular novelists is tempered by the statement that "we by no means prohibit all fiction."[36]

---

34. Anon., "Character: How It Is Formed and What Is Worth," *Evangelical Magazine* (1866), 376.

35. Dale, "Amusements," *Good Words* (1867), 331; Jay, *Religion of the Heart*, 2.

36. Anon, "Character: How It Is Formed and What Is Worth," *Evangelical Magazine* (1866), 376.

Nineteenth-century complaints about the novel were accompanied by more constructive and hopeful ideas about the form. Take, for instance, an 1859 review in *The Christian Observer,* perhaps the best-known mainstream periodical of the evangelical party in the Church of England: "Novel writers and story builders are just now, to a marvellous extent, the educators of Great Britain. . . . Instead, then, of decrying a kind of literature which has so many charms for the young . . . how much wiser to attempt, so far as we may, to raise the standards of works of fiction."[37] Or consider an essay on "Sensational Literature," published in the same periodical a few years later: "*Fiction* is not an evil in itself. It may, no doubt, be readily abused, and made a vehicle for conveying poison to the mind; but a good story may be invented or feigned, and then employed for the benefit of society."[38] Neither of the evangelicals cited object to fiction per se, though in both cases the writers are suspicious of the novel and critical of some its manifestations. But they still worry about the novel's efficacy, its lack of transparency, and the competing motivations of the authors who write it. Other evangelicals turned to the Bible to support new forms of storytelling. As an anonymous reviewer in the dissent-oriented periodical, *The Evangelical Magazine,* put it in 1864: "There are those who think all fiction wrong; we respect their feeling, but we cannot help thinking their judgement most mistaken. Teaching parables is the most instructive and impressive of all teaching, and we can scarcely conceive of any one rising from the perusal of such works as Miss Muloch's, Miss Manning's, and Miss Yonge's, without much of good impression and purpose."[39]

Bebbington observes that "there was probably always more opposition in theory than in practice" to novels, and he goes on to note how, by "the end of the century, a whole fictional genre, the so-called Scottish 'Kailyard School,' existed to convey a Christian message."[40] But the use of fiction by evangelicals was apparent well before the late nineteenth century. In chapter 3, I detail the uses to which novels are put in the pages of *Good Words,* a mid-century journal with a professed evangelical ambition, but we can also find related examples elsewhere: the fiction published by the Religious Tract Society's *The Leisure Hour* and *Sunday at Home*; the novels that were prominent in *The Quiver,* an evangelical journal committed, in the words of its subtitle, to "the Defence of

---

37. Anon., "Religious Stories: The Ministry of Life. By Maria Louisa Charlesworth," *The Christian Observer* (1859), 56.
38. Anon., "Sensational Literature," *The Christian Observer* (1865), 810.
39. Anon., "Brief Notice of Books," *Evangelical Magazine* (1864), 603.
40. Bebbington, *Evangelicalism in Modern Britain*, 131. For further discussion of the Kailyard school, albeit without Bebbington's focus on evangelicalism, see Nash, *Kailyard and Scottish Literature.*

Biblical Truth and the Advancement of Religion in the Homes of the People";
and the large number of Victorian publishers who identified as evangelical and
included fiction in their lists.[41]

We should remember, as well, that evangelicals were part of the extensive
reading public that consumed novels so readily. While nineteenth-century
publishers often sought to demarcate different audiences, their attempts were
rarely matched by reality, and the ecclesial elasticity of evangelicalism noted at
the start of this introduction means that many evangelicals read and enjoyed
the novels attacked by some of their brethren.[42] Given the number of articles
in evangelical journals encouraging believers to reflect on their reading habits, there was clearly a perception among evangelicals that their brothers and
sisters in Christ were reading fiction, and the concerns expressed in those
articles offer more of those many instances in which members of evangelical
congregations turn out to be less theologically conservative than some of their
leaders. In addition to reading novels, a number of evangelicals turned their
hand to writing it. Evangelical novelists of the nineteenth century included
Charlotte Elizabeth Tonna, Mary Martha Sherwood, Caroline Lucy Scott,
Emily Sarah Holt, Elizabeth Rundle Charles, Maria Louisa Charlesworth, and
Emma Worboise. Miriam Burstein reminds us that these, and many others,
played "a crucial role in nineteenth-century religious and popular culture,"
and Trisha Tucker notes their popularity: "Some of their novels sold hundreds
of thousands of copies, were widely reviewed and read on both sides of the
Atlantic, and were translated into multiple languages."[43]

Tucker touches on an important issue when she criticizes those, myself
included, who do not talk about these evangelical writers in our accounts of
religion and the nineteenth-century novel. Her own exploration of this fiction,
of which we get a taste in the article just cited, explains how "scholars have
continued the trend of linking Evangelicalism to 'feminine' values and implicitly or explicitly, disparaging those values."[44] Tucker's approach offers a useful
way forward, for while the fiction of Charlotte Elizabeth Tonna and company
are unlikely to find many current readers, evangelical or otherwise, who are

---

41. John Hatchard of Piccadilly, for example, was the printer of *The Christian Observer* and the main publisher for the Clapham Sect. And Charles Mudie, of Mudie's Circulating Library, was another prominent evangelical.

42. "On the one hand, Evangelical groups pioneered niche marketing long before commercial advertisers began to copy them. . . . On the other hand, the Religious Tract Society worried that publications targeted too precisely could draw invidious distinctions." Price, *How to Do Things with Books in Victorian Britain*, 164–65.

43. Burstein, *Victorian Reformations*, 2. Tucker, "Gendering the Evangelical Novel," 83.

44. Tucker, "Gendering the Evangelical Novel," 86.

rushing to restore them to the canon, they still possess cultural significance.[45] Nevertheless, I have decided against writing about evangelical fiction here.[46] Because this is a book about how evangelicalism came to shape the Victorian novel more generally, and why this is important for us to think about today, I do not want to write about fiction that is now routinely ignored and would do little to advance the primary thesis of this book. I happen to believe that the writers I discuss wrote better novels than the evangelical writers I ignore, but this is not an important argument or one that I am trying to defend, for the primary rationale behind my choice of texts is seeking common ground with a community of literary scholars who are yet to be convinced about why evangelicalism matters at all to their stories of the Victorian novel.

TWO POTENTIAL DEAD ENDS

Seeking common ground with other scholars of Victorian literature does not always mean replicating their practice, and it is worth saying more about two potential approaches to my topic that I have deliberately not taken: reading evangelicalism with reference to its involvement with the British Empire and seeking to understand the movement through the novels of George Eliot. To begin with the former, it may seem strange to some readers that I have so little to say about the religious movement's participation in the imperial project. Anna Johnston begins her study of the London Missionary Society by noting how "the historical conjunction of the evangelical revival and the second British Empire suggests certain cultural, intellectual, and ideological relations between the two," and the critical tradition since the late twentieth century has tended to concur, believing that the evangelical commitment to mission can and should be explained through the movement's collusion with imperialism.[47] It is certainly the case that evangelicals were committed to spreading the gospel overseas, with a large number of missionary organizations established in the nineteenth century, and this work was inevitably connected to the expansion of empire and British attempts to "civilize" those who thought and acted differently.

---

45. For Bryan B. Rasmussen, for instance, Tonna's significance lies in her use of "evangelical spiritual autobiography . . . as a mode that underscores the extent to which the self intersects with rhetorical practices and cultural and political crises." Rasmussen, "From God's Work to Fieldwork," 182.

46. In chapter 3, I discuss fiction that appeared in the evangelical magazine *Good Words*. But my interest is in showing how and why the literary mission of this periodical accommodated narratives that lacked unambiguous evangelical statements.

47. Johnston, *Missionary Writing and Empire*, 15.

While evangelicals were committed to mission abroad, they were also keen to evangelize those within the British Isles. Attending church or expressing some sort of general attachment to the Christian faith was never deemed sufficient for evangelical believers: the religious awakening they experienced and found so edifying individually was a phenomenon they wanted to lead others into, not least because they believed that the eternal state of one's soul hung on whether or not a person had genuinely turned to God and accepted his forgiveness. Hence the profusion of para-church activities in Victorian Britain, from small group Bible studies to the May Meetings at London's Exeter Hall, which were all designed to extend the gospel beyond the confines of a traditional church service. Evangelicals were continually looking for new opportunities to evangelize those at home, with the periodical *Good Words* proudly announcing in 1860 that "our readers are probably aware that nearly all the theatres in the lower part of London have been opened for religious services; and are attended once or twice on Sundays by immense crowds of the working classes resident in the surrounding localities."[48] These activities were continuous with missionary activity abroad, and if we think about evangelism primarily as a work directed overseas, we can fail to see how the same evangelistic impulse permeated the domestic life that preoccupied the majority of Victorian novels. The evangelical commitment to mission could be seen at home and abroad. Thus, when Elaine Freedgood tells us that "the imperialized nature of Britain in this period is evident most starkly in the material world of the novel," we might look for a similar foreign-domestic connection when it comes to missionary activity.[49]

Although missionary activity is inseparable from the imperial project, there is a danger in treating the two as synonymous. I do not deny that evangelical motivations were often influenced by imperialistic ambitions, at least at some level, but it is simply not true that a desire for cultural domination was the sole reason for evangelicals engaging with mission as enthusiastically as they did. And it is worth remembering, too, that some evangelicals were opposed to the imperial project. Timothy Larsen makes a convincing case for differences within the evangelical response to Governor Eyre's brutal repression of the 1865 Morant Bay Rebellion in Jamaica, and this is far from being the only instance of evangelical reservations about empire.[50] While much of the more specialized work on nineteenth-century religion and empire reg-

---

48. Anon., "Preaching on the Stage," *Good Words* (1860), 189.
49. Elaine Freedgood, "The Novel and Empire," in Kucich and Taylor, eds., *The Oxford History of the Novel in English*, 3:379.
50. Larsen, *Contested Christianity*, chapter 12. Also, see Cox, "Were Victorian Nonconformists the Worst Imperialists of All?" 243–255.

isters the complexity of missionary collusion with and divergence from the imperial project, the relentless ideological critique favored by scholars such as Patrick Brantlinger and Catherine Hall continues to dominate much of our thinking in literary studies about the work of evangelicals.[51] My main reason for staying away from the subject of empire is that our reflections on the imperial project often end up dominating our reading and effacing the other motivations that fed into evangelical practice. This is not an inevitable outcome, and I value the work of those scholars who find more constructive and complex ways of thinking through the relation of evangelicalism to empire.[52] But my desire to create new paths for our thoughts about evangelicalism and the novel means avoiding paradigms that have often resulted in evangelicals being painted as the bogeymen of the nineteenth century.

If my lack of attention to empire strikes readers as one gap in this book, then the lack of a chapter on George Eliot is likely to seem another. When describing my project to colleagues, there have been several occasions when I have been asked whether there was going to be a chapter on Eliot. My short answer—no—has typically been met by quizzical looks or follow-up questions as to why this is so. This seems curious, for while my choice of authors is along canonical lines, Eliot is not the only novelist missing: I find no place for the Brontë sisters, Thomas Hardy, or Elizabeth Gaskell, either. Yet their absence does not elicit the same concern as the lack of a chapter on Eliot. It is easy to see the potential attraction of an author who created characters such as Mr. Bulstrode and Dinah Morris, wrote *Scenes of a Clerical Life* (1857), and, over the course of her own life, vehemently rejected the evangelical beliefs with which she grew up. "Eliot's enduring commitment to all that is good in individuals and in society" can, says Vance, be seen as "a legacy of her more conventionally religious past" and is part of the reason why "her work demonstrate[s] the continuing importance to the shape and substance of the novel of the religious traditions of her time."[53] Jay is more explicit about the nature of Eliot's religious debt and its consequences for her writing, claiming that "Eliot's doctrine of realism owed more to her Evangelical background than has previously been suggested."[54] And Barry Qualls finds roots in the puritan/evangelical tradition when he cites John Bunyan and "the later reli-

---

51. See Brantlinger, *The Rule of Darkness*; Hall, *Civilising Subjects*.

52. See, for example: Porter, *Religion versus Empire?*; Gilley and Stanley, *The Cambridge History of Christianity, Vol. 8*; Cox, *The British Missionary Enterprise since 1700*; and Werner, *Missionary Cosmopolitanism in the British Nineteenth Century*. For a more specific example of crossover with my own work in this book, see McKelvy, "The Importance of Being Ezra."

53. Norman Vance, "Religion and the Novel," in Kucich and Taylor, eds., *The Oxford History of the Novel in English*, 3:490.

54. Jay, *Religion of the Heart*, 209.

gious writers that followed" him as important for Eliot's sense of herself as a teacher.⁵⁵

My decision not to focus on Eliot is at odds with the choices made by other scholars. Cunningham has a chapter on Eliot in his study of dissent, focusing on *Adam Bede* (1859), and Jay, beginning the chapter on Eliot in *The Religion of the Heart,* looks back to the first section of her book and notes how the author "has repeatedly emerged as paramount among major novelists in the accuracy and subtlety with which she used her experience of Evangelicalism."⁵⁶ I have heard similar comments at conferences, from scholars who, unlike Jay, continue to identify personally with the evangelical tradition. The rationale usually revolves around how Eliot's sympathetic and detailed portraits offer more fertile soil for evangelical faith than Dickens's caricatures, and we see a similar line of reasoning in the admiration that many nineteenth-century evangelicals had for an author whose use of a pseudonym initially led her to be mistaken as a clergyman. Though circumspect about the overall view of religion presented in *Adam Bede,* a reviewer for *The Christian Observer* admitted the work "to be a better book than the mass of novels," claiming that "is more life-like" and "*truer,* than the old circulating library trash."⁵⁷ There were multiple reasons why nineteenth-century evangelicals valued the veracity of realism, including the way in which they thought it enabled a less mediated form of religious instruction. One could read Eliot and learn lessons for life, from the value of godly living to the struggles of acting with integrity and the dictates of one's conscience. Evangelicals typically saw veracity as the means to an end rather than the goal in itself, for the reader was still required to identify the significance of the events they encountered in fiction and translate the lessons for their own life. And the position of the author and/or narrator regarding faith was also seen to play a guiding role, which is why evangelicals were so frequently anxious about who was telling the story. If there is a degree of naivety in the evangelical preference for realism, then, it involves more than a belief that the realist novel simply records history.

Recognizing this complex evangelical preference for realism allows us to draw a parallel with contemporary scholarship on the Victorian novel, which typically follows suit, albeit for different reasons. Contemporary explorations of the ethical implications of Eliot's sympathy are significantly different than the moral reading promoted by evangelical reviewers in the nineteenth century. But the commitment to realism is shared, and both communities have to deal with the problems that verisimilitude can cause. If nineteenth-century

---

55. Qualls, *The Secular Pilgrims of Victorian Fiction,* 140.
56. Jay, *Religion of the Heart,* 208.
57. Anon., "Recent Semi-Religious Works of Fiction," *The Christian Observer* (1860), 29.

evangelicals could approach realism with a more involved hermeneutic but still get overtaken by the apparent truthfulness of the events described, then perhaps modern scholars are at risk of doing likewise. We are all liable to miss aspects of the discrepancy between the world of fiction and the world that we inhabit, even though our reading so often presumes that we have this discrepancy in hand.

For all Eliot's cosmopolitan sympathy, intellectual brilliance, and skill as a novelist, she still only gives us a version of reality. The point is hardly original: Eliot herself reminds us of it throughout her fiction, commenting on the limits of those instruments we employ to help us see more clearly—"even with a microscope directed on a water-drop we find ourselves making interpretations which turn out to be rather coarse"—and insisting on the perspectival nature of all attempts to understand the world.[58] Josephine McDonagh is right to point out how, in *Middlemarch*, "the narrative attempts to distance itself from the very terms in which it has established its own [clinical] project," yet the penetrative power of Eliot's gaze continues to attract readers.[59] Critics may have given up on the idea that Eliot achieves or seeks objectivity in her narrative, but they remain committed to the idea that this novelist sees more clearly than anyone else because of the way she stands apart from the things she describes. Karen Chase wonders, "Who besides Eliot has been better aware of the alteration of objects given a change in perspective[?]"; Elizabeth Deeds Ermath, writing about the "complex treatment of perspective," observes that "George Eliot has few equals—perhaps no equals"; and George Levine insists that "George Eliot, more than most, explored the possibilities of detachment and tested the most forceful objections to it."[60]

Thus, when Eliot turns her gaze to religion, it is no surprise that the majority of readers think she is most likely right. Eliot's efforts to reveal the authentic mechanisms of religious belief are evident throughout *Middlemarch*, a novel Jameson reads as an "immense deconstruction of the ideology of providence as such, a tracking down of its religious overtones and undertones, and an almost surgical exploration of its results and effectiveness."[61] Simon During locates evangelicalism as one of the specific targets for Eliot's critical gaze, declaring it to be "under sustained critique in the novels" and highlight-

---

58. Eliot, *Middlemarch*, 75.
59. McDonagh, *George Eliot*, 38.
60. Karen Chase, "Introduction," in Chase, ed., *Middlemarch in the Twenty-First Century*, 4; Elizabeth Deeds Ermath, "Negotiating *Middlemarch*," in Chase, *Middlemarch in the Twenty-First Century*, 111; Levine, *Dying to Know*, 175.
61. Jameson, "The Experiments of Time: Providence and Realism," in Moretti, ed., *The Novel*, 2:119.

ing Bulstrode as a character whose commitment to conversion fails to register how that belief "can be used as an instrument of power, to foster patronage and support networks against the larger social interest."[62] Admittedly, there are more likeable evangelical characters elsewhere in Eliot's oeuvre, but the significance of Bulstrode to Eliot's wider account of evangelicalism does not rest on whether or not we like him. Indeed, Eliot goes out of her way to encourage readers to censure their initial distaste. Having first been led to loathe Bulstrode's pomposity and self-importance, we are then encouraged to be more sympathetic toward the crippling sense of guilt that accompanies his failures. Eliot continues to pull the hermeneutical strings as she makes this shift, granting Bulstrode some insight into his inner turmoil but using free indirect discourse when narrating his prayers to remind readers that she understands his predicament more clearly than he:

> For Bulstrode shrank from a direct lie with an intensity disproportionate to the number of his more direct misdeeds. But many of these misdeeds were like the subtle muscular movements which are not taken account of in the consciousness, though they bring the end that we fix our mind on and desire. And it is only what we are vividly conscious of that we can vividly imagine to be seen by Omniscience.[63]

What proves so detrimental for evangelicalism in Eliot's writing is not that certain characters are likeable or otherwise but that she presents herself as occupying the best vantage point for understanding what they are really thinking.

Even if we are not reading Eliot for what she might reveal directly about belief, the weight of explanatory detail she provides can overwhelm other possible views of the world. In the context of a different argument to the one I am proposing here, Levine explains how "novels devoted to details, context, and character give less the illusion of manipulation than those in which what will happen is the driving force of the narrative," and I think we sometimes miss the secular undercurrents that pervade Eliot's fiction.[64] Jon Singleton notes how Eliot's critique of faith "emerges only gradually," with her continued interest in the language of faith slowly revealing itself to be part of "an empirical, critical method for testing the effects of faith in various socialized

---

62. Simon During, "George Eliot and Secularism," in Anderson and Shaw, eds., *A Companion to George Eliot*, 439.
63. Eliot, *Middlemarch*, 536.
64. Levine, *Realism, Ethics and Secularism*, 191.

and embodied contexts."[65] Eliot's exploration of theological belief turns out to be an extended exercise in secular critique, albeit one infused with Ludwig Feuerbach's ongoing interest in religious language. Yet we continue to look to Eliot to explain the workings of evangelical faith. To adapt the central idea of Feuerbach and indulge in a more speculative line of thought, I wonder whether some critics are drawn to Eliot because she functions idealistically as the sort of thinker they aspire to be, a detached observer with divine powers to see the world as it truly is.

Whatever the actual motivations at work when scholars invest so heavily in Eliot's intellectual project, my point is that we need to be more cautious about accepting what she says about the inner workings of nineteenth-century evangelicals, not because her view is always wrong but because hers is not the only reading available. It is significant, I think, that the appeal to Eliot as a way forward for those interested in evangelicalism has not led to a wider renewal of critical interest in evangelicalism. Eliot's treatment of the movement turns out to be a dead end: while she writes about evangelicals with moments of sympathy and a volume that leads us to think that she will reveal more about the movement than other novelists, her accounts continually seek to replace evangelicalism with other explanatory accounts.[66] Writing about the bias against religion within modern western thought, Talal Asad calls attention to how it is frequently "assumed that there is always an unconscious motive to a religious act, a motive that is therefore secular."[67] On Eliot's reading, evangelicalism can be explained most fully through a secular language that she helps to develop, and those who accept her sophisticated accounts are left with no reason to continue considering evangelicalism as a resource for thinking about the world. The result is that the voice of evangelical religion is marginalized: we are left examining faith from the outside and rejecting the possibility that this particular expression of the church might prove capable of speaking to contemporary literary scholarship. When it comes, then, to understanding the role of evangelicalism in the development of the Victorian

---

65. Singleton, "Malignant Faith and Cognitive Restructuring," 240.

66. To be clear, turning to Eliot does not have to prevent us from thinking about evangelicalism. Nadia Valman makes a compelling case in *The Jewess in Nineteenth-Century British Literary Culture* for the afterlife of evangelical conversion in the structural design of *Daniel Deronda* (1876), and she is not alone in demonstrating the value of continuing to reflect on Eliot's engagement with the Christian faith. But while the link Valman makes between conversion narratives and the Jewish discourse of *Daniel Deronda* is thoughtful and suggestive, she does acknowledge that Eliot's version of the conversion narrative is "secularized" (150) and "not theological" (159). For further discussion of how the sacred and secular combine in Eliot, see McKelvy, *The English Cult of Literature: Devoted Readers, 1774–1880*; Rainof, *The Victorian Novel of Adulthood*; Lecourt, *Cultivating Belief*.

67. Asad, *Formations of the Secular*, 11.

novel, it is probably time for a new story in which empire and Eliot are no longer our principal guides.

A NEW STORY

Laying down the old guides can help us approach evangelicalism with a more expansive vista, one capable of recognizing how the movement's understanding of the divine word pervaded mainstream Victorian literary culture. Ultimately, I am less concerned with providing a specialist's field guide to evangelicalism than I am in encouraging this more encompassing vision. My work offers a less rigidly secular account of the novel than historians of the form have often put forward, and this has implications for our ongoing reading of this literature. As the chapters that follow delve into the relationship between evangelicalism and the novel, we will see how existing lines of thought in literary studies are put into new perspective and shown to be as religious as they are secular. The bildungsroman is recast as a theological story rather than unambiguous evidence of secularization; the attempt to narrate the story of our lives from year to year, to quote Charles Dickens's editorial agenda for *All the Year Round*, comes to be understood as echoing and competing with the evangelical story that was so formative for the Victorians; the decisions of the publishing industry are shown to be motivated by religious factors as well as commercial interests; and the question of affect, which has been so prominent for literary studies in recent years, becomes rooted in one of the Christian settings that proved so influential for the Victorian era. This is the sort of vocabulary we need, one that stops instantiating a simplistic secular/religious binary and instead seeks to register how complex secular-religious formations give rise to the evangelical tonalities that sound in ostensibly secular texts.

Despite the transformations of religion in modernity, the influence of evangelicalism on the Victorian novel remained active and was not just a secular residue from a once-religious age. My choice of texts is designed to make this clear by showing how mainstream novelists who did not identify as evangelical continued to grapple with evangelical ideas. In the case of William Makepeace Thackeray's *Vanity Fair* (1848), the engagement with John Bunyan's *The Pilgrim's Progress* (1678) and the personal activism so prominent among evangelicals encourages readers to assess the novel's implications for the lives of those who read it. While Thackeray's satirical style rejects the codified and rigid morality that many literary scholars have come to associate with evangelicalism, his novel's on-going conviction in how fiction can affect readers is indebted to an evangelical belief in the power of words and their life-giving power to bring about personal transformation. And in the following chapter, I turn to Charles Dickens's *A Tale of Two Cities* (1859), showing how the conversion tale favored by evangelicals made its way into the narrative design of arguably the most famous of all Victorian novelists and an author who exerted considerable influence on his peers through the pages of *All the Year Round*.

The contextual importance of periodicals for the novel is part of the story that I tell. This aspect is most pronounced in my chapter on the journal *Good Words*, a periodical that enlisted the novel to help communicate a message of salvation through the atoning work of Christ on the cross. The emphasis on sharing the good news of Christ was vital to the evangelical movement, hence the shared etymology of the words evangelism and evangelicalism, but the means used to achieve this end were never straightforward, and this proved to be the case with the fiction that appeared in *Good Words*. Two of the contributors to the periodical in the 1860s, Ellen Wood and George MacDonald, wrote works that questioned, respectively, the evangelical story of salvation by faith and the more rigid theological identity of the evangelical movement itself. While their motivations were very different, the outcome in both cases confirmed that the novel was not simply an empty vessel that could mediate ideas transparently, but, rather, a form that shaped the evangelical message by insisting that the gospel could be told and read in a greater multitude of ways. What becomes clear in the pages of this periodical is that evangelicalism was changed by its engagement with the form of the novel. My point, however, is that this uncomfortable process of transformation was part of evangelicalism's understanding of itself as a movement committed to embracing innovation and change in order to make the gospel known; the transformation was not, in other words, a marker of secularization.

Turning to Wilkie Collins's *The Moonstone* (1868) and reading it in the light of evangelical debates about biblical hermeneutics in the 1860s enables me to show how another of the evangelical priorities spoken of by Bebbington, biblicism, made its presence felt in a work of fiction that has not typically been thought of as religious in orientation. As my chapter on this novel explains, we are not simply considering how the novel comes to reject a religious perspective in which it no longer believes. *The Moonstone* may be highly critical of evangelical hermeneutics, but it prefers the communal aspect of that tradition to the more specialized modes of interpretation favored by Higher Critics and subsequently taken up by professional literary scholars in the modern academy, who share the belief that texts need historically trained experts who can recover an original moment of understanding. The question of how we read is also integral to the concluding chapter of this book, on Samuel Butler's *The*

Way of All Flesh (1903). Reflecting on why evangelicalism has been treated by literary scholars in the way that it has, I link the privileged role of ironic distance in Butler's narration to the contemporary hermeneutic practice of the many literary critics that have followed in his footsteps. Like Butler's narrator, Overton, modern literary critics typically prefer to stand apart from what is read. They do so because they think distance (and the irony that enables it) grants an epistemic superiority over the knowledge of those who get too close to subjects and allow personal feelings to affect their understanding.[68] Drawing on recent work by Rita Felski and others on the limits of critique, my chapter suggests that our preference for distance has roots in the late Victorian (and Modernist) attempt to throw off an evangelical heritage that emphasizes our personal proximity to and involvement with the books that we read. While that motivation may be less pressing for contemporary critics than it was for authors such as Butler, our widespread failure as critics to deal with the religious threads of our own story is an obstacle to reading the Victorian novel. This is partly because the manifest theological content of the Victorian novel needs to be taken seriously and partly because religion has never completely vanished from the subsequent history of literary criticism, a factor made apparent through the examples and texts that Michael Warner draws on when he writes so insightfully about the "pious labour" of critical reading.[69] However much we might try and pretend otherwise, evangelicalism needs to be recognized as part of the story that we tell about the Victorian novel.

---

68. There is probably some disagreement between the line of thought I advance here and the impulse of Deidre's Lynch's insistence in *Loving Literature* that "our bookish activities need not always be a forum for interpersonal relations." The disagreement is softened, however, by her focus on the love of literature as the primary site for thinking about those interpersonal relations (this is not the mode of interpersonal relations I have in mind here), and her thoughtful account of the "central role that affective labor—our ways of feeling, then, as well as knowing—has been assigned within English studies." Lynch, *Loving Literature*, 23, 1.

69. Michael Warner, "Uncritical Reading," in Gallop, ed., *Polemic*, 36.

CHAPTER 1

The Pilgrim's Progression to *Vanity Fair*

There is little doubt that nineteenth-century evangelicals had concerns about the novel. One anonymous contributor to an 1864 issue of the *Evangelical Magazine* asked readers to think again about their choice of reading lest the "literature of the day" lead to "spiritual lethargy and decay," and similar worries about the effect of reading fiction were articulated in evangelical pulpits, pamphlets, and periodicals.[1] It is easy to see why subsequent generations of literary critics, for whom literature poses no such concern, have dismissed these complaints as an anachronistic response to the rise of fiction in modernity and read them as evidence of how little evangelicalism has to offer our contemporary histories of the novel. But there is a more complex story to be told, one in which evangelicalism is not just a mere footnote. Evangelicals read and wrote fiction throughout the nineteenth century, as I noted in the introduction. And, as I will discuss at greater length in chapter 3, the movement's pragmatic commitment to mission encouraged other evangelicals to explore the evangelistic uses to which the novel might be put, an example of the ingenuity of means that Joseph Stubenrauch locates at the heart of nineteenth-century evangelicalism.[2] Whatever worries evan-

---

1. Anon., "Cleaving to the Dust," *Evangelical Magazine* (1864), 792.
2. See Stubenrauch, *The Evangelical Age of Ingenuity*.

gelicals may have harbored about fiction, they still wrote, produced, and consumed novels, often in large numbers.

What is needed, then, is a more capacious and constructive account of the relationship between evangelicalism and the novel, one that can register the tensions without positioning literary form and religious movement as polar opposites. We might answer this call by talking at length about the evangelical novelists of the period. But, as I explained in the introductory chapter, my fear is that such a move would, ultimately, do little to break down the division that exists in the mind of many critics between evangelical believers and the better-known Victorian authors who repeatedly expressed criticism of the "religious world" in their fiction. Instead of taking this route, my preference is to start by recognizing that preachers and novelists in the nineteenth century were more familiar with one another than their complaints suggest and consider how these complaints reveal a range of shared ideas and practices. This chapter turns to William Makepeace Thackeray's *Vanity Fair* (1848), reading it by way of John Bunyan's *The Pilgrim's Progress* (1678) and arguing that Thackeray's novel is rooted in and shaped by the evangelical tradition. Entertaining this idea requires a suspension of some of our underlying beliefs about the fundamental difference between the period's best-known novelists and the community of readers who sometimes sought to police the reading of their fiction. Only then can we start to consider a different story, one in which evangelical thought is seen to be integral to the way that Victorians thought about the novel.

THE ANXIETY OF INFLUENCE

Evangelical anxieties about the novel were not monolithic. On those occasions when evangelicals criticized the form in explicit terms, a wide variety of reasons were put forward. Some worried that fiction would distract readers from "more spiritual" pursuits, particularly the reading of scripture. Others, such as George McCrie, feared the apparently innocuous means by which the novel could convey "false" religious ideas: "because sound theologians are smiling at the flimsiness of the argument . . . they forget the fascination by which it is recommended."[3] Elsewhere, fellow evangelicals seemed to have had an array of additional concerns: were clerical figures represented in a respectful manner that encouraged confidence in the leaders of the church; were fictional accounts of lapses in individual morality punished in a manner that might

---

3. McCrie, *The Religion of Our Literature*, ix.

reinforce the value of godly living; and would literary accounts of immoral activity prove overly attractive and entice readers into sin? The list of worries about fiction is extensive, and the further down the list we read, the less points cohere. Evangelicals were not always clear about the reasons for their anxiety. In several instances, the language used to complain about the novel is vague, and the reasoning is less assured theologically than we find in many other areas of evangelical writing. Evangelical theology was usually expressed in a straightforward style, reflecting a belief that the good news of the gospel was best served by simplicity and plain speech rather than elaborate thought. But when it came to writing about fiction, terms such as impropriety and immorality were bandied about, with little attempt to explain why some material should be deemed spiritually uplifting and other material dangerous.[4] To return to a quotation used in the previous chapter, the conviction of the judgement that "if a man would build up for himself a strong and useful character, he must read very sparingly fiction of any kind" was not accompanied by any sort of clear explanation as to why this was so.[5] As a result, we are left to try and determine what might be going on.

A fuller account of why evangelicals were anxious about the novel can be found in the chapters that follow. However, one aspect seems central from the outset: evangelicals were concerned because they believed that books had an effect on those who read them. Their understanding of the Word of God as "quick, and powerful, and sharper than any two-edged sword, piercing even to the dividing asunder of soul and spirit, and of the joints and marrow" (Heb. 4:12) laid the foundation for thinking of all words as efficacious in some sense.[6] Although evangelicals saw the Bible as unique, their view of how it worked, particularly scripture's capacity to transform the lives of those who read and heard its words, led them to think about all language in related terms. Words could change the lives of readers, hence the continual question about the sort of works one listened to and read. This belief in the transformative power of words underwrote the centrality of the sermon in evangelical church services,

---

4. Patrick Brantlinger reminds us of the sharp-yet-questionable distinctions employed by Hannah More, whose "'Cheap Repository Tracts' and her improving novel, *Coelebs in Search of a Wife* (1809), are also intended as 'antidotes' to the 'poison' of novels and other dangerous reading material." Brantlinger, *The Reading Lesson*, 6.

5. Anon., "Character: How It Is Formed and What It Is Worth," *Evangelical Magazine* (1866), 376.

6. I differ from Isabel Hofmeyr on this point. She argues that the evangelical commitment to the power of the written word was driven by an imperial agenda, whereas I see an earlier explanation, beginning in scripture and gaining force during the Reformation, when the power of the spoken word through preaching took on a quasi-sacramental role. See Hofmeyr, *The Portable Bunyan*, 18–20.

Anglican and dissenting, and also explains the evangelical commitment to other forms of written publication, from tracts to a myriad of other publishing forms. Writing about the extensive evangelical involvement in popular science publishing during the nineteenth century, Aileen Fyfe explains how evangelicals saw "print as an aid to devotion" and "a divine gift for spreading the word of God."[7] This commitment to print included fiction, which was less distinct from nonfictional evangelical writing than we might think. Evangelical tracts and published sermons regularly employed stories and anecdotes, many of which were apocryphal, and even the most conservative evangelicals did not claim that Christ's stories of the Prodigal Son or Good Samaritan relied on a historical precedent. While evangelicals typically displayed a preference for more factual writing over fiction, they were not intrinsically opposed to the latter, and their willingness to use story as a means to an end led to several evangelicals putting their own hand to the writing of fiction.

If the growth of print culture in the nineteenth century encouraged evangelicals to engage with a literary form they had long been nervous of, there were earlier models on which they could draw. The most prominent fictional text in evangelical circles was *The Pilgrim's Progress*, which Isabel Hofmeyr insists "stood second only to the Bible" in nonconformist circles.[8] Although Bunyan's text was particularly important for nonconformists, it was revered across the evangelical tradition, in part because it offered "a language to talk about the emotional and personal experience of religion."[9] Writing for the Anglican evangelical periodical *The Christian Observer* in 1861 and complaining about some of the novels published elsewhere, one critic highlighted the privileged position of Bunyan's work in the period: "Fiction, when properly employed, may serve the highest and noblest ends; of this the *Pilgrim's Progress* is an admirable example."[10] One of the reasons why Bunyan's novel is so revealing for us as critics of the nineteenth century is that it complicates the idea of audiences divided by their reading of religious material on the one hand and their reading of "secular" novels on the other. Bunyan appealed to evangelicals and nonevangelicals alike. His work was reprinted extensively: directly, in new editions, and indirectly, in adaptions such as Mrs. Sherwood's *The Indian Pilgrim* (1818). There were also what Mary Hammond describes as "didactic" editions, which "seem to be performing the function of a domestic

---

7. Fyfe, *Science and Salvation*, 10, 12.
8. Hofmeyr, *The Portable Bunyan*, 58.
9. Ibid., 59.
10. Anon., "Review of *Lady Elinor Mordaunt*," *The Christian Observer* (1861), 482.

sermon."[11] Perhaps more significant though was the textual afterlife of Bunyan, in the various transnational forms examined by Hofmeyr, and in the world of the nineteenth-century novel, where, as Emma Mason points out, his work haunted the "plot-lines, pedagogies and affective subtexts."[12]

It is hard to think of a more striking example of the Victorian novel's debt to *The Pilgrim's Progress* than *Vanity Fair*. Norman Vance tells us that "it was Bunyan's imaginative realization of a familiar theme in the idea of 'Vanity Fair' in *The Pilgrim's Progress* that gave Thackeray his best-remembered title and a controlling metaphor for his novel to go with it."[13] Thackeray describes the worldliness of Bunyan's "Vanity Fair" scene at length in his own novel and reinforces the textual link established through his title when he describes Brussels as a place "where all the Vanity Fair booths were laid out with the most tempting liveliness and splendor."[14] The metaphoric connection established through both novels' preoccupation with the world of "Vanity Fair" is extensive and far reaching, but there are further ways of thinking about how the two works relate. These include other thematic parallels, such as the mutual interest in (anti-) pilgrimage. While Bunyan's protagonists make their way along a definite though circuitous path, in a manner frequently seen as a step toward the modern bildungsroman, the pilgrims' reliance on divine aid for their journey is at odds with the subsequent emphasis on the role of human agency in stories of individual development. Thackeray's novel offers another ambiguous approach to the development of the self when his characters struggle to go anywhere successfully. *Vanity Fair* is, as the subtitle reminds us, "a novel without a hero," and its characters consistently fail to realize their life goals. Reflecting on Amelia's misguided decision to marry George Osborne, the narrator echoes the language of Bunyan when he describes the journey his character is making and the novelist's account of such a journey: "Was the prize gained—the heaven of life—and the winner still doubtful and unsatisfied? As his hero and heroine pass the matrimonial barrier, the novelist generally drops the curtain, as if the drama were over then: the doubts and struggles of life ended. . . . But our little Amelia was just on the bank of her new country, and was already looking anxiously back."[15]

---

11. Mary Hammond, "*The Pilgrim's Progress* and its Nineteenth-Century Publishers," in Owens and Sim, eds., *Reception, Appropriation, Recollection: Bunyan's* Pilgrim's Progress, 104.

12. Emma Mason, "The Victorians and Bunyan's Legacy," in Duncan-Page, ed., *The Cambridge Companion to Bunyan*, 159.

13. Norman Vance, "Pilgrim's Abounding: Bunyan and the Victorian Novel," in Owens and Sim, eds., *Reception, Appropriation, Recollection: Bunyan's* Pilgrim's Progress, 71.

14. Thackeray, *Vanity Fair*, 340.

15. Ibid., 318–19.

Amelia's concerns at the world she leaves behind would almost certainly have reminded nineteenth-century readers of Christian and Christiana looking back with their own anxieties as they make their way to a new land. Nineteenth-century readers brought up on Bunyan might also have identified two formal debts to the Puritan writer as they read Thackeray's novel: the way in which a commentary on the narrative is prominent in both texts and the texts' mutual proclivity for allegorical names. Bunyan's annotations to his text are mirrored by the frequent interjections of Thackeray's narrator regarding the story he tells; in both cases, the technique reminds us that the world we are reading about is not the only one there is.[16] Allegory lends itself to the realization that reading crosses worlds, and only slightly less explicit than Bunyan's Christian and Christiana escaping the City of Destruction and encountering figures such as Pliable and Worldly-Wise are Thackeray's morally compromised Steyne (stain), the quick-witted Becky *Sharp*, the harsh pupil discipline provided by Dr. Swishtail, and the aptly named auctioneer, Hammerdown.

Although the connections between *The Pilgrim's Progress* and *Vanity Fair* are significant on their own terms, what matters more for the argument of this chapter is the extent to which both novels have come to be seen as major landmarks in the development of the realist novel. Wolfgang Iser explains that "Christian's story is one of an increasing self-awareness, and in this respect it is indisputably a novel, or at least a novel-in-the-making. Self-awareness requires experience, and this is what Christian gains in his confrontation with the world. In the novel, experience is the keynote of the action, whereas in the epic and allegory everything was subsidiary to the idea."[17] The evangelical emphasis on an individual's experience of God proves crucial to uniting this modern emphasis on the self with the Christian tradition, and it is no surprise that experience of the present empirical world is also at the forefront of *Vanity Fair*, with the novel following *The Pilgrim's Progress* in the use of certain realist techniques—including extensive description and a close examination of the interior life of characters—to describe this world. Like Bunyan's work, though, we are reminded that the seen world is not all there is: realism is disrupted throughout Thackeray's novel, not by any supernatural reference but by the mirrors that "inscribe the unseen workings of consciousness," an intrusive narrator, and the frequent reminders of the unreality of the world we are reading about.[18]

---

16. Although I make reference to a single narrator throughout this chapter, I am aware that he takes on very different personas over the course of *Vanity Fair*.

17. Iser, *The Implied Reader*, 28.

18. Brink-Roby, "Psyche: Mirror and Mind in *Vanity Fair*," 126. Later in her essay, Brink-Roby notes the link between glass and mirrors in *Vanity Fair* and the "mirror as an emblem of moral religious self-knowledge" in Bunyan (see 146n32).

There is nothing new or contentious about noting the complex and sometimes contradictory contributions of Bunyan and Thackeray to the realist tradition. George Levine reminds us: "Lurking in the workings of realism is an element of earlier kinds of narratives, exemplary tales, for example, or allegory, what Michael McKeon has described as a 'pedagogical end,' that is, the teaching of precept by example."[19] What is contested, however, is the question of whether the contributions of the Christian religion and the earlier literary forms associated with it remain important for the realist novel or are an inconsequential leftover that can be consigned to the background. For Levine, the answer is clear. His insistence that realism is "predominantly a secular form" continues Georg Lukács's classic description of the novel as the "epic of a world that has been abandoned by God," and he finds even less religious meaning than Lukács in the world portrayed by Victorian writers.[20] Levine anticipates the argument I am making at the start of this chapter when he pauses briefly to consider the lingering presence of Bunyan's work in *Vanity Fair* and its possible significance for our understanding of religion and the novel, but he goes on to dismiss the idea that the presence might have religious weight:

> *Vanity Fair* is a good representative of nineteenth-century realism just because it doggedly insists on confining its narration to the doings of "Vanity Fair." While the very determination to do that and to invoke Bunyan's place can reasonably enough suggest the possibility of a divine if hidden presence in the world or at least of genuine piety, Thackeray's novel treats religion as it treats commercial culture—it is simply a fact of this lower world.[21]

Levine is not alone in the conclusion he reaches. His Rutgers colleague Barry Qualls makes a similar argument when he observes how Rebecca Sharp "ends precisely as so many early pilgrims: 'Virtue Rewarded,' the chapter title announces. But her booth, her reward, is in Vanity Fair. Only the language, with its traditional images from emblematic topography, recalls an older belief in God's intervention in history in order to save."[22]

Yet (evangelical) religion is no simple fact, and its persistence in the Victorian novel cannot be passed over so quickly. The main problem with the

---

19. Levine, *Realism, Ethics and Secularism*, 188.
20. Ibid., 198; Lukács, *The Theory of the Novel*, 88.
21. Levine, *Realism, Ethics and Secularism*, 200.
22. Qualls, *The Secular Pilgrims of Victorian Fiction*, 7. In the acknowledgements for his book, Qualls notes his debt to Levine. The reference to his colleague reminds us just how much influence Levine has had on secular readings of the Victorian novel during the last four decades.

argument Levine and Qualls make is its reliance on extreme transcendence, understood within a narrow and limited frame. In their account, the presence of religion as an active category of thought requires unambiguous reference to the supernatural, the afterlife, the ineffable, and anything else devoid of earthly content. It is hard to know how, in any period of history, the Christian religion might have fulfilled such criteria. The doctrines of the Incarnation and Creation insist that any and every expression of the Christian faith has something to say about the present world and its relation to God. This is particularly important in modernity, where the emphasis on what Charles Taylor has termed the immanent frame ties thinking about transcendence even more closely to immanence. Shaped by its emergence in the early stages of modernity, evangelicalism is willing and able to ascribe divine significance to everyday events.[23] Thus when *Vanity Fair* describes Mr. Crawley reading sermons and pamphlets about the Corn Laws, the mixture is not to be interpreted as a straightforward sign of his compromised religiosity, even if his subsequent actions fall short of the evangelical ideal. An ability to find religious meaning in every area of life is fundamental to the Christian faith, and the decision by Thackeray's narrator to stay away from overtly religious forms of discourse does not have to be viewed as a secular direction for the novel. The narrator notes the difficulty of isolating his story's religious leanings when he writes:

> Sick-bed homilies and pious reflections are, to be sure, out of place in mere story-books, and we are not going (after the fashion of some novelists of the present day) to cajole the public into a sermon, when it is only a comedy that the readers pays his money to witness. But, without preaching, the truth may surely be borne in mind, that the bustle, and triumph, and laughter, and gaiety which Vanity Fair exhibits in public, do not always pursue the performer into private life, and that the most dreary depression of spirits and dismall repentances sometimes overcome him.[24]

The "But" here is easily missed, and critics such as Levine risk making the same mistake as contemporaries of Thackeray by focusing on the ungodli-

---

23. See Taylor, *A Secular Age*, chapter 15. I refer to Taylor here because of the importance of his work on this topic and, more generally, because of my admiration for his thinking about religion and secularity in the modern world. But my one major criticism of Taylor's work revolves around his reliance on an immanent/transcendent binary, which always risks casting premodern Christianity in rarified transcendent terms and wrongly construing what a more religious age might have looked like.

24. Thackeray, *Vanity Fair*, 227.

ness of *Vanity Fair*. In a letter to Robert Bell, who had protested against the "foul atmosphere" of the novel, Thackeray explained that his "object" had been "to indicate, in cheerful terms, that we are for the most part an abominably foolish and selfish people, 'desperately wicked' and all eager after vanities."[25] Although we might want to question the motivations behind the gloss that Thackeray gives to one of his detractors, suspicion about what we are reading is a useful cue on this occasion for deciding what we ourselves should make of the "worldly" content of this nineteenth-century novel.

J. Russell Perkin notes several factors that prompt us to consider the theological ramifications of Thackeray's novel. These include Thackeray's evangelical upbringing, his subsequent commitment to a theology Perkin identifies as "broad church," the inclusion and significance of a preacher on the illustrated cover of *Vanity Fair*, the religious references in Thackeray's letters and journalism, the novel's use of biblical texts such as Ecclesiastes and the Parable of Dives and Lazarus, and Thackeray's intertextual debt to Bunyan. Turning to Mikhail Bakhtin's theory of novelistic dialogism to clarify that he sees Christian belief "as one of the numerous languages of *Vanity Fair*," Perkin describes the religious dimension of the novel as "implied" and insists that it "neither rejects nor affirms Christianity. . . . It is up to the reader to decide."[26] I sympathize with Perkin's position given the novel's narrative complexity and the likely reluctance of many readers to think of Thackeray theologically. Yet I want to make a stronger claim by highlighting *Vanity Fair*'s debt to evangelical thought and reading it as evidence for the wider influence of evangelicalism on the mainstream Victorian novel. To support this claim, the remainder of the chapter is organized into three parts: an argument that the burden the reader is asked to bear by Bunyan and Thackeray is rooted in and shaped by the evangelical tradition; an exploration of the evangelically inflected "message" of *Vanity Fair*, which, despite its accompanying skepticism, asks us to see the present world with different eyes; and a concluding suggestion that learning to look for the signs of religion and its transformation in modernity, as Danièle Hervieu-Léger encourages, might lead to a more theologically nuanced account of how evangelicalism shaped the world of the Victorian novel.[27]

---

25. Quoted in Ray, "Vanity Fair: One Version of the Novelist's Responsibility," 94.
26. Perkin, *Theology and the Victorian Novel*, 35, 54. The chapter from which these quotations are taken is entitled "The Implied Theology of *Vanity Fair*."
27. Hervieu-Léger, *Religion as A Chain of Memory*, 29.

THE BURDEN ON THE READER

Critical disagreements as to whether *Vanity Fair* should be interpreted primarily as a secular or religious text continue an older set of debates about *The Pilgrim's Progress,* a work praised for a variety of reasons and rewritten for different ends. Although the theological content of *The Pilgrim's Progress* is more overt than it is in *Vanity Fair,* Bunyan's book has not always been read with the Christian religion in mind. "When books travel," explains Hofmeyr, "they change shape. They are excised, summarized, abridged, and bowdlerized by the new intellectual formations into which they migrate."[28] Assessing the reception of *The Pilgrim's Progress* in nineteenth-century Britain, Vincent Newey insists that the "process most regularly reflected in works that recollect Bunyan is that of secularisation, whether as loss . . . or as opportunity."[29] Many Victorians who identified as Christian and found spiritual sustenance in Bunyan's writing would have disagreed with Newey's claim, however, and while nineteenth-century readings should not automatically be privileged over recent interpretations, they do remind us of the historicity of all critical reading and the limits of our interpretative vistas. Our willingness to interrogate the judgments passed down to us becomes especially important when we consider that Newey's nontheological reading is shared by much of the post-Victorian critical tradition. That tradition has often sought justification for its nonreligious emphasis in Coleridge's famous distinction between Bunyan's theology and art, a distinction "that has had a profound (if in some ways also baneful) influence right up to our present day."[30] If theology and art can be separated, many scholars reason, then it becomes possible to look at one without thinking too much about the other.

There are key exceptions to this critical neglect of Bunyan's theology, the most significant of which is Michael Davies's *Graceful Reading: Theology and Narrative in the Works of John Bunyan* (2002). Attempting to deal with the "complex literary issues of narrative construction and textual manipulation . . . through (and not in spite of) the tenets of a theology that is so frequently amputated from them," Davies seeks to reconstitute the theological background and correct a popular but overly simplistic view of Bunyan's Calvinism as harsh, condemnatory, and restrictive. Davies insists that there is a "salvatory imperative" to *The Pilgrim's Progress* and details how the intended work

---

28. Hofmeyr, *The Portable Bunyan,* 2–3.
29. Vincent Newey, "Bunyan's Afterlives: Case Studies," in Owens and Sims, eds., *Reception, Appropriation, Recollection,* 28.
30. Owens and Sim, "Introduction," *Reception, Appropriation, Recollection,* 18.

of the narrative is to enable readers to appreciate the graceful operation of Christian salvation:

> In order to read one's self and the Word "grace-fully," according to the experience of faith, Bunyan primarily asserts that a very different hierarchy of understanding must be invoked by the believer, one involving not a worldly, carnal reason nor a merely intellectual comprehension of salvation but one that is largely irrational, unworldly, and illogical: this demands a reading of "things unseen" via the light of the Spirit, not of the mind. It is this need to read the self in terms of an unworldly faith that Bunyan's narratives always, and often quite forcefully, encourage in the reader.[31]

Davies's argument is helpfully attuned to the processes of reading as well as more overtly theological matters. Yet his insistence on restoring a seventeenth-century Puritan context to our reading can, as Beth Lynch observes, risk "focusing on the textual agenda, rather than the textual experience of the narratives in question."[32] This is most apparent toward the end of *Graceful Reading* when Davies complains about the "subsequent reception of *The Pilgrim's Progress* (both in literary studies and amongst its many general readers of the last three centuries) as either a forerunner of the novel or an imaginatively didactic children's story." This reception, Davies insists, "says as much about its deradicalization as a Nonconformist text as it does about the cultural climates in which such misreadings have been authorized since the book's initial publication."[33]

The problem with insisting on a reading of *The Pilgrim's Progress* governed by the contextual framework of historical theology and authorial intent is its intolerance of other experiences of reading. What are we to do with those who read the text with something else in mind—whether that be the missionaries who, according to Hofmeyr, sought to use Bunyan for imperial ends; those involved with the emergence of English literature as an academic discipline, who saw the writer as a cornerstone of Englishness; or others still, who follow Coleridge in preferring the art of Bunyan over his theology?[34] How are we to engage with their readings? Up until his conclusion, Davies finds room for different readers and creates space for their views alongside his interest in

---

31. Davies, *Graceful Reading*, 4, 6, 7.
32. Lynch, *John Bunyan and the Language of Conviction*, 6–7.
33. Davies, *Graceful Reading*, 290–91.
34. Hofmeyr discusses the role of Bunyan in the emergence of English literature as a discipline in chapter 10 of *The Portable Bunyan*.

the shape of the narrative. Drawing on Stanley Fish's theory of interpretative communities, Davies explains:

> What the text [i.e., *The Pilgrim's Progress*] teaches the reader is that interpreting the texts of the Word and the self in the light of a faith in a doctrine of grace is inseparable from a revolution in what Fish refers to as one's "perceptual habits." What *The Pilgrim's Progress* continually underscores in fact, is that interpreting and understanding correctly in spiritual matters is subject to and conditional upon an experimental knowledge of faith in grace that has little to do with conventional processes of rationalization or epistemology. It is for this reason that a character like Talkative is given such an important role in *The Pilgrim's Progress*.[35]

The reference to Fish is revealing and explains how Davies can make room for the reader whilst also seeking to regulate his or her reading. Davies's argument here follows a similar trajectory to Fish's arguments in *Surprised by Sin* (1967) and an article on *The Pilgrim's Progress* published by Fish just a few years later (1971). In these early works, Fish emphasizes the experience of reading but locates it within a scheme that the author anticipates and directs through his or her writing. Our growing realization that the Pilgrim's journey is "antiprogressive" is seen by Fish as part of a deliberate attempt to subvert "its basic figure" and encourage readers to see that the "truth about the world is not to be found within its own confines or configurations, but from the vantage point of a perspective that transforms it," a perspective which, for Bunyan, insists on God's agency in directing our journeys rather than our own ability to make them.[36]

For a critical generation familiar with the essential tenets of reader-response theory, it is easy to find fault with the accounts of reading provided here by Fish. Our own very different readings of texts suggest that readers are not as malleable or obedient as authors and scholars might sometimes hope, and when the next stage of Fish's writing (i.e., the essays of the 1970s, which led to the publication of *Is There a Text in This Class?* in 1980) alerted us to the ways in which interpretative communities construct meaning as much as finding it, there was an understandable question about where the emphasis on the reader could take us. Some of Fish's most vociferous detractors took his argument for the power of the interpreter to heart by reading him in a way he did not intend and claiming that he was encouraging a state of anarchy

---

35. Davies, *Graceful Reading*, 250–51.
36. Fish, "Progress in *The Pilgrim's Progress*," 265, 270.

in which readers were free to read texts in any way they chose. Others were quick to spot Fish's concern with the limited agency of the reader, understood in his earlier work by thinking about manipulative authors and then, in *Is There a Text in This Class?*, with reference to all powerful interpretative communities. Faced with an apparent interpretative dead end in the work of Fish that left little space for thinking about the very reader that his work claimed to be interested in, many critics took the opportunity to go back to business as usual, relying on a hermeneutic that concerned itself with recovering what a text meant for its initial audience.[37]

I am aware how much is left out of this potted history, including the more recent critical interest in historical accounts of how Victorian texts were read and the extensive work on affect that has been prominent over the last decade or so.[38] Deidre Lynch provides an erudite account of how the growing awareness that our "reluctance to engage the affective attachments that have connected readers to the institutions of English has inhibited us from bringing our histories of aesthetics between 1750 and 1850 into dialogue with accounts of this century as a pivotal epoch in the history of emotion, intimacy and sexuality."[39] All too often, however, the uncomfortable idea that readers, you and me included, are implicated in and shaped by the novels we read gets left behind as our criticism seeks refuge in historical surveys of the reading experience and the effect of that reading on others, in "what nineteenth-century readers and writers *thought* they were doing."[40] The tendency is apparent in Leah Price's *How To Do Things with Books in Victorian Britain* (2012): attentiveness to the reader gives way to an interest in nonreading, "thing theory," and the different ways in which books were distributed, sold, and handled. Price's work is brilliant, mesmerizing, and theoretically innovative; a major contribution to book history and literary criticism; and a book that pushes readers to think differently at every turn. But her emphasis on the nonreaderly side of our interaction with books can end up providing yet another excuse to avoid coming to terms with our own participation in the reading of the Victorian literature that we discuss.[41]

---

37. See chapter 4 for further discussion of the relationship between nineteenth-century biblical hermeneutics and the ongoing preference in literary studies for readings based on historical recovery.
38. See, for instance, McKelvy, *The English Cult of Literature*; Dames, *The Physiology of the Novel*; Ablow, ed., *The Feeling of Reading*; and Lynch, *Loving Literature*.
39. Lynch, *Loving Literature*, 11.
40. Rachel Ablow, "Introduction," in Ablow, ed., *The Feeling of Reading*, 3.
41. Price writes: "The tract did not create what Roger Chartier calls 'communities of readers,' much less what Stanley Fish calls 'interpretive communities'—if only because to be inter-

Not only does the work of Fish offer a vital point of connection between literary studies and the important philosophical hermeneutical questions discussed by Hans-Georg Gadamer and Paul Ricoeur; it also provides tools for reflecting on the type of reading that people like me undertake in our work as literary scholars. Scholars like to present the results of their professional reading in ways that make the story they tell sound authoritative, but our interpretative contribution to the stories we tell involves choices that can be contested. While our interpretative contributions are sometimes unconscious (hence Fish's emphasis on the communities that shape us), our agency is always at work when we make sense of a text. The toll of such work may help explain why recent Victorian scholars such as Andrew H. Miller and Leah Price continue to find value in talking about the "burden" of reading, despite their theoretical distance from older accounts of the role of the reader.[42] If readers remain involved in the reading (or nonreading) of books then there is a reason to examine the work this involves.

Although the size of *Vanity Fair* might seem to be the most immediate burden for readers coming to Thackeray's novel for the first time, the work of interpretation is framed otherwise as Thackeray's narrative expands the burden-of-the-book motif that we find in *The Pilgrim's Progress*. Kevin Seidel points out that the "close association that Bunyan creates between the scriptures and his own writing prevents 'the Book' in the opening scene" from being a burden "equated [solely] with either *Pilgrim's Progress* or the Bible."[43] This textual ambivalence is continued in *Vanity Fair* as Thackeray imagines the burden of reading his text as an exemplar of the broader burden we bear when reading fiction. Kate Flint tells us that "*Vanity Fair* is, famously, a novel in which the burden of interpretation is left up to the reader. . . . What is more, *Vanity Fair* is a novel which persistently draws attention to the process of reading itself. . . . The attitudes towards reading which are alluded to in the text intersect with widely circulating debates about reading in the 1840s: debates found in literary magazines and medical textbooks, in conduct manuals and religious tracts, as well as within fiction."[44] With these debates in mind, Thackeray imagines reading to be work as much as pleasure; his novel challenges us to consider the effect of reading, to grapple with the interpretative

---

preted, tracts would actually have had to be read." Price, *How to Do Things with Books in Victorian Britain*, 151–52.

42. I am thinking here of the title of Miller's *The Burdens of Perfection* and the chapter on the "Burden of the Book" in Price's *How To Do Things with Books in Victorian Britain*. See also Lane, *The Burdens of Intimacy: Psychoanalysis and Victorian Masculinity*.

43. Seidel, "Pilgrim's Progress and the Book," 510.

44. Kate Flint, "Women, Men and the Reading of *Vanity Fair*," in Raven, Small and Tadmor, eds., *The Practice and Representation of Reading in England*, 246–47.

choices involved, and to come to terms with the personal disclosures reading forces upon us. When the narrator concludes ironically that we "can shut up the box and the puppets, for *our* play is played out," he appears to be giving us permission to silence the revelations as much as telling us that they are at an end.[45]

More than most other Victorian novels with something to say about reading, *Vanity Fair* emphasizes the personal burden of interpretation. The term "personal" is problematic, I realize, and it is a topic I will return to in the concluding chapter. For now, the reference should be understood as referring to our reflections on what a particular text means for "me," the shifting, elusive, and constructed subject who reads a given novel. How do I think about the emotions and choices that follow from my engagement with a text, to the extent that I reflect on them at all? Rather than encouraging us to think that reading novels is all about a distant view of others, Thackeray's narrative insists on our proximity to the stories we read. This proximity can be discomforting, as in the moment where many readers in the academy are forced to join with Victorian readers in confronting the middle-class assumptions they bring to their reading of Rebecca Sharp: "The world is a looking-glass, and gives back to every man the reflection of his own face. Frown at it, and it will in turn look sourly upon you; laugh at it and with it, and it is a jolly kind companion; and so let all young persons take their choice."[46] Our "choice" as readers includes considering the attitudes we bring to the novel. In contrast to the emancipatory vision of reading proffered by the bildungsroman, Thackeray figures reading as burdensome and difficult. When Lord Steyne thinks he has penetrated Rebecca Sharp's performance and found her to be "unsurpassable in lies," he reveals himself to be equally entangled in a misunderstanding of his own motivations and position.[47] But Thackeray's analogy of the novel as a looking glass means that we have to think through the personal implications of this reading and consider whether the blemishes we find so readily in Lord Steyne are also reflected in the stains that mark our own state of heart.

Thackeray's preface to *Vanity Fair* warns that we will find ourselves actively "walking through" the "exhibition" as we read the novel.[48] In the letter to Robert Bell quoted from already in this chapter, Thackeray goes on to tell his interlocutor that having taken readers through the exhibition of *Vanity Fair*, he wants "to leave everybody dissatisfied and unhappy at the end of the story" as "we ought all to be with our own and all other stories. Good God, don't I

---

45. Thackeray, *Vanity Fair*, 878, emphasis mine.
46. Ibid., 15.
47. Ibid., 664.
48. Ibid., 1.

see (in that may-be cracked and warped looking glass in which I am always looking) my own weaknesses, wickednesses, lusts, follies, shortcomings?"[49] Whether or not Thackeray's preoccupation with sin is as clear-cut as his narrator and letter suggests, his novel does seem concerned with prompting in readers something more than just light-hearted amusement at the faults of others. Despite admitting that there is plenty to entertain us in the novel, the narrator insists that "the general impression is one more melancholy than mirthful": "When you come home, you sit down, in a sober, contemplative frame of mind, and apply yourself to your books or your business."[50]

A preference for applying oneself and being "doers of the word and not hearers only" was integral to evangelicalism.[51] The emphasis on application was evident in the movement's activism, its preference for reading scripture with an eye to the personal implications for one's daily life, and its distrust of theological investigation that appeared esoteric or too heavily theorized. Thackeray's talk of applied reading does not make him an evangelical, any more than his use of Bunyan does, but its presence at the start of *Vanity Fair* and the repeated calls for readers to consider the personal implications of their reading suggest that the evangelical movement had more influence on his novel than has been appreciated hitherto. Although scenes such as the one in which Mrs. Kirk questions Amelia to see whether she was "awakened" and a "professing Christian" can fool us into thinking that the narrator is unaffected by the evangelical tradition he describes, the evangelical tradition taught Thackeray to appreciate the effect of reading, and this lesson is replayed throughout *Vanity Fair* as we are prompted to wake from moral complacency and comprehend the compromised state of our souls.[52]

Writing in a different setting about a more overtly religious story, one evangelical commentator wrote: "With Bunyan's Pilgrim in our eye, we cannot doubt the possible utility of this kind of writing."[53] For Thackeray, to open the pages of any novel and be involved with its narrative was a potentially transformative act, not because of general moral lessons that might be learned along the way but because the mental space enabled through novel reading could enable an investigation of the self and one's sinful state. Although John Calvin, Martin Luther, and a long list of other Protestant theologians insisted that identifying one's sinful state was only possible through the work

---

49. Qtd. in Ray, "Vanity Fair: One Version of the Novelist's Responsibility," 94.
50. Thackeray, *Vanity Fair*, 1.
51. Anon., "Working Christians," *The Evangelical Magazine* (1866), 88.
52. Thackeray, *Vanity Fair*, 331.
53. Anon., "Religious Stories: The Ministry of Life. By Maria Louisa Charlesworth," *The Christian Observer* (1859), 56.

of God's Holy Spirit, evangelicals typically emphasized human participation in the work of self-reflection and associated God's work more with the salvation that could be received once individuals had repented of what they had done wrong. In so much as reading could contribute to a realization of one's sin, books were a burden that made an impression on one's spiritual journey. Evangelicals may have been concerned that books might affect readers in undesirable ways but the underlying reason for that concern—the recognition that there is a personal burden to reading—was a perspective that Thackeray shared with evangelicalism and one that he made integral to *Vanity Fair*.

THROUGH DIFFERENT EYES

Is it reasonable to suggest that *Vanity Fair*'s concern with reading is linked to the book-as-burden motif we find in *The Pilgrim's Progress* and see repeated throughout nineteenth-century evangelicalism? Patrick Parrinder thinks not, insisting that "Thackeray wishes to be thought the least Puritanical of all novelists."[54] It is easy to see why we might want to distance the author of *Vanity Fair* from the puritan concern that "metaphors make us blind" and subsequent nineteenth-century evangelical anxieties about the morality of the literature by which "the *mind* of the nation is, so to speak, moulded and stereotyped."[55] The narrator of *Vanity Fair* seems to delight in the immoral acts and persons he describes, or at least to delight in their potential for shocking readers. Reminding us that "this history has 'Vanity Fair' for a title, and . . . Vanity Fair is a very vain, wicked, foolish place, full of all sorts of humbugs and falseness and pretensions," the narrator dismisses the option of preaching strongly against immorality and teases readers about the vice he has planned for his novel: "I warn my 'kyind friends,' then, that I am going to tell a story of harrowing villainy and complicated—but, as I trust, intensely interesting—crime. . . . The present Number will be very mild. Others——but we will not anticipate *those*."[56] Although the novel's antiheroine is never apprehended, many of the "immoral" activities that take place in *Vanity Fair* are punished within the narrative or described in ways that acknowledge the wrongdoing involved. Yet the novel's refusal to emphasize these judgments, the narrator's apparent fascination with the crimes described, and the ironic and sometimes flippant mode of narration combine to give Thackeray's novel a different

---

54. Parrinder, *Nation and Novel*, 234.
55. Bunyan, *The Pilgrim's Progress*, 46; Anon., "The Literature of Our Day," *The Christian Observer* (1862), 281.
56. Thackeray, *Vanity Fair*, 95–96.

tone and feel from Bunyan and much of the nineteenth-century evangelical tradition.

While a critical distinction between the attitude of evangelical moralists and the narrator of *Vanity Fair* appears justified, there is, as so often proves the case when reading the Victorian novel, another perspective available.[57] To describe Thackeray as existing in opposition to Puritanism, or to distinguish too strongly between Thackeray and his contemporary evangelicals, is to offer the sort of counsel that we find coming from the mouth of Bunyan's Mr. Worldly-Wiseman. When Mr. Worldly-Wiseman notes his acquaintance with "Legality," a man that "hath skill to cure those that are somewhat crazed in their wits with their burden," and directs Christian toward this figure as a means of relieving him of his religious burden, he sounds as though he knows what the Christian faith is really all about and is qualified to explicate its reading habits.[58] But Bunyan quickly insists otherwise. In a similar vein, the initial ease with which we might distinguish between *Vanity Fair*'s amoral stance and the moral agenda of evangelicalism relies on a theological misunderstanding of evangelicalism's ethical position. Although I will leave a fuller discussion of evangelicalism's theology of goodness until chapter 3, when I consider the work of the periodical *Good Words*, we can anticipate this later discussion by noting two things: first, Thackeray's novel is more interested in ethics than its light-hearted tone has led some readers to believe, and second, there is more to evangelical ethics than policing a limited range of personal activities.

For a book written by an author alleged to be so far from Puritanism, *Vanity Fair* is surprisingly moral in its perspective.[59] Despite the refusal to moralize in the didactic mode expected by his implied audience, Thackeray's narrator repeatedly urges readers to think through the ethical ramifications of what they are reading. On one oft-cited occasion, the novel's narrator takes the moral high ground and critiques the ethical inconsistency of his implied readership:

> We must pass over a part of Mrs Rebecca Crawley's biography with that lightness and delicacy which the world demands—the moral world, that has,

---

57. Explaining how the novel form helped Victorians pursue a moral perfectionism influenced by the evangelical tradition and overcome the skepticism that threatened to disable the will, Miller argues: "Studying what it is to have a point of view; studying what it is to change a point of view; and engineering such a change: these are the tasks the novel set for itself as it participated in the period's perfectionism." Miller, *The Burdens of Perfection*, 55.

58. Bunyan, *The Pilgrim's Progress*, 62.

59. John Sutherland acknowledges that many commentators have found Thackeray's text to be "a powerfully moral novel." Sutherland, "Introduction" to the Oxford World's Classics edition of Thackeray, *Vanity Fair*, xxv.

perhaps, no particular objection to vice, but an insuperable repugnance to hearing vice called by its proper name. There are things we do and know perfectly well in Vanity Fair, though we never speak them. . . . It is only when their naughty names are called out that your modesty has any occasion to show alarm or sense of outrage, and it has been the wish of the present writer, all through this story, deferentially to submit to the fashion at present prevailing, and only to hint at the existence of wickedness in a light, easy, and agreeable manner, so that nobody's fine feelings may be offended.[60]

For the narrator of these words, the problem with contemporary morality is not its ethical orientation but rather that its moral vision does not go far enough.

Thackeray's attempt to impress upon readers the limitations of their moral vision is in line with the underlying theology of evangelical morality, even if that theology was not always obvious when evangelicals made some of their more austere moral judgments. For evangelicals, the question of whether a particular action should be judged right or wrong was less important than the perceived disjunction between the fallen state of the world and the kingdom of God. Convinced that human sinfulness was rooted more deeply than specific sins of commission or omission, evangelicals sought to view the world with different eyes and encouraged individuals to reflect on the state of their heart and question whether the pursuit of social norms was consistent with the demands of the gospel. The difficulty of that question may explain why evangelicals sometimes found it easier to pronounce on discrete areas, such as perceived sexual immorality, but even when evangelical morality did become limited in its concerns, it still continued to emphasize the state of one's heart over the outward act. Evangelicalism may not have been the only tradition to locate personal transformation at the center of its ethical vision but there are more than enough references in *Vanity Fair*—the link to Bunyan, the narrator's comparison of himself with a preacher, and so on—to suggest that the narrator's attempts to challenge our moral sense owes much to the evangelical tradition. Our overwhelming sense that Thackeray is not on the side of the evangelicals makes it hard to appreciate this debt. Yet disliking a group of people does not prevent someone from being influenced by them, and the language of evangelicalism is evident throughout, as when Thackeray's narrator notes drily that "remorse is the least active of all moral senses—the very easiest to be deadened when wakened: and in some never wakened at all."[61]

---

60. Thackeray, *Vanity Fair*, 812.
61. Ibid., 534.

The evasiveness of Thackeray's narrator was a problem for those evangelicals who found the range of ethical positions in fiction difficult and wanted a more explicit and stable moral code in their reading material. Many midcentury evangelicals approached morality from a largely conservative standpoint, asking whether the literature of the day was "lawful, useful and safe for Christian minds" and an appropriate means of finding one's "moral bearings."[62] Yet to believe as evangelicals did that the Kingdom of God called individuals to reorientate their view of the world and confront the deeply rooted nature of their sinful understanding was consistent with the emphasis in *Vanity Fair* on pointing out our faults rather than telling us precisely how to live. The novel's focus on alerting readers to what was wrong with the world was a perspective consistent with the evangelical tradition, and in other settings, evangelicals would have nodded their heads in agreement when reading the insinuation that Rebecca's Sharp habit of going to church, busying "herself in works of piety" and having her name on "all the Charity Lists" were not trustworthy signs of a genuine Christian faith.[63] Although nineteenth-century evangelicals were more comfortable with action than theoretical reflection, they believed the former to be a sign of an inward reality and remained acutely aware that the appearance of goodness needed careful discernment. They knew, in other words, that things were not always as they seemed. In this respect, at least, the rooting out of evangelical hypocrisy by some Victorian novelists can be seen as continuing evangelical practice as much as confronting it. Indeed, it may be that the competition implied by this convergence—as some novelists took on a role previously thought to be the preserve of the preacher—played a role in inciting evangelical suspicions about the work that novels undertook.

Allegory was the central means by which Bunyan challenged his audience to see the world differently and observe a spiritual reality beyond the world we experience through the senses. Carolynn Van Dyke reminds us that "the crisis that initiates the pilgrimage is, in fact, Christian's discovery of himself in two worlds at once."[64] Describing the different states that coexist throughout *The Pilgrim's Progress*, Davies explains: "Allegory is supremely suited to Bunyan's ontological poetics because by nature, it would seem, allegory acts to make the reader self-conscious about interpretation while enabling the author to dramatize such procedures of interpretation in the very action of the narrative."[65] By urging readers to think about two orders of signification, allegory ensures that they are made aware of their need to interpret the things

---

62. Anon., "The Literature of Our Day," 280.
63. Thackeray, *Vanity Fair*, 877.
64. Van Dyke, *The Fiction of Truth*, 170.
65. Davies, *Graceful Reading*, 222.

they read and see how "human words are creatures of the moment, even, as are the bodies of those who speak the words; fleetingly they are present and then they pass away."[66] But the apparent unity and simplicity of allegory also seeks to keep the hermeneutical task uncomplicated, a factor that was especially important for a Protestant movement committed to the idea of truth as plain and self-evident. Although Thackeray's use of allegory is less extensive than his seventeenth-century predecessor, and arguably part of a more complex hermeneutical strategy, he shares Bunyan's recognition that literature can help us see the world differently. Thackeray adds other visual cues to his use of allegory, from the illustrations that play such an important role in the novel to a choice of vocabulary that plays on the slippage between the *scenes* acted out and the things that are *seen* by readers. Like *The Pilgrim's Progress* and the evangelical tradition that held Bunyan's book in such high regard, the narrative of *Vanity Fair* constitutes an attempt to view the world through different eyes.[67]

In certain respects, *Vanity Fair* is more willing than Bunyan and his theological descendants to turn the critical gaze upon religious groups and practices. Complaining about a group of genteel ladies who "were severe and Evangelical, and held by Exeter Hall," Thackeray's narrator suggests that the evangelical tradition has become so introspective and enamored by charismatic pulpit performances that it is no longer able to see the world through different eyes.[68] But focusing on the novel's exposure of religious activity can blind us to the way in which all areas of life and every person in the novel are marked by a failure of critical vision. Thackeray embraces the ontological poetics used by Bunyan and reminds us that the whole of humanity struggles to see the "true" state of things. Rebecca Sharp's eyes are said to be capable of shooting someone dead with a glance, but her ocular power has limited reach when it comes to seeing beneath the machinations of others; Rawdon Crawley's suspicion of his wife makes him "very watchful," but he still fails to see what is really going on between his wife and Lord Steyne; and even the novelist, who, as "it has been said before, knows everything," is led to admit the limitations of any claim to an all-knowing eye.[69] By likening himself to "the Manager of the Performance [who] sits before the curtain on the boards, and

---

66. Jeffrey, *People of the Book*, 69.
67. I am arguing here for a degree of continuity with the training in discernment that Christian undergoes in *The Pilgrim's Progress*: "Part of the discernment he attains is stylistic, particularly in the way that he learns to see through deception." Roger Pooley, "Plain and Simple: Bunyan and Style," in Keeble, ed., *John Bunyan: Conventicle and Parnassus*, 101.
68. Thackeray, *Vanity Fair*, 782.
69. Ibid., 16, 667, 453.

looks into the Fair," the narrator of the "Before the Curtain" preface figures himself as part of the world he describes, acknowledging that he is no more able than his characters to see things as plainly as he would like.[70]

The way in which Thackeray's novel recognizes the potential deceitfulness of all written documents has far reaching consequences. As Brantlinger points out: "If Vanity Fair—that is, society—is counterfeit, then so is its supposedly creditworthy reflection, *Vanity Fair*."[71] But there is a long-standing religious tradition of attending to sinfulness even though one's vantage point is also fallen. Following the logic of Fish in his reading of Bunyan, we might say that the recurring failures to see the world clearly in *Vanity Fair* are part of the process by which we learn to see the world through different eyes: "There is in *The Pilgrim's Progress* an inverse relationship between visibility and reliability, and Christian's first conversation with Evangelist not only establishes this relationship, but implicates the reader in it."[72] A similar relationship exists in *Vanity Fair*, with the things that appear most transparent, including Dobbin's love for Amelia, proving to be otherwise as the events of the novel unfold. In the case of Becky, ostensible signs of wealth and affection are shown to be false, and the pattern gradually trains us to be skeptical of all that this world offers. Although Judith Fisher argues that Thackeray's "'world without God' . . . must be understood as having resulted from the absence of a dominant system; that is, a world in which no one voice is *known* to be right," the evangelical tradition, especially in its dissenting Calvinist manifestation, often saw skepticism toward human knowledge and social appearances as a sign of the religious conscience rather than evidence for the secular view imagined by Fisher.[73] As Becky becomes an inadvertent guide to the misleading claims of modern society, and we are made aware of our own lack of direction, readers are trained in the tradition inaugurated by Bunyan. John Schad writes: "If Becky's wandering mimics our experience of reading *Vanity Fair* then we too are cast going nowhere, a possibility with which we have always read in that our novel's very title implies a failure to arrive, the failure to arrive at the Celestial City."[74]

A novel that trains readers to see the world through Christian eyes provides a different experience to the one that Levine finds in *Vanity Fair* when he insists on its empirical commitment to the simple facts of this lower world. Indeed, the reading education provided by Thackeray is markedly differ-

---

70. Ibid., 1.
71. Brantlinger, *The Reading Lesson*, 131.
72. Fish, "Progress in *The Pilgrim's Progress*," 272.
73. Fisher, *Thackeray's Skeptical Narrative*, 10.
74. Schad, "Reading the Long Way Round: Thackeray's *Vanity Fair*," 29.

ent from the process detailed by Chris Otter, who, writing in another context, describes how nineteenth-century individuals were trained to view the world scientifically: "The liberal subject was a self-judging being, rational and objective. Vision provided the phenomenological structure for such potential, providing the impression that judgment was being formed wholly from within the body rather than from a complex perceptual interaction with the world. This is the structure necessary for empiricism, induction, and those approaches to reality generically termed *scientific*."[75] A Christian view of the world is not necessarily opposed to a scientific one; and I do not meant to imply that the vision detailed by Otter is the only form of scientific training available.[76] My point, rather, is that the skepticism of *Vanity Fair* does not necessarily mean what Levine, Fisher, and others suggest; it can instead be seen as a continuation of the religious training of the reader's eye provided by *The Pilgrim's Progress*.

TELLING RELIGIOUS STORIES ABOUT THE VICTORIAN NOVEL

The suggestion that *Vanity Fair*'s interest in the personal ethics of reading can (or should) be viewed as a consequence of evangelicalism is one that I expect some readers to contest. For many, the story of modernity is one in which religion has been left behind, and Levine has been at the forefront of those who have extended this view to our reading of the nineteenth-century novel. I have referred to Levine at several points already, in recognition of the significance and influence of his scholarship on the novel, and, like many others, I see him as one of the great commentators on the Victorian realist novel. But that does not mean agreeing with all that he has to say, and I am not persuaded by the arguments he makes for the form's inherent secularity. Turning to the episode in *Vanity Fair* when the narrator refuses to repeat or overhear the prayers of Amelia, Levine concludes: "The narrator closes the door on Amelia's prayers because, he claims, these are not the province of Vanity Fair, but it would be no stretch to suggest that Thackeray himself closed off a representation of that kind of piety just because it would change the nature of the novel itself."[77] Yet

---

75. Otter, *The Victorian Eye*, 48.
76. Otter notes the parallel between the liberal subject who can see for his or herself and the Protestant tradition of thinking about the world as "unveiled to all, and not in need of deciphering by privileged hermeneuts" (48). The evangelical emphasis on worlds and words being self-evident is a subject I return to in chapter 4.
77. Levine, *Realism, Ethics and Secularism*, 221.

the amiable and fluent nature of Levine's writing style masks how much of a stretch we are being asked to make. Thackeray's narrator describes Amelia's prayers as "secrets," but her devotions are not wholly different from the type of prayer advocated by Jesus in the Gospels—"But thou, when thou prayest, enter into thy closet, and when thou hast shut thy door, pray to thy Father which is in secret" (Matt. 6:6)—and they are certainly in line with the more internal forms of piety favored by nineteenth-century evangelicals. Furthermore, Levine's equation here of secrecy with avoidance fails to engage with the complex role that the private realm, in all its forms, plays in the nineteenth-century novel. If we admit the possibility of religion into our thinking rather than explaining away every instance of belief, and if we use markers of Christianity as a prompt for searching out other forms of evangelical influence in the novel, we end up with a very different account than the one provided by Levine.

Evangelicalism does not have a monopoly on the idea that reading shapes and is shaped by our beliefs. We might think, for instance, of the habitual practices of reading encouraged by other Christian traditions, such as the Oxford Movement; the rhythms of rereading that Deidre Lynch links to devotional practice but considers in the context of canon formation and the development of English literature; and the widespread "confusion of the religious and the literary" that William McKelvy explores so carefully in *The English Cult of Literature: Devoted Readers, 1774–1880* (2007).[78] Yet the particular evangelical interest in the effect of reading books offers an important means of registering the movement's influence on the Victorian novel. This, in turn, has the potential to disrupt the regularity with which scholars write evangelical religion out of the story they tell about the period's fiction. While some evangelical interpretative communities might wonder whether these omissions are deliberate, as seems to be the case with Levine, the reasons for the lack of reference to evangelicalism are usually more benign. All of us miss things when we tell stories, and we typically miss the aspects that we find unremarkable, confusing or difficult to fit into our existing view of the world. The stories we tell about the novel, like the stories the novel tells us, are shaped by the teleological impulses of readers as much as the events recorded in the narrative. If some accounts of realism can lead us to think that we stand apart from the stories we read, other expressions of the nineteenth-century novel, such as the ones given to us by Thackeray, remind us that our presuppositions affect our reading.

Becky's reading in *Vanity Fair* exemplifies the widespread tendency to read in our own idiosyncratic ways. It is noticeable, for example, how she reads

---

78. McKelvy, *The English Cult of Literature*, 127. See the discussion of Keble's *The Christian Year* in King, *Imagined Spiritual Communities*, chapter 4, and the exploration of how rereading shaped constructions of the canon in Lynch, *Loving Literature*, chapter 4.

Arabian Nights and *Guthrie's Geography*, two books foregrounding their own sense of direction, with a bias to her future situation and the perceived need to secure a husband.[79] Her reading reorients the texts, and although Becky prides herself on the ability to fabricate tales by making them appear "neat, simple and artless," the narrator suggests elsewhere that her skill as a storyteller is also the quality that marks her tales as false.[80] When Becky attempts to persuade Pitt Crawley that her relationship with Lord Steyne is innocent, the narrator implies she is lying by telling us that she presents a "perfectly connected story."[81] There are traces, here, of a long-standing puritan and evangelical suspicion of artfulness. But this does not mean that the complaint is without merit. Histories of the novel that rely on crude expressions of the secularization thesis and presume that all of the novel's major qualities—its novelty, its temporality, its immanence, its range of perspective, its material emphasis, and its concern with nationhood—are evidence for the loss of religious belief, are subject to the same criticism. They narrate a story that is too neat in its reorientation, too perfectly connected, and one that fails to take adequate account of the diffuse grammar and vocabulary of the Christian faith.

Qualls tell us that the Victorians who lacked "Bunyan's [religious] assurance" and "held all the more tenaciously to his language" continued to think in terms of journeys even though they no longer saw the world as the Puritans did: "They [the Victorians] were determined to shape the facts of this world into a religious topography, making a path towards social unity in this world an analogue to Christian's progress towards the Celestial City."[82] As the previous discussion in this chapter has made clear, I am not convinced that the Victorians lacked Bunyan's assurance in the manner described by Qualls, nor am I convinced that their beliefs (or ours) can be jettisoned so easily. But I do want to follow Qualls in using *Vanity Fair* to map out a religious path through the world of the Victorian novel, recognizing as I do so that too neat a religious story can result in a mirrored version of the very problem I find in Levine's secular account of the novel. My hope, then, is to offer an evangelical account of the novel that is confident enough to command our attention yet still open to secular interruptions and readings that are less theologically inclined. Thackeray's turn to a dramatic metaphor at the start of his novel proves helpful on this count. Although the characters in *Vanity Fair* lack Christian and Christiana's acute sense of following a providential path, Thackeray's decision to frame the events of his novel as a piece of

---

79. Thackeray, *Vanity Fair*, 26.
80. Ibid., 834.
81. Ibid., 694.
82. Qualls, *The Secular Pilgrims of Victorian Fiction*, 12.

drama continues the imagery of Bunyan's work, with pilgrims on a preordained journey transformed into puppets directed by an omniscient narrator. Thackeray's puppets may be less conscious of playing a part within a broader religious schema, but the spiritual consciousness of Bunyan's pilgrim has less salvific efficacy than we often presume. Moreover, Hans Urs von Balthasar's five-volume *Theo-Drama* and Kevin Vanhoozer's reworking of this material in an evangelical theological context make it clear that the trope of drama has multiple theological possibilities for our understanding of agency as it plots the interaction between God, individual agents, and the world as stage. Given the importance of evangelicalism for the mid nineteenth century, it seems reasonable to search out ways in which the truth of the Christian story is "not simply stated but shown, tried, and proven" in Thackeray's novel, even though the narrative might be read differently.[83]

Although evangelicalism is only one part of the more complex world imagined in *Vanity Fair*, it remains integral to many of the scenes, and the novel would no longer be recognizable if every allusion or reference to this particular religious movement was excised. What is more, the theological overtones of the text's drama would have been intensified for Victorian readers who encountered Thackeray's work after and alongside other explicitly Christian commentary regarding the spiritual significance of life's events. Readers used to reading about life events in terms of their theological meaning would likely have honed in on the more overt references to religion in *Vanity Fair* and read them differently than those modern readers for whom "religion is no longer a primary fact of experience."[84] Rather than presuming that the world of the novel was a replacement for religion, readers used to thinking of themselves as pilgrims on a spiritual journey would have had little problem in looking for ways to accommodate their religious beliefs within new settings. The idea of a new setting for religion is made explicit in the memorable scene where Becky reenacts her experience of being evangelized by Lady Southdown:

> Becky acted the whole scene for them. She put on a nightcap and gown. She preached a great sermon in the true serious manner: she lectured on the virtue of the medicine which she pretended to administer, with a gravity of imitation so perfect, that you would have thought it was the countess's own Roman nose through which she snuffled. "Give us Lady Southdown and the

---

83. Vanhoozer, *The Drama of Doctrine*, 101. I should point out that Vanhoozer is not thinking about *Vanity Fair* when he describes the drama of doctrine in this way.

84. I am quoting here from a review by Margaret Russett of the introduction to nineteenth-century religion and literature that I cowrote with Emma Mason. See Margaret Russett, "Recent Studies in the Nineteenth Century," 950.

black dose," was a constant cry amongst the folks in Becky's little drawing-room in May Fair. And for the first time in her life the Dowager Countess of Southdown was made amusing.[85]

For some, Becky's performance merely confirms *Vanity Fair*'s secular take on religious society. This is a plausible interpretation, but other ones are possible too, and may even prove preferable. We might see Becky's mockery as a more focused attack on heavy-handed approaches to evangelism or as a criticism of Lady Southdown's tendency to treat her tracts as human medicine for the soul (rather than relying on the convicting power of the Holy Spirit). Alternatively, we might decide that our prior knowledge of Becky means that we laugh at her as well as with her, thus questioning whether it is her performance or ours that is the one under greatest scrutiny.

Becky's mimicry provides us with a metonym of *Vanity Fair*'s relationship to the evangelical tradition, with the mimicry capable of being seen as reinforcing or destabilizing faith. The narrator of *Vanity Fair* does not tell us much about the reaction of Becky's audience beyond noting their general amusement and, perhaps more crucially, their desire to see more. We are left to decide for ourselves what they (or we) will take away from the performance. Although nineteenth-century evangelicals tended to be uncomfortable with such moments of ambiguity in fiction, their belief that a genuine understanding of the Christian story is predicated on heartfelt internalization followed by practical application shaped the way in which many Victorian readers understood the performances that take place in *Vanity Fair*. In addition to insisting that readers have a burden to see beneath glittery appearances and providing training so that readers might see the world through different eyes, Thackeray's novel follows evangelicalism in recognizing that single scenes, such as the one Becky performs for her assembled congregation (and the ones that Christian and Christiana go through in Bunyan's tale), need to be understood within a larger tableau. Thackeray differs from evangelicalism in his understanding of what that grand narrative involves, and also in the light-hearted tone through which he typically describes it. But *Vanity Fair*'s debt to evangelicalism remains visible, encouraging us to pay closer attention to the role that the Christian tradition plays here and elsewhere in the Victorian novel.

---

85. Thackeray, *Vanity Fair*, 528.

CHAPTER 2

Dickens's Tale of Conversion

How should we respond to the Christian references that confront us in Charles Dickens's *A Tale of Two Cities* (1859)? The question is given greater urgency by the book's eschatological language, the plot's relocation of otherwise incidental historical details within a carefully orchestrated apocalyptic drama, and the narrator's altar-call-like appeal to our emotions. It is difficult to read that "it was the best of times, it was the worst of times" and think that this is just another story, despite the numbing effect of this quotation's subsequent familiarity. The novel's semantic debt to the Book of Revelation—twin cities, persecution, violence, judgment, martyrdom, resurrection, and so on—provides further confirmation that something revolutionary is unfolding on the page and beckoning us to respond. By the time we get to Sydney Carton's salvific sacrifice, we have been threaded into a tale where the biblical and theological allusions are, like the register knitted by Madame Defarge and her compatriots, seemingly without end. Dr. Manette is "recalled to life," Mr. Jerry Cruncher is known as the "resurrection man," Mrs. Cruncher intercedes through her flopping, Barsad is described as "one of the greatest scoundrels upon earth since accursed Judas—which he certainly did look rather like," and the Monseigneur's evil activity is said to be like "reading the Lord's Prayer backwards for a great number of years."[1] An inverted Eucha-

---

1. Dickens, *A Tale of Two Cities*, 70, 223.

rist is conjured up early on when red wine is spilt on the ground, drunk by those passing by and linked to the blood that will be spilt in the time to come. But by the end of the novel, the symbolism of blood sacrifice has returned to a more ostensibly orthodox Christian reading, as the story of Carton's atonement is remembered and passed on. While the narrator insists that the world he describes is one in which "La Guillotine" has "superseded the Cross," the narrative as a whole seems at pains to suggest otherwise.[2]

If the last fifty years have largely confirmed Robert Alter's 1969 claim that *A Tale of Two Cities* has "given serious critics of Dickens more trouble than any other of his novels," then it may well be that the text's religious references are to blame.[3] The heavy use of Christian allusion presents an obvious stumbling block to those who want to insist on a resolutely secular Dickens, and it is tempting for such readers to link some of the faults commonly attributed to the novel—"lacking humour, overusing coincidences, relying on incident rather than dialogue, descending into melodrama, and self-indulgently repeating tired metaphors and imagery"—with aspects of the evangelical tradition.[4] For many, the novel's references to Christianity seem too obvious and too earnest to merit further critical comment. And it is not just advocates of a secular Dickens who have struggled to account for the novel's religious preoccupations. Norris Pope includes just one passing reference to the novel in *Dickens and Charity* (1978); Thomas Vargish manages only three pages in the course of an extended chapter on Dickens in *The Providential Aesthetic in Victorian Fiction* (1985); and Dennis Walder has little to say about any of Dickens's last three completed novels in *Dickens and Religion* (1981). When Walder does turn his attention to *A Tale of Two Cities*, he seems genuinely bemused, noting the "explicit, even systematic expression of Dickens's religious views" in the novel but doubting "how far Dickens really holds the belief expressed at the end" and worrying about the "improbability" of the final act of self-sacrifice.[5] Janet Larson's silence on the subject of *A Tale of Two Cities* is even more glaring, because of the detailed and extensive readings that characterize the rest of *Dickens and the Broken Scripture* (1985). Though attentive to the intertextual presence of the Book of Revelation in *Little Dorrit*, she ignores the equally important and arguably more striking uses to which this biblical text is put in *A Tale of Two Cities*.

---

2. Ibid., 260.
3. Alter, "The Demons of History in Dickens's *Tale*," 135.
4. Paul Davis, "A Tale of Two Cities," in Paroissien, ed., *A Companion to Charles Dickens*, 413.
5. Walder, *Dickens and Religion*, 198.

Although recent work by Ilana M. Blumberg (2013) and Jan-Melissa Schramm (2012) offers significant steps forward in appreciating how *A Tale of Two Cities* "orients itself so thoroughly in the Christian inheritance," most readers of their work and mine continue to lack the theological tools needed to make sense of what the novel might be doing through its engagement with the Christian tradition.[6] The solution to this problem that I want to explore in this chapter involves thinking about Dickens's use of the evangelical conversion narrative. My argument, in short, is that Dickens uses evangelical conversion narratives—tales in which multiple parts are reordered and reread into a coherent story that looks to Christ's death on the cross as the site of personal transformation—as a model for ordering the tumultuous events described in *A Tale of Two Cities* and narrating a story of transformation. Initially, this claim might seem limited, a return to George Orwell's older concern about using personal transformation as an "alibi" to avoid endangering "the *status quo*."[7] But Dickens's use of conversion narratives as a means of responding to the challenges of fragmentation has broader implications, revealing the extent to which evangelicalism shaped the nineteenth-century novel.[8] As well as offering a fictional solution to the chaos of the French Revolution, Dickens saw the potential of conversion narratives to bring together the fragmented and competing voices that sought the public's attention in the pages of his periodical *All the Year Round*.[9] By writing his own metastory about how the fictional voices of the period fitted together and should be understood, Dickens ended up rivaling the stories told by evangelicals, not because he was seeking to replace the scriptural sources on which they drew but because the affective power of the new story that he told competed with evangelical proclamations of the gospel. Having come to appreciate the affective power of evangelical

---

6. Blumberg, *Victorian Sacrifice*, 62; Schramm, *Atonement and Self-Sacrifice in Nineteenth-Century Narrative*, chapter 4.

7. George Orwell, "Charles Dickens," in *Inside the Whale and Other Essays*, 31.

8. Emily Walker Heady helps us appreciate the redemptive ambition of evangelical accounts of conversion when she observes that the transformation involved "is not merely a private, internal change, but an epistemological re-posturing that orients the convert vis-à-vis the world in which he lives." Heady, *Victorian Conversion Narratives and Reading Communities*, 8.

9. My claim that evangelical conversion narratives offer a solution to the fragmentation of serialization differs from the position articulated by Sarah Winter, who reads *The Old Curiosity Shop* as disassociating "the new medium of serial fiction from an Evangelical providentialist epistemology, with its view of literacy as a means of social control and of reading as a means of conversion." Winter, *The Pleasures of Memory*, 147. For another recent critical point of comparison, see the work of Gowan Dawson, who makes a case for the influence of the paleontologist Richard Owen on Dickens: the reconstruction of dinosaur bones "must have seemed an especially attractive skill to a novelist eager to disclose the underlying design of his own seemingly ill-proportioned serial fiction." Dawson, "Dickens, Dinosaurs, and Design," 764.

conversion narratives, Dickens sought to deliver his own superior version. In doing so, he reveals both his debt to evangelicalism and his efforts to supplant the movement's efforts. Rather than following Carolyn W. de la L. Oulton and others, then, in thinking about evangelical thought primarily as an influence that Dickens was trying to throw off, I argue for the generative role that evangelical belief plays in Dickens's understanding of his role as a novelist.[10]

EVANGELICAL CONVERSION IN *A TALE OF TWO CITIES*

In a letter to Wilkie Collins, dated October 6, 1859, Dickens explained his thoughts on how a narrative ought to be plotted: "I think the business of Art is to lay all the ground carefully, but with the care that conceals itself—to shew, by a backward light, what everything has been working to—but only to SUGGEST, until the fulfilment comes. These are the ways of Providence—of which ways, all Art is but a little imitation."[11] The quotation is a familiar one and has been the subject of many critical discussions, including the one provided by Vargish in *The Providential Aesthetic in Victorian Fiction*. Vargish explains how providential ideas are translated into fiction: for example, authors describing events that seem coincidental but which subsequently become intelligible as the narrative progresses, and "*inconsequent actualization* . . . the fulfilment or realization of a desire or fear by causal sequences which the characters do not initiate or control."[12] Because his aim is to study the "fictional representation of providence at work in the world," rather than religious discourse, Vargish gives minimal space to the theological debates that surrounded references to providence in the nineteenth century.[13] He does trace a shift in the nineteenth century away from natural theology as a means of comprehending God's perfect design, but for much of the book, Vargish allows providence to stand as a stable and uncontested theological idea.

Yet the question of how God governs the world has long been the subject of theological debate and exploration. Different ideas about providence are present throughout the Jewish and Christian scriptures, and recur throughout church history. In the Protestant tradition, many of the debates are structured

---

10. Oulton, *Literature and Religion in Mid-Victorian England*; Walder, *Dickens and Religion*; Winter, *The Pleasures of Memory*. Simon Dentith highlights the Murdstones in *David Copperfield* as "a version of Evangelicalism that Dickens was keen to repudiate." Dentith, *Nineteenth-Century British Literature Then and Now*, 70.

11. Dickens, Letter to Wilkie Collins (October 6, 1859), in Storey, ed., *The Letters of Charles Dickens*, 9:128.

12. Vargish, *The Providential Aesthetic in Victorian Fiction*, 10.

13. Ibid., 2.

around the historic disagreement between two Reformers, John Calvin and Jacobus Arminius, who argued, respectively, for an emphasis on God's control and an emphasis on human free will.[14] These positions continued to make their presence felt in the nineteenth century, through Calvinism and Methodism, but they were not the only means of thinking about providence. The doctrine raised, and was addressed through, other questions. For instance, did God govern the world through the natural order, as evangelicals such as Thomas Chalmers and William Wilberforce thought, or did he work through special acts of intervention, as Edward Irving, William Booth, and the Seventh Earl of Shaftsbury claimed? One's answer to this question had consequences for an array of other theological issues, from science to intercessory prayer.[15] Thus debates about providence were not confined to the formal study of theological doctrine but had major implications for how Christian believers thought about other issues, including economics, social welfare, and education.

Although Vargish shows some awareness of the complexity of providence, his casual translation of the term into the language of literary narrative does tend to come at the cost of theological nuance. A similar problem can be found in other late twentieth-century literary criticism dealing with the nineteenth-century novel. Audrey Jaffe's influential and perceptive study of omniscience in Dickens offers even less theological engagement than Vargish, and when Jerome Meckier reads providence in terms of Dickens's rivalry with Wilkie Collins, theology is relegated to the background as he considers the different ways in which both writers "investigate the paradox underlying the use of catastrophe in melodramatic realism: appointed times and the end of roads that have been travelled in darkness always arrive suddenly for the irresponsible and unaware. They are then called catastrophes and invested with unearthly significance, even if, upon reconsideration, they are seen by the novelist familiar with the ways of providence to have been inevitable and long overdue."[16]

When Meckier seeks to explain the theological referent in the letter by Dickens quoted at the start of this section, he highlights the influence of Thomas Carlyle, a figure who certainly exerted a considerable influence on Dickens when the latter sat down to write his fictional account of the French

---

14. The influence of Calvin on the nineteenth century is relatively familiar to scholars of Dickens, though many make the mistake of thinking that Calvinism and evangelicalism are synonymous. Not all evangelicals in the period held to the teachings of Calvin.

15. For more on the economic consequences of different evangelical views about providence, see Hilton, *The Age of Atonement*.

16. Meckier, *Hidden Rivalries in Victorian Fiction*, 250. See also Jaffe, *Vanishing Points: Dickens, Narrative, and the Subject of Omniscience*.

Revolution. In general terms, there is nothing remiss in Meckier's claim that "Dickens's letter to Collins about providence is strongly Carlylean in flavor." Yet this flavor cannot be described adequately as "essentially [a] Christian pattern of salvation following travail," and the lack of accompanying gloss is a problem given that theological accounts of God's plans for and governance of the world are extremely complex and involved.[17]

Dickens's description of all things working toward a climactic moment of revelation constitutes a particular view of providence, one that is rooted in evangelical theology and its emphasis on individual conversion.[18] For evangelicals, the point at which Jesus is acknowledged as a personal savior is the prompt for a widespread reinterpretation of one's whole life, with everything becoming an anticipation or consequence of this climactic moment.[19] Of course, reinterpreting one's own history in the light of a new event is not unique to evangelical Christianity. Bruce Hindmarsh's important study of the rise of the conversion narrative in the early modern period acknowledges how these tales of conversion "emerged as part of a larger cultural turn towards autobiographical writing in the Renaissance."[20] But, as he goes on to show, evangelicalism did not just repeat the Western elevation of the self: it actively concentrated everything around a single moment of transformation. Accentuating the transformational stories of its Puritan and Pietist forbears, evangelical conversion narratives became the defining features of the Evangelical Revival in the 1730s and 1740s. By the start of the nineteenth century, the tradition of personal stories "characterized by an overwhelming sense of the spontaneity of divine grace" had undergone a "process of proliferation and elaboration," helping the form become "firmly established" in British cultural life.[21]

By emphasizing the death of Jesus Christ on the cross and our need to respond to this event, evangelical conversion narratives understood providence primarily as a story about personal regeneration through Christ. All Christian traditions situate the person and work of Jesus at the center of their view of history, but evangelicalism's emphasis on Christ's salvific work and our need to respond personally to this event focuses one's grasp of the divine plan on a specific and climactic moment. Summarizing this core evangelical idea, David Bebbington explains: "The reconciliation of humanity to God

---

17. Meckier, *Hidden Rivalries in Victorian Fiction*, 97.

18. For a more recent critical instance of someone failing to register the specifically evangelical way in which Dickens writes about providence, see Colledge, *Dickens, Christianity and The Life of Our Lord*, 42–43.

19. Evangelicals coined the idea of Christ as a "personal savior," and the term gained increasing currency from the middle of the nineteenth century.

20. Hindmarsh, *The Evangelical Conversion Narrative*, 18.

21. Ibid., 321, 322.

... achieved by Christ on the cross is why the Christian religion speaks of God as the author of salvation."[22] Everything in evangelicalism's reading of the story of salvation pivots on the work of Christ on the cross, the "very foundation of Christianity" as John Cumming, George Eliot's bête noire, put it.[23] Old Testament prophecies are read typologically, as anticipations of Christ's redemptive act or as proofs that Jesus was who he said and thus able to offer atonement through his death; the New Testament is seen, more easily than its scriptural predecessor, as the story of Christ's victorious death on the cross.[24] And everything since, including the considerable social and philanthropic activity of evangelicalism in the nineteenth century, is referred back to the events at Calvary. The Rev. John Venn's call for "the *Gospel* [to] be regarded as the only real and universal remedy—the only instrument for regenerating the world" was repeated by evangelicals throughout the nineteenth century, with the gospel message continually looking to Calvary and our need to respond to the redemption bought through Christ's sacrifice.[25] Writing in 1855, Mortlock Daniell put it this way: "The truth is, the gospel comes so near, knocking as it were at the heart of every man, that every man must either *receive* it or *reject* it. . . . If he receives the gospel he is saved, not by his own works. He did not atone for his own sins. . . . He consented to God's only way of saving sinners."[26]

Although Bebbington's summary of evangelicalism lists crucicentrism and conversion separately, the two aspects are closely related, as he readily acknowledges. Writing about regeneration, the Rev. Canon John Ryle explained the meaning of the cross for converted individuals: "There are two distinct things which the Lord Jesus Christ does for every sinner whom He undertakes to save. He washes him from his sins in His own blood, and gives him a free pardon:—that is his justification. He puts the Holy Spirit into his heart, and makes him an entirely new man:—that is his Regeneration." Ryle continues: "The two things are both absolutely necessary to salvation . . . [and] never separate."[27] William Pollock makes a similar point about the personal and life-changing consequences of Christ's death on the cross: "While 'Imputation' in the abstract, signifies simply the act of reckoning . . . in the language of theology, 'imputation' is rather employed, for the most part, to convey the specific notion of crediting one with that which is not properly his own, but

---

22. Bebbington, *Evangelicalism in Modern Britain*, 14.
23. Cumming, *The Atonement in Its Twofold Aspects*, 21.
24. For further discussion of the evangelical use of typology, see Landow, *Victorian Types, Victorian Shadows*.
25. Anon., *Things That Accompany Salvation*, 87.
26. Daniell, *The Christ of Holy Scripture*, 176.
27. Rev. Canon John Ryle, "Regeneration," in Garbett, ed., *Evangelical Principles*, 132–33.

that which is transferred from another to his credit, in the sight and by the act of God. . . . 'Imputation' lies at the very foundation of the whole scheme of the gospel."[28] For Ryle, Pollock, and a much larger body of evangelicals, the cross cannot be reduced to an abstract piece of doctrine; it is to be understood personally rather than via more theoretical approaches to theology.

Schramm draws out the personal consequences of the atonement for the Victorians by connecting the doctrine with nineteenth-century conceptions of sacrifice and showing how this informs a range of nineteenth-century novels. *Atonement and Self-Sacrifice in Nineteenth-Century Narrative* (2012) includes a compelling chapter on *A Tale of Two Cities*, which situates the sacrifice that Carton makes in the novel against the backdrop of Anglican debates in the 1850s over the meaning of the atonement. Whereas some theologians argued that the death of Jesus was a general expression of God's love for the world, others, including most evangelical Anglicans, insisted that there could be no salvation unless that death was understood specifically as an act of substitutionary atonement, the belief that the crucifixion of Christ fulfills God's demand for human sin to be atoned for by another. Demonstrating how the plot of *A Tale of Two Cities* sides unexpectedly with those evangelicals who agreed with the Baptist minister Charles Spurgeon in thinking that "the whole substance of salvation lies in the thought, that Christ stood in the place of man," Schramm explores the different ways in which the novel figures substitution.[29] My focus here is slightly different, however.[30] Rather than thinking primarily about the theological, legal, and ethical implications of vicarious experience in narrative, I want to take up a question that Schramm asks in the conclusion of her book, when she wonders whether the use of "the rhetoric of sacrifice" means that novels such as "*A Tale of Two Cities* somehow perform the work of religion in the period."[31] Without wanting to slip into Arnoldian modes of thought and think of literature as a replacement for religion, I do think that the Victorian novel as imagined by Dickens takes on a quasi-religious function and does so because of the way in which its narrative structure

---

28. Anon., *Things That Accompany Salvation*, 104.

29. Spurgeon, "The Anxious Inquirer," *The Christian Guest* (1859), 75.

30. Despite this difference in emphasis, my work remains in close conversation with Schramm's. There is also a degree of overlap with Blumberg's work, although her study is more focused on the ethical implications of religious sacrifice. In arguing for the importance of the atonement to *A Tale of Two Cities*, all three of us differ, I think, from the position of Oulton, who claims that the "resolution to the novel supersedes the doctrine of Atonement through personal emulation of Christ's sacrifice." Oulton, *Literature and Religion in Mid-Victorian England*, 66. The need for personal emulation was inseparable from the evangelical understanding of the Atonement.

31. Schramm, *Atonement and Self-Sacrifice in Nineteenth-Century Narrative*, 234.

and purpose have been shaped by evangelical ideas about conversion and its story of transformation.

There are a number of transformations in *A Tale of Two Cities*: Sydney Carton's sacrifice, Jerry Cruncher's decision to abandon grave robbing, Barsad continually switching sides, Charles Darnay's renunciation of his family's abuse of power, and the French Revolution as a whole. Some prove more meaningful and/or lasting than others, yet the critical tradition has been reluctant to give any of these incidents much credence. This is partly the result of continuing sympathy with Orwell's older complaint about Dickens being "a change of heart" man and the view that Dickens's commitment to personal transformation is more apposite to earlier works such as *A Christmas Carol* (1843) than the complex social investigations thought to mark Dickens's later work.[32] It is also the result of an ongoing suspicion in critical circles about religious claims of any sort, including those surrounding conversion. I discuss the reasons for and consequences of this suspicion further in the concluding chapter, but for now it is enough to note that dismissing the transformations in *A Tale of Two Cities* as insignificant because they are implausible ignores the way in which nineteenth-century evangelicals understood religious conversion. Writing for *The Christian Guest*, the Rev. David E. Ford declared: "Often have I heard the remark that little dependence is to be placed on sudden conversion. But real conversion must always be sudden, and in fact instantaneous."[33] Although some fellow evangelicals were less convinced that conversion had to be instantaneous, all agreed that it was a divine act rather than something that could be explained through natural causes: "Dismiss from your minds for ever the common idea that natural theology, moral suasion, logical arguments, and an exhibition of truth, are sufficient of themselves to turn a sinner from his sins. . . . It is a strong delusion."[34] By presenting an unlikely transformational event and impressing its consequences on us through an apocalyptic mode of narration, Dickens confirms his narrative debt to evangelicalism. Like the evangelical preachers of his day, Dickens invites readers to heed the message of salvation and be transformed. It is not always clear what we are being called to convert to, because, in the final instance, Dickens does not share evangelicalism's more precise conviction of what the gospel entails. Yet the narrative

---

32. Orwell writes: "It seems that in every attack Dickens makes upon society he is always pointing to a change of spirit rather than a change of structure. . . . Useless to change institutions without a 'change of heart'—that, essentially, is what he is always saying." Orwell, "Charles Dickens," in *Inside the Whale and Other Essays*, 30–31. Orwell's comment is repeated and discussed further by Walder in *Dickens and Religion*, chapter 5.

33. Ford, "Conversion, as a Matter of Experience," *The Christian Guest* (1859), 505.

34. Rev. John Ryle, "The Work of the Holy Ghost," in Anon., ed., *Things That Accompany Salvation*, 127.

of conversion is present in many of the scenes that occur in *A Tale of Two Cities* and, more importantly, shapes the climax to which everything else leads.

The suggestion in *A Tale of Two Cities* of salvation hinging on something greater than a plausible notion of human good work marks a break from Dickens's comments elsewhere, most famously in the letter to the Rev. David Macrae, where Dickens wrote of his endeavor "to exhibit in all my good people some faint reflections of the teaching of our great Master [Jesus], and unostentatiously to lead the reader up to those teachings as the great source of all moral goodness."[35] Years before the American writer Charles Sheldon published his book *In His Steps* (1896) and consolidated such talk of Jesus as the great moral example, *A Tale of Two Cities* surprises us by conceiving of salvation as the evangelicals saw it: an act of substitutionary atonement, in which, as the last chapter of the novel puts it, "The Footsteps Die Out for Ever."[36] The footsteps that die out are Carton's, but they are also presumably meant to bring to mind Dr. Manette, the great physician, who spends so much of the novel pacing up and down. Describing Manette's influence in Paris, the narrator tells us: "Among these terrors, and the brood belonging to them, the Doctor walked with a steady head: confident in his power, cautiously persistent in his end, never doubting that he would save Lucie's husband at last. . . . Silent, humane, indispensable in hospital and prison . . . he was a man apart."[37] As the text continues, Dr. Manette becomes increasingly convinced of his redemptive power. When he appears at Charles Darnay's first trial in France and wins a short-lived victory for his son-in-law, Dr. Manette comforts his daughter with the words: "Don't tremble so. I have saved him."[38] In case we should miss the theological import of this event, the narrative goes on: "He had accomplished the task he had set himself, his promise was redeemed, he had saved Charles."[39] These references are in keeping with Dickens's emphasis elsewhere on the good works that different people do in imitation of Christ, works that are seen as infinitely preferable to the empty rhetoric of the evangelical Mr. Chadband in *Bleak House* (1852–53). But as the story continues in *A Tale of Two Cities*, good works prove inadequate to bring about salvation and are seemingly overtaken by an evangelical account in which one person has to suffer and die for the guilt of another.[40]

---

35. Charles Dickens, Letter to Rev David Macrae [1861], in Storey, ed., *The Letters of Charles Dickens*, 9:556.

36. For an illuminating discussion of Sheldon's book, see Jackson, *The Word and Its Witness*, chapter 3.

37. Dickens, *A Tale of Two Cities*, 260.

38. Ibid., 273.

39. Ibid., 274.

40. It would be misleading to draw too strong a distinction here, with Schramm arguing persuasively for the ways in which nineteenth-century conceptions of individual sacrifice were

Unlike the redemption offered by Jesus, Carton's sacrifice saves just one man (though we might concede that it also encompasses Charles's family, who are reunited with their son-in-law, husband, and father). Although the restricted scope of the salvation in the novel might be said to expose the limits of the analogy between Carton's sacrifice and Christ's death on the cross, the debt of *A Tale of Two Cities* to the evangelical conversion narrative is not easily dismissed. For evangelicals, the offer of salvation through Christ came with certain restrictions, either on the grounds (for the Calvinists) that God had already destined who was to be saved and who was to be damned, or because some people chose to reject the gift of salvation on offer. While one of the most popular evangelical summaries of the gospel was John 3:16—"For God so loved the world, that he gave his only begotten Son, that whosoever believeth in him should not perish, but have everlasting life"—the promise of salvation for those who believed implied that there were damning consequences for those who did not believe. Many evangelicals were keen to point out that two verses later John's Gospel continues: "He that believeth not is condemned already" (John 3:18). Reminding readers of the threat of eternal punishment that hangs over those who ignored the offer of salvation, John Cumming underlined the consequences that accompany the evangelical understanding of the gospel: "The word of salvation becomes either 'the savour of life,' or it is 'the savour of death.' May God, in his mercy, grant it be not unto us the latter."[41] *A Tale of Two Cities* is full of more earthly reminders of judgment on sinners, most notably in the violent ends met by Marquis St. Evremonde and Madame Defarge, but also through the registrations knitted by Defarge and her fellow revolutionaries in a book that parodies the Lamb's book of life. It may be that Dickens has evangelicalism in mind, albeit subconsciously, when he has Defarge tell his wife that her policy of "extermination is good *doctrine*" and the narrator describe how Madame Defarge's "hearers derived a horrible enjoyment from the deadly nature of her *wrath*."[42]

The final chapter of the novel compounds the sense that Madame Defarge's book of judgment competes for souls with the Lamb's (or perhaps more accurately Dickens's) book of life. Madame Defarge may be dead by the time that we read about Carton's sacrifice, but her demonic spirit lives on: the chapter begins with three references to the number six (two references to "six tumbrils," followed by a reference to "six carts"), 666, marking Vengeance as a new

---

modeled on a theological example. But the distinction was certainly felt by many evangelicals in the nineteenth century, who resisted a gospel of good works and insisted on the efficacy and uniqueness of Christ's salvific work on the cross.

41. Cumming, *Look to Jesus*, 64.
42. Dickens, *A Tale of Two Cities*, 322, 324, emphasis mine.

manifestation of the Antichrist who continues to lead souls to destruction.[43] On one level, there is nothing exclusively evangelical about Dickens's allusion to the biblical struggle in Revelation between Christ and the Antichrist; on another level, however, the competition for human souls returns us to a recognizably evangelical conception of history, in which the ultimate concern is the fate of individual souls. Vengeance and her coterie register another twenty-three lives in this chapter, a sizeable number but less than half the deaths detailed two chapters earlier. By contrast, the book of life records the metaphorical resurrection of the seamstress with whom Carton shares his final moments, and, beyond this individual, it envisions a "beautiful people rising from this abyss."[44] We are encouraged to think about everything in terms of the damned and the saved, with the emphasis falling on the hope carried by those who, having heard the story of Carton's sacrifice, embrace his promise that "whosoever liveth and believeth in me shall never die."

RELIGIOUS ECHOES AND THE ORGANIZING POWER OF THE EVANGELICAL STORY

A Tale of Two Cities confronts us with the Christian language of salvation at every turn. These references can sometimes be harder for contemporary critics to grasp than they were for Victorian readers more familiar with the evangelical message. But there are plenty of moments where the novel's investment in the content of the Christian tradition is made explicit. Take, for instance, the scene in which Carton's decapitation by the guillotine is juxtaposed with a quotation from the Gospel of John: "I am the Resurrection and the Life, saith the Lord: he that believeth in me, though he were dead, yet shall he live: and whosoever liveth and believeth in me shall never die."[45] Although the quotation is one of the novel's most memorable sentences, it is unclear who is speaking—the words are left unattributed and contained within a discrete paragraph. We might be listening to the Bible, but we might just as easily be listening to the *Book of Common Prayer,* which includes the quotation from

---

43. Ibid., 353. On Jan 13, 1860, *All the Year Round* published an article called "The End of the World," attacking (evangelical) figures such as Dr. John Cumming for trying to calculate the identity of the Beast (666) described in the Book of Revelation. In a different context and following a markedly different reading, John Bowen provides a persuasive and highly original account of the significance of the numbers in the novel. See "Counting On: *A Tale of Two Cities,*" in Jones, McDonagh and Mee, eds., *Charles Dickens,* A Tale of Two Cities *and the French Revolution.*

44. Dickens, *A Tale of Two Cities,* 357.

45. Ibid., 357. See John 11:25–26.

John's Gospel in its burial service for the dead. Earlier in Dickens's text, we are told how Sydney Carton heard these "solemn words . . . read at his father's grave," but the ambiguity of the father figure in a novel that goes on to type Carton as a Christ-like savior leaves more questions than answers when the father's words reverberate at Carton's execution.[46] The subsequent timing of the quotation, immediately after the death of the seamstress yet before the execution of Carton, suggests that we might be listening to Carton's last words. Or perhaps the quotation should remain unattributed, rather like the "disembodied, imaginary monologue" that immediately follows, which, according to Richard Menke, deliberately "surmount[s] the boundaries of space and time to include everybody's story."[47]

This unmoored quotation prompts us to think through the role that Christianity plays in Dickens's novel. Writing about *The Old Curiosity Shop*, Sarah Winter argues that "Dickens attempted to undermine the authority of religious fictions in order to appropriate their project to shape, and even to reconstitute, the ideas and actions of the reader in the service of achieving larger moral, political, and social goals."[48] And Larson offers a similar line of thought in her monograph, explaining how Dickens seeks to break apart the biblical text through selective quotation across his oeuvre: sometimes the novelist uses scripture to "stabilize his fictions," and sometimes he sees his primary response to the word of God as a work of "reconstruction."[49] Implicit throughout Larson's study is the idea that this work of reconstruction is secular. The heterogeneity and multivocality in Dickens's fictional engagement with scripture is presumed to break apart a text that, in its Christian setting, Larson views as univocal and no longer sustainable, having come under sustained critical examination in the eighteenth and nineteenth centuries. Evangelicalism, as such, does not feature in Larson's account, but her line of thought renders the work of this religious movement redundant, an antiquated and ultimately futile effort to maintain a Christian narrative that was no longer able to address the needs of the age. There is a danger, though, in presuming that sustained critical attention by an author always fractures an otherwise stable Christian story, and it is misleading to think that those moderns outside a community of faith are the only ones capable of undertaking the work of reconstruction. When Larson tells us that "these new conventions, new ways of reading the Bible, were inherently more unstable than the old conventions by virtue of their being in formation, widely debated, and under threat

---

46. Dickens, *A Tale of Two Cities*, 298.
47. Menke, *Telegraphic Realism*, 130.
48. Winter, "Curiosity as Didacticism in *The Old Curiosity Shop*," 30–31.
49. Larson, *Dickens and the Broken Scripture*, 313.

from without," she risks conflating one set of religious reading habits with all religious reading habits.[50] Although parts of the Christian tradition have sometimes pursued a singular and fixed reading of the Bible, the tradition as a whole reveals a set of beliefs in continual flux and constantly subject to new lines of thought.

While evangelical theology was energetic and pragmatic enough to accommodate many of the changes to cultural life in the eighteenth and nineteenth centuries, its emphasis on a simple and personal reading of the biblical story left it uncomfortable with narrative ruptures. Evangelicals were always seeking to put the different parts of divine history back together, whether through biblical harmonization strategies, an emphasis on unchanging core doctrine, or via conversion stories that ordered every narrative event into a coherent whole. Conversion stories, in particular, offered a clear strategy for ordering broken parts, even though this strategy was not always as effective as the rhetoric suggested. Evangelical conversion narratives sometimes seemed to leave out elements that did not fit, and, on other occasions, they drew attention to the "wrong" things (i.e., the dramatic accounts of wrongdoing rather than the moment of resolution). Nor was the narrative sequence as final as it initially seemed. One only has to think, for example, of Victorians such as Thomas Cooper, whose life included moments of conversion and un-conversion, to appreciate that the narrative trajectory could be reversed.[51] Yet for all these problems, evangelicals remained committed to narrative unity and believed in the redemptive vision it offered.

Dickens often shared this preference for narrative unity in his fiction. Although he complained repeatedly about the narrowness and closure of certain evangelical ideas, such as the doctrine of total depravity, and wrote works in which a polyphonic voice can often be heard, he sympathized with the vision of narrative unity modeled by evangelical accounts of conversion and valued its capacity for articulating an ambitious redemptive vision that could deal with the chaos of the modern age. This can be seen in the design of *A Tale of Two Cities*, particularly when it comes to the echoes that constitute such an important trope in the novel. When the French Revolution finally breaks out, the chapter is titled "Echoing Footsteps," and Lucie sits in the house "listening to the echoing footsteps of years." Some of the sounds she hears are hopeful, such as a "child's laugh" that recalls the "Divine friend of children"; others are more menacing.[52] The latter become more prominent as the chapter moves

---

50. Ibid., 314.

51. On the unconversion and conversion of Thomas Cooper, see Larsen, *Crisis of Doubt*, chapter 4.

52. Dickens, *A Tale of Two Cities*, 200.

from the domesticity of a "wonderful corner for echoes . . . where the Doctor lived" to the sounds coming from across the English Channel. Urging themselves on to the Bastille, the revolutionaries are characterized aurally: "With a roar that sounded as if all the breath in France had been shaped into the detested word, the living sea rose, wave on wave, depth on depth, and overflowed the city to that point. Alarm-bells ringing, drums beating, the sea raging and thundering on its new beach, the attack begun."[53] The problem with the revolution on this reading is not that everything it has to say is bad, but rather that, cumulatively, its message has descended into disorder and discord.

If we listen carefully to the revolutionary sounds in the "Echoing Footsteps" chapter, we can hear references to the Book of Revelation, a revolutionary and apocalyptic text which, as I have noted already, suits the novel's predilection for interpreting everything in terms of salvation and judgment. The number of Dickens's chapter may well be significant in this respect. "Echoing Footsteps" is chapter 21 of Book 2, anticipating, perhaps, the hopeful message of chapter 21 in the Book of Revelation.[54] At the moment when Dickens's story is in danger of being drowned out by revolutionary violence, his text alludes to a time when there is "no more sea" and in which "God shall wipe away all tears from their eyes," having made "all things new."[55] This note of hope offers a counterpoint to the noise of the revolution, which "had almost destroyed their [Defarge, the turnkey, and Jacques Three's] sense of hearing" and which threatens to overwhelm the auditory capacity of the reader. "Everywhere was tumult, exultation, deafening and maniacal bewilderment, astounding noise, yet furious dumb show."[56] The problem is not just that revolutionary noise is too violent for the hearing of readers but also that too many echoes become incoherent. In this respect, the references to the Book of Revelation act not only as a source of hope but also a means of restoring a recognizable story amid the increasing disorder.

The Book of Revelation seeks a story that can make sense of the disruptions of history and incorporate everything into a coherent narrative.[57] At least this is how the book was typically read by evangelicals in the nineteenth century: at one end of the evangelical theological spectrum, John Cumming

---

53. Ibid., 200, 205.
54. The periodical form of the novel also had this numbering. The August 27, 1859, installment in *All the Year Round* subtitled the serialized part: "Book the Second. The Golden Thread. Chapter XXI. Echoing Footsteps."
55. Revelation 21:1, 4, 5.
56. Dickens, *A Tale of Two Cities*, 207, 206.
57. This is one of the reasons why Thomas Carlyle borrows so heavily from the Book of Revelation when describing the French Revolution. For further discussion on this point, see Brooks, *Signs for the Times*, chapter 2.

treated the Book of Revelation as a prophetic manual for interpreting current historic events; at the other end, more academically minded Victorian evangelical theologians saw the Book of Revelation as a symbolic conclusion to the world's story of salvation.[58] For all the substantial differences in these readings, the unity and closure of John's vision are valued in both instances. Yet the different evangelical commentaries on the Book of Revelation also attest to the difficulty of comprehending what John's Apocalypse has to say: the weight of textual echoes and allusions in this biblical text militates against any single explanatory account. The final book of the Bible may seek to establish narrative order, but it does so through a style of writing that creates disorder for the reader in other ways. Thus, when Dickens looks to the Book of Revelation for an answer to the chaos of history, he encounters the very problem he is seeking to address—a multiplicity of echoes whose frequency renders any definitive meaning inaudible.

Echoing the biblical text creates difficulties for Dickens in *A Tale of Two Cities*, not least because of the way in which the scriptures have been read by others. Although Dickens was not opposed to everything that evangelicals said about the Christian story, there were several areas where Dickens sought to depart from this message, and as the sound of religion in the novel is detached from some its theological roots, the result can start to lose coherence. Aware that the scriptural echoes in *A Tale of Two Cities* need to be moored through other means, Dickens looks for additional organizing stories to ensure that his biblically inflected response to the French Revolution does not descend into chaos. At the start of the "Echoing Footsteps" chapter, he introduces a simple quasi-providential schema when he writes of Lucie's "golden thread." But in a repeat of the problem of *Bleak House*, where the carefully controlled narrative of Esther struggles to see beyond the domestic sphere, Lucie's control is confined to the world at home. When events in France force the narrative to move outside the domestic sphere and face the return of a "howling universe," Dickens turns to another personal organizing story.[59] In place of Lucie's domestic care, we are given the revenge narrative of Madame Defarge: "As a whirlpool of boiling waters has a center point, so, all this raging circled around Defarge's wine-shop."[60] Madame Defarge's personal tale allows Dickens to acknowledge the horrors of history without losing sight of a meaningful narrative, and he is able to use the personal dimension of her story to reject the possibility that history is uncontrolled chaos.

---

58. John Cumming's publications on the Book of Revelation include *The Great Tribulation*.
59. Dickens, *A Tale of Two Cities*, 209.
60. Ibid., 204.

In many ways, Dickens depends on the personal realm to restore narrative cohesion. Even the revolutionary forces that appear out of control in the novel are thought about in personal terms: the uncanny description of every male revolutionary as "Jacques" implicitly reminds readers that the mob has a name, and while the novel describes the guillotine as a "retributive instrument" of judgment that counts (rather than names) the lives it ends, the accompanying personification—"the figure of the sharp female called La Guillotine"—retains the idea that all events depend ultimately on human agency.[61] But personal stories have to take account of social complexity, as Dickens acknowledges throughout his fiction. Recognizing the threat of revolutionary incoherence and disorder, Dickens links his talk of echoes in the "Echoing Footsteps" chapter to another disembodied image: footsteps that have lost their way. Unlike the footsteps that normally direct us where we want to go, the footsteps at this point in *A Tale of Two Cities* go nowhere and are, in the words of the narrator, "headlong, mad and dangerous."[62] The early description of Dr. Manette's shoemaking as an involuntary response to the trauma of his imprisonment acknowledges the struggle for oppressed people to make their way in the world. Later on, the discovery that "Charles Darnay had set his foot according to Doctor Manette's reiterated instructions" is the prelude to finding that there is no salvation in "the same cautious counsel [that] directed every step that lay before him [Darnay], and [which] had prepared every inch of his road."[63] The footsteps that can be heard in the "Echoing Footsteps" chapter are less hopeful still, and eventually take their place alongside other disconnected body parts. Although the mob moves as one, their limbs are curiously disconnected, from the feet that rush from place to place, to the arms without "agency," which "crookedly quivered and jerked, scores at a time."[64] At the end of the chapter, the "seven gory heads" impaled on pikes reinforces our sense of dismemberment, as well as alluding to the inhuman beast that haunts John's vision in the Book of Revelation.[65]

Aware of the competing claims of cohesive personal stories, and the chaos of noisy echoes and dismembered limbs, the final chapter of *A Tale of Two Cites* turns for a solution to a more explicit evangelical form of narrative, one that imposes its own order on the sometimes-unruly voices of the biblical text. Carton's sacrifice invites readers to consider the parallel with Christ's

---

61. Ibid., 357, 259.
62. Ibid., 204, 210.
63. Ibid., 269.
64. Ibid., 204.
65. Ibid., 210. Also, see Revelation 17.3b: "And I saw a woman sit upon a scarlet coloured beast, full of names of blasphemy, having seven heads and ten horns."

death on the cross. For Dickens, the parallel offers a means of harmonizing the sounds that have been heard hitherto and reconnecting the broken body parts the narrative has just been describing: "The murmuring of many voices, the upturning of many faces, the pressing on of many footsteps in the outskirts of the crowd, so that it swells forward in a mass, like one great heave of water, all flashes away."[66] The moment of revelation that "flashes" upon us transforms the "mass" hysteria of the crowd into a more cohesive story of regeneration associated with a different type of "mass." As the tale comes to an end, the noise of revolution gives way to a discernible story that can be passed on to future generations ("I heard him tell the child my story"), and the directionless footsteps of the mob are replaced by a new tale of "a man winning his way up in that path of life which once was mine."[67] While Dickens retained significant reservations about the content of evangelical conversion narratives, he saw the form's potential.

ALL THE YEAR ROUND AND DICKENS'S PLAN OF SALVATION

As well as using the evangelical conversion narrative to help order the fragments in *A Tale of Two Cities,* Dickens looked to this religious form to facilitate his vision for *All the Year Round.* Serialization had long been part of Dickens's publishing strategy, but the emergence of the new periodical in 1859, out of the ashes of his fallout with Bradbury and Evans over control of *Household Words,* brought with it a more ambitious idea of how serialized fiction in a weekly periodical might come to enjoy a central place in the lives of the reading public. *A Tale of Two Cities* was the first serialized novel in *All the Year Round* and was published in weekly installments between April 30, 1859, and November 26, 1859. The editorial note printed in the last installment, on a page that saw both the end of *A Tale of Two Cities* and the beginning of *A Woman in White,* read as follows:

> We purpose always reserving the first place in these pages for a continuous original work of fiction, occupying about the same amount of time in its serial publication, as that which is just completed. The second story of our series we now beg to introduce to the attention of our readers. It will pass, next week, into the station hitherto occupied by *A Tale of Two Cities.* And it

---

66. Dickens, *A Tale of Two Cities,* 357.
67. Ibid, 358.

is our hope and aim, while we work hard at every other department of our journal, to produce, in this one, some sustained works of imagination that may become part of English Literature.

Featuring contributions by major writers such as Wilkie Collins, Edward Bulwer-Lytton, and Elisabeth Gaskell, *All the Year Round* included an epigraph from Shakespeare on each title page and gave prominence to Dickens's role as conductor. Taken together, this amounted to a major statement about Dickens's literary standing.[68] Yet the language on the title page goes further than a claim to canonicity and literary fame. *All the Year Round* also claims to be "*the* story of our lives, from year to year" and, in reworking the quotation from *Othello* that it uses for its epigraph, the periodical changes the "story of *my* life / From year to year" to include all our lives.[69]

By designing Dickens's new periodical in the way that he did, *All the Year Round* took on a priestly or preacher-like role, with the aim of "intervening regularly in the lives of his readers."[70] At a point in Victorian life where the Bible was still the main guiding narrative for much of the population, Dickens's "continuous work of fiction" made a bold claim when it promised to articulate the "story of our lives, from year to year." The publishing rhythm of the journal was clearly meant to establish a new habit of reading (weekly publication, all the year round), and the liturgical intimations lent support to the fear of some evangelicals that the Bible might be in danger of losing its position at the center of cultural life.[71] While we should be cautious about how we read these concerns, for the reasons outlined in the previous chapter, there was widespread anxiety among evangelicals about the reach of serialized fiction and the effect that this might have on people's reading habits. What becomes clear on examining *All the Year Round* is that this concern was not wholly without foundation.

Dickens seems to have shared evangelicals' sense that the narrative provided through his own authorship and editorial oversight might rival the religious story they told. This possibility emerges from the language Dickens used in a letter to John Foster, dated October 6, 1860. Listen to the strong religious overtones in the vocabulary Dickens uses when explaining how a decline in

---

68. Wynne discusses the literary ambition of *All the Year Round* in *The Sensation Novel and the Victorian Family Magazine*, 22–28.
69. Shakespeare, *Othello*, I.iii.128–29, emphasis mine.
70. Andrews, *Charles Dickens and His Performing Selves*, 16.
71. In making this claim, I am indebted to Schramm's suggestion that Dickens "created works which spoke to the heart of the nation with an almost liturgical power." Schramm, *Atonement and Self-Sacrifice in Nineteenth-Century Narrative*, 180.

All the Year Round's sales led to the serialization of his new work as a replacement lead novel for Charles Lever's unpopular *A Day's Ride*: "The sacrifice of *Great Expectations* is really and truly made for myself. The property of *All the Year Round* is far too valuable, in every way, to be much endangered. Our fall is not large, but we have a considerable advance in hand of the story [by Lever] . . . and there is no vitality in it, and no chance whatever of stopping the fall."[72] Dickens's view of himself as savior extended beyond *All the Year Round*, but the view of himself as creator, governor, preserver, and redeemer was certainly evident in the editorial decisions he made when conducting the periodical.[73] Lillian Nayder argues that the periodical continued a controlling trend that Dickens had established earlier at *Household Words*, where he directed the management team around him and "conceived of himself as one who grants legitimacy to works of fiction." This editorial control did not lessen when one periodical finished and another began, as Nayder points out: "Dickens's power to legitimate was brought home to both him and Collins during their exchange over Reade's *Griffith Gaunt*, with Dickens explaining what he would—and would not—'pass' as the editor of *All the Year Round*."[74]

Dickens's desire to control every aspect of *All the Year Round* was likely exacerbated by the recent memory of losing control of *Household Words*. If this is the case, then the periodical can be said to follow the direction of the opening novel in maneuvering everything around a sacrificial death and looking toward the new life that this enables. Other theological ideas are conveyed through the language Dickens chooses to describe his latest editorial position. The reference to Dickens as the periodical's "conductor" not only reinforces the sense in which he is trying to orchestrate a new rhythm of family reading; it conveys how the editor's influence coexists with the voices of those who contribute to the periodical.[75] This model of coexistence parallels a popular evangelical trope for explaining God's providential work in saving humanity.[76] Faced with the difficulty of explaining how human agency fitted into God's

---

72. Dickens, Letter to John Forster (October 6, 1860), in Storey, ed., *The Letters of Charles Dickens*, 9:320.

73. Consider, for example, his work with fallen women at Urania Cottage, discussed by Jenny Hartley in *Charles Dickens and the House of Fallen Women*. Hartley reads Dickens's management at Urania Cottage more benevolently than I do.

74. Nayder, *Unequal Partners*, 158.

75. Contemporaries of Dickens were aware, however, that Dickens's description of himself as a conductor needed to be treated with suspicion. Alexander Smith observed: "There is a certain weekly journal conducted by a master of fiction, which seems to be entirely written by the editor; certain portions when the editor is at his best, other portions when his eyes were weary." Smith, "Literary Work," *Good Words* (1863), 742.

76. See, for example, the title of two of W. Arnot's four talks on Romans 6:13 (evening three, "Instruments of Righteousness—How They Are Formed," and evening four, "Instruments

plan of salvation (e.g., Did God need humans to proclaim his message? Did humans need to repent to enable God's forgiveness?), evangelical discussions of the gospel frequently used the term "instrumentality." W. Dalton could explain that "conversion, as to its cause and origin, is of God, but instrumentally it is the work of man," and John Venn could switch the source of agency, without any real disagreement, and insist that the gospel was "the only real and universal remedy—the only instrument for regenerating the world."[77] Like Dickens's talk of "conducting" the periodical, references to instrumentality offered evangelicals a language for explaining how different elements might play their part within a divinely orchestrated scheme.

While the parallel with God might seem to position Dickens as a secular rival to his divine counterpart, it makes more sense to think of him as a competitor of the evangelical preachers of his day. There is little to suggest that Dickens ever thought of himself as taking over from God, but there is a strong body of evidence to support the idea that Dickens saw himself as a rival to some of the other prominent Christian voices of his age. Valentine Cunningham is right to describe Dickens as an author who preaches through his novels and rivals other Protestant "teachers and preachers of righteousness."[78] While the novelist differs from many of his ecclesial rivals by rejecting the suggestion that he is channeling words from on high—those who lay claim to such "spiritual revelations," such as Mrs. Joanna Southcott, are objects of amusement from the very start of *A Tale of Two Cities*—there were plenty of evangelical preachers who rejected the idea of extemporary preaching and delivered their message with a level of effort and skill that Dickens thought he could surpass.[79]

Unlike the "sonorous sermon" announced by Mr. Lorry's watch, the message Dickens preaches is one he believes to be efficacious and capable of transforming the lives of his readers: "For tears at the end, the ending in tears—tears of the characters, tear-inducements for readers—are the repeated outwards signs [for Dickens] of the Christ spirit."[80] We can see Dickens's interest in preaching for a response in both the climactic moments of *A Tale of Two Cities* and the public readings he gave during the last decade of his life. As Malcolm Andrews explains, the message of these readings and its delivery

---

of Righteousness—How They Are Used" in "At Home in the Scriptures: A Series of Family Readings on the Sunday Evenings of December," *Good Words* (1862), 758–66.

77. In Anon., ed. *Things That Accompany Salvation*, 216, 87.

78. Cunningham, "Dickens and Christianity," in Paroissien, ed., *A Companion to Charles Dickens*, 271.

79. Dickens, *A Tale of Two Cities*, 1.

80. Ibid, 16; Cunningham, "Dickens and Christianity," in Paroissien, ed., *A Companion to Charles Dickens*, 260.

were constructed with great care: "He meticulously designed the set and props for his Readings; he determined the choice of repertoire, the venues, and the dates and times of performances. In effect, in this form of delivery of his work, he was author, publisher, and adaptor: he had absolute power over the transmission of his own material."[81] The preparation and design of these reading were remarkably similar to the care with which Dickens conducted his own novel and other people's fiction in the pages of *All the Year Round*. In every case, Dickens was exploring effective means of making his voice heard: "The assertive voice and the sense of a powerful managerial presence in orchestrating the fiction must account for much of the success of Dickens as a serial novelist: both were, of course, central to the success of the Readings."[82]

While Andrews does not write directly of the novelist as a new preacher for his time, the connection is one that Dickens himself encourages in "The Uncommercial Traveller: Two Views of a Cheap Theatre." Published in *All the Year Round* on February 25, 1860, the essay records Dickens's experience of going to watch a play at the Britannia Theatre on a Saturday evening and then listening to a sermon given by the evangelical Rev. Newman Hall at the same theater the next day.[83] In light of Dickens's ongoing interest in communicating his message as effectively as possible, it is unsurprising that the efforts of some evangelicals to find a different environment for their message should have attracted his attention. It is also worth noting how closely the studious description of the pulpit and its setting—"The chandeliers in the ceiling were lighted; there was no light on the stage. . . . In the centre . . . in a desk or pulpit covered with red baize, was the presiding minister"—accords with the set Dickens developed for his own readings.[84]

In his account of the two performances he hears at the theater, Dickens emphasizes the four thousand or so who come to the Sunday performance and welcomes the decision to take a religious message to the masses. His criticism of some of the techniques used in the sermon includes, apparently without irony, a complaint about the use of unrealistic character, yet he praises the "large Christianity of his [the preacher's] general tone."[85] In the final para-

---

81. Andrews, *Dickens and His Performing Selves*, 28.
82. Ibid, 30.
83. Dickens does not name Hall in his article. The gloss comes from a report in the *Record* newspaper (January 30, 1860). See the head note to the reprint of "The Uncommercial Traveller: Two Views of a Cheap Theatre" in Slater and Drew, eds., *The Dent Uniform Edition of Dickens' Journalism*, vol. 4.
84. Ibid., 58. Compare this description with Andrews, *Dickens and His Performing Selves*, 126–46.
85. Dickens, "The Uncommercial Traveller: Two View of a Cheap Theatre," in Slater and Drew, eds., *The Dent Uniform Edition of Dickens' Journalism*, 60.

graph, Dickens introduces a "third head, taking precedence of all others, to which my remarks on the discourse I heard, have tended."[86] Highlighting the models for preaching to be found in the New Testament, he urges all Sunday preachers to imitate them and overcome the difficulty of the "verse-form" in the King James Bible by "setting forth the history in narrative, with no fear of exhausting it."[87] Up until this point, the case for including Dickens's own writing within the call to repeat and reimagine the biblical story remains ambiguous. But when Dickens goes on to list a series of resurrection incidents in the Gospels, starting with the widow's son and the ruler's daughter (Luke 7; Matthew 9) and finishing with the raising of Lazarus from the dead (John 11), the parallel with the central motif of *A Tale of Two Cities* becomes more obvious and prompts the question of what this advice for preachers might mean for the novelist who gives it.

Drawing his essay to a conclusion, Dickens writes: "Let the preacher who will thoroughly forget himself and remember no individuality but one, and no eloquence but one, stand up before four thousand men and women at the Britannia Theatre any Sunday night, recounting that narrative to them as fellow creatures, and he shall see a sight!"[88] The idea that a novelist might be best suited to instruct preachers how to preach is startling. It is not, however, the only major claim Dickens makes in the essay. Given the increasingly large audience for his own material, Dickens's advice for Hall and his associates to simply imitate the New Testament can be seen as advice that Dickens no longer thinks he needs to heed himself. This is not to say that Dickens gives up on the Christian gospel, nor do I think that he is questioning the right of others to proclaim a story of salvation. But I do think that his own tales and their telling have, in his eyes at least, started to overshadow the story that the evangelical church proclaims.

Those in the evangelical community who were critical of Dickens were right to see his agenda for converting religion into fiction as a potential rival to their own proclamations of the biblical story. Yet Dickens's approach to storytelling retained a surprising amount of common ground with the approach of the evangelical community. Both favored narratives around a unifying moment of revelation. Although evangelicals often seemed keen to defend the authority of scripture by rendering it static, their emphasis on proclaiming the gospel suggests that they recognized the drama of the biblical narrative and the importance of people's participation in it. Evangelicals shared with Dickens a belief that words meant most when they were heard and responded to,

---

86. Ibid, 61.
87. Ibid, 62.
88. Ibid.

and the novelist's preoccupation with conversion is indebted to those within this religious movement. Thus while there are many options open to us as we try to come to terms with Dickens's talk of the Christian religion, I think Cunningham is right to characterize the novelist's work as forcefully as he does: "The preacher as Resurrection Man, giving new life to certain old Bible narratives, re-narrating the Bible as a set of resurrection narratives, doing sermon as narrative and narrative as sermon: this is, we can well believe, Dickens's vision of himself, as the only effective Christian preacher for his time."[89]

---

89. Cunningham, "Dickens and Christianity," in Paroissien, ed., *A Companion to Charles Dickens*, 275.

CHAPTER 3

Good Words and the Great Commission

*W*riting in *The Call to Seriousness: The Evangelical Impact on the Victorians* (1976), Ian Bradley insists that evangelicals "were prepared to try anything if there was some chance that it might lead to a soul being saved."[1] For all the significant developments over recent decades in our understanding of Victorian evangelicalism, Bradley's observation is one with which we still need to come to terms. What mattered most for evangelicals was the gospel, the message that Jesus had died on the cross to save sinners from their sin. There was nothing unusual about Thomas Binney describing this message as "the full statement of evangelical truth," and fellow Victorian evangelicals regularly insisted that all one had to do to receive this salvation was to accept the personal import of this "good news."[2] Every effort was made to keep the details as to what this acceptance entailed straightforward. Unbelievers were encouraged to acknowledge their sin, ask God's for-

---

1. Bradley, *The Call to Seriousness*, 34.
2. Thomas Binney, "Our Sunday Evenings in May," *Good Words* (1861), 302. Noting the integral link between evangelism and evangelicalism, Mark Noll explains: "The English word 'evangelical' comes from a transliteration of the Greek noun euangelion, which was used by the writers of the New Testament to signify the glad tidings—the good news—of Jesus' appearance on earth as the Son of God to accomplish God's plan of salvation for needy humans. . . . Thus, 'evangelical' religion has always been 'gospel' religion, or religion focusing on the 'good news' of salvation brought to sinners by Jesus Christ." See Mark Noll, "What Is 'Evangelical'?" in McDermott, ed., *The Oxford Handbook to Evangelical Theology*, 20–21.

giveness, and place their trust in Christ. The Scottish evangelical clergyman, Norman Macleod, was one of many midcentury evangelicals who sought to affirm the simplicity of this message: "For Christianity, we repeat, is not a mere system of morals or of doctrines, apart from a living Person; but is Jesus for us, Jesus to us, Jesus in us, Jesus ours, and with Him all things, now and for ever!"[3]

It was inevitable that this simple gospel message would sound different when it was translated into fiction. The Victorian novel was not, as I have been arguing throughout this book, an inherently secular form. But its long, complex, and mutable nature—a set of qualities exacerbated through publication in periodicals—was at odds with the heavily distilled account of the biblical story favored by evangelicals.[4] The tension did not stop evangelicals from seeking to co-opt the novel for evangelistic purposes, however, and a belief that the novel might help communicate the gospel was part of a broader evangelical enthusiasm for all aspects of print culture. Evangelicals quickly understood how the rise of cheap print could help them communicate their message. Declaring that "the beginning of the nineteenth century marks an epoch of revival in the Protestant [evangelical] Church," Macleod pointed to a growth in missionary organizations, identifying ten missionary societies at the beginning of the century and fifty-one by the time of his article in 1862. He then went on to draw attention to the extensive publishing work of the Religious Tract Society:

> That Society was formed in 1799. During the first year of its operations . . . it had issued 200,000 tracts. What is its present working power? . . . Its annual distribution of tracts . . . [is] 21,407,803. . . . What a mighty agency has this been for the dissemination of religious truth! How extensive the influence, how grand the immortality, which the printing press, employed with such evangelical Christian zeal, secures to the labours of men of God.[5]

Macleod was not alone in realizing how much a burgeoning publishing industry had to offer evangelicals, and the Religious Tract Society was one of a large number of publishers to utilize print in an effort to proclaim the gospel. Graham Law identifies "evangelicals" as "among the first groups" in the nineteenth century "to exploit the possibilities of the mass production and distribution of

---

3. Macleod, "What If Christianity Is Not True?," *Good Words* (1862), 129.

4. Deborah Wynne explains how periodicals encouraged dialogue between different contributors and forms, including the novel, and offered "sites of simultaneity." Wynne, *The Sensation Novel and the Victorian Family Magazine*, 20.

5. Macleod, "Missions in the Nineteenth Century," *Good Words* (1862), 261–62.

reading matter," and Aileen Fyfe's study of the Religious Tract Society reveals how evangelical publication readily embraced several types of writing, including science.[6]

Despite their considerable investment in print culture, evangelical reservations about what people read did not go away. As one anonymous contributor to the *Evangelical Magazine* put it: "How much of the literature of the day is there, of which we may read whole columns, without there being suggested a single thought to quicken the life of our soul?"[7] For evangelicals involved with writing and producing literature of their own, the desire to quicken the soul, to "write stories [not] merely as a literary man, to give amusement, or as works of art only, but . . . [to] always keep before me the one end of leading souls to know and love God,"[8] raised the question of how far one might go in accommodating their message to the age in which they lived. To what extent could the story of Jesus be reimagined and retranslated for the Victorian era? We tend to presume that this was only a question for missionaries who sought to take their message abroad, but the dilemma was just as real for those who sought to proselytize at home. Although the evangelical insistence on a simple core message seemed to discourage latitude in the translation of the gospel into the cultural forms of the day, the determination to help others understand the heart of the gospel also led to an appreciation of the flexibility and freedom offered by fiction.

The tension between wanting to think about their message as faithful to an original and straightforward gospel yet capable of adapting to the needs of a new audience is evident in *Good Words*, the midmarket family periodical that is the focus of this chapter. Published by Alexander Strahan and edited by Norman Macleod, *Good Words* experimented with the use of different literary forms, including the novel. Material was written by evangelical and nonevangelical writers, and utilized for evangelistic ends by the publisher and editor. In the first section of this chapter, I examine the evangelical orientation of *Good Words* more closely, showing how elements within the periodical that have sometimes been interpreted as secular were consistent with evangelicalism. *Good Words* was not the only periodical of the period to experiment with fiction and other less overtly religious forms of writing.[9] Yet it stands out as a valuable case study, not least because of its title, which provides a useful opportunity for reevaluating the contribution of evangelical thought to the

---

6. Law, *Serializing Fiction*, 8; see also Fyfe, *Science and Salvation*.
7. Anon., "Cleaving to the Dust," *The Evangelical Magazine* (1864), 792.
8. D. Macleod, *Memoir of Norman Macleod*, 2:110.
9. See the *Leisure Hour* and the *Quiver*, for instance.

Victorian novel. Although evangelicals insisted that the gospel concerned the good news of unearned salvation through Christ, the movement was often better known as the century's moral guardian, and it is the latter rather than the former that has left the stronger legacy in critical thought about the novel. In the second section, I explore the novel Ellen Wood contributed to *Good Words* and show how easy it was for the evangelical order of things to grow confused, with the talk of salvation being overtaken by moralistic discourse. This was not, though, the only outcome of having nonevangelical novelists write for the periodical. The final section examines the contribution of George MacDonald, a writer who did not think of himself as an evangelical but shared many of the movement's theological interests, nonetheless. MacDonald's involvement with *Good Words* prompts questions about where the limits of evangelicalism lie. What emerges from his contribution is the possibility that some of the theological breadth commonly associated with the so-called liberal turn of the broad church might be better understood within the context of an evangelical faith that valorized theological reform and the openness required by the radical challenge of the gospel. Anyone willing, in the words of Bradley, to "try anything if there was some chance that it might lead to a soul being saved" was likely to risk their religious identity in the process of proclaiming that message. To put it another way, if a movement really was committed to being "all things to all men, that I might by all means save some," as both the Apostle Paul and Macleod declared, it had to be willing to sacrifice a more stable sense of its religious identity along the way.[10]

THE GOSPEL OF *GOOD WORDS*

Following a brief appearance in an earlier incarnation (the *Christian Guest*, published in 1859), *Good Words* first appeared in 1860. Published by Strahan, a Scottish publishing entrepreneur, and edited by Macleod, a well-known evangelical moderate in the Church of Scotland, the periodical was aimed at the crowded family market, offering, to quote its George-Herbert-inspired motto, "good words [that] are worth much and cost little." The words cost slightly more from January 1861, when the periodical moved from weekly to monthly publication with a new price of sixpence, and they began to come from some of the best-known writers of the period. Contributors to *Good Words* in the 1860s included John Hollingshead, Holman Hunt, Charles Kingsley,

---

10. See 1 Corinthians 9:22b: "I have become all things to all people so that by all possible means I might save some," and the citation of Norman Macleod in Donald Macleod, *Memoir of Norman Macleod*, 2:110.

George MacDonald, H. L. Mansel, J. E. Millais, Dinah Maria Mulock, Margaret Oliphant, Samuel Smiles, Lord Alfred Tennyson, Anthony Trollope, and Ellen Wood. Although the content of each issue varied, there was typically a serialized novel across the year (from the likes of Oliphant, MacDonald, and Wood), short essays on anything from science to travel writing, poems, illustrations, the occasional short story, and one or more overtly theological pieces.[11] The theological contributions varied in content and style and were not exclusively evangelical, yet most issues of the journal included a serialized contribution from an evangelical heavyweight such as Henry Alford, C. J. Vaughan, or Thomas Guthrie.

According to Patricia Srebrnik, whose book on Strahan remains an invaluable guide to the periodical's workings, the decision to move *Good Words* to monthly contribution was a deliberate attempt by the Scottish publisher to reposition *Good Words* as a competitor to *Cornhill*.[12] If Strahan's recollections are to be believed, the idea of competing with *Cornhill* had an even earlier history. Writing retrospectively, Strahan drew attention to the fact that: "It so happened that Part I of 'Good Words' was published on the same day as Part I of the 'Cornhill Magazine.'"[13] Whether by intention or accident, the two periodicals competed for an overlapping market and had comparable sales figures in the early years: at the start of 1862, *Good Words* was selling around seventy thousand copies, only slightly less than *Cornhill*'s eighty thousand copies. Talking about the two journals together helps us appreciate the ambition and scope of the publication produced by Strahan and Macleod, as well as reminding us that *Cornhill* was not as secular as much of the subsequent history of Victorian periodicals has implied.[14] Although *Cornhill* did not include

---

11. In recent years, critics have become more interested in some of the different forms and genres that appeared in *Good Words*. See Kooistra, "'Making Poetry' in *Good Words*," and Ehnes, "Religion, Readership and the Periodical Press."

12. Srebrnik, *Alexander Strahan*, 37–47. Elsewhere, Mark Turner follows Srebrnik in comparing *Good Words* with *Cornhill*, although he also makes a persuasive case for comparing the weekly predecessor of *Good Words* with Dickens's *Household Words*. See Turner, *Trollope and the Magazines*, chapter 2.

13. Strahan, *Norman Macleod*, 10.

14. I am deliberately referring to *Good Words* as the joint work of Strahan and Macleod. Although Srebrnik's book on Strahan offers an authoritative guide to the workings of *Good Words*, she has a tendency to overplay her subject's involvement with the periodical. For example, we are told that Strahan's letters to John Hollingshead "demonstrate that although Macleod occasionally exercised the right of veto over manuscripts, it was Strahan who performed the bulk of the actual editorial work" (42). Yet the evidence cited does not justify the claim. While Strahan may have corresponded with Hollingshead and while he was clearly willing to make decisions without consulting his editor, Macleod handled a number of other contributors, from Anthony Trollope to J. M. Ludlow. The toll this exacted on Macleod is confirmed by his brother: "As the next twelve years were the last [i.e., 1860–72], so they were

the same sort of evangelical homilies that featured in *Good Words*, it regularly addressed "religious" matters, with essays such as Matthew Arnold's "Pagan and Christian Religious Sentiment" (April 1864) and an unsigned piece by Dinah Mulock on "Sermons" (January 1864). It was not unusual for people to read both journals, and a number of contributors, including Mulock and MacDonald, moved freely between the publications.[15] Moreover, a letter from MacDonald to his wife, likely written in the early 1860s, suggests that MacDonald discussed with George Smith the possibility of taking on the editorship of the *Cornhill* in the same decade that would later see the author of *Phantastes* (1858) emerge first as a regular contributor to *Good Words* and then as editor of *Good Words for the Young*.[16]

Although *Good Words*'s combination of explicitly theological writing with material that is less recognizably religious was not wholly unique, it is still striking enough to make us think about what we associate with the terms sacred and secular. This sort of reflection was certainly present in the journal itself, with Macleod presenting the following editorial note at the end of the December 1860 issue: "When I accepted the Editorship of this Magazine, my principal motive was the desire to provide a Periodical for all the week, whose articles should be wholly original, and which should not only be written in a Christian spirit, or merely blend 'the religious' with 'the secular,' but should also yoke them together without compromise." Macleod believed there was a long-standing theological precedent for his desire to break with the secular/religious divide that emerged as the major framework of modern secularism, but this did not mean that his endeavor to yoke different elements together was straightforward. For Mark Turner, one of a small number of

---

the most laborious and most important of his life. In addition to his onerous pastoral duties, he now accepted the editorship of *Good Words*. The voluminous correspondence which that office entailed necessary occupied much of his time." D. Macleod, *Memoir of Norman Macleod*, 2:95.

15. References to the MacDonald family reading both journals can be found in the George MacDonald Collection at the Beinecke Library, Yale. See Gen MSS 103, Box 7, folder 235 (letter from George MacDonald to Louisa, dated April 1860, concerning the *Cornhill*) and folder 237 (letter from Lily to Louisa, dated March 5, 1862, concerning *Good Words*).

16. See George MacDonald Collection, Beinecke Library, Yale, Gen MSS 103, Box 7, folder 238. MacDonald's letter to his wife includes: "I saw Mr Smith yesterday, and gave him a copy of my lecture. I found him full of delight with *Phantastes*. . . . But he could not give me much hope about the Editorship, & I have taken less than he gave. . . . As soon as Moir heard that I was a competitor, he said to Smith that if he stood in my way he would withdraw at once. But that could not be you know, for it does not follow that they would choose me if he withdrew, seeing that that there are very few Editors in London who have not applied for it. Moir will have a good chance, Smith says." While the letter is undated, it has been sorted alongside other material from 1863–64. The *Cornhill* is not mentioned by name, but it is difficult to think what other periodical MacDonald could be referring to.

critics to have written on *Good Words,* the journal's combination of religious and secular material generated considerable anxiety among those in charge and explains many of the changes in format that occurred during the first few years.[17] Alongside the move to monthly publication already mentioned, these changes included the introduction of named contributors, the increasing space given over to advertisements, and the changing layout of the title page. Analyzing these alterations, Turner concludes that *Good Words* suffered from "unstable identity" in its early years.[18]

To reflect further on Turner's conclusion, we need to go back to his starting point: the decision that Macleod took in 1863 to reject Trollope's *Rachel Ray,* a novel that the editor had previously commissioned for publication in *Good Words.* As Turner points out, this rejection of Trollope's novel was heavily motivated by the growing criticism that Macleod's periodical was receiving from some of his fellow evangelicals in 1863. Leading the criticism was the *Record,* a theologically conservative Anglican evangelical newspaper, which complained:

> There is a "mingle-mangle" . . . of persons, as well as of things, in *Good Words,* against which we indignantly protest. There is a spurious liberalism prevalent in the present day, which rejoices in seeing persons of the most opposite and antagonistic opinions brought to work, speak, or write together. . . . We think this has a direct tendency to the utter confounding of truth with error; and we are convinced that in all such compromises the truth loses all that error gains, and that all the gain is on the side of error.[19]

By criticizing MacLeod's "mingle-mangle," the *Record* was seeking to affirm a dualism that it believed to be present in the New Testament: an absolute distinction between light and dark, good and evil, the sheep and the goats. What the *Record* found so disconcerting about *Good Words* was the way in which it dealt with material that could not be categorized using this formula. How, for example, were the biblical commentaries (sacred) from Stanley (associated with the broad church and largely considered secular) to be viewed? And what status was to be accorded to the fiction (secular) contributed by some of the

---

17. Turner, *Trollope and the Magazines,* chapter 2.

18. Ibid., 59. In contrast to Turner's observation that the advertising base for *Good Words* in the 1860s "relied mostly on secular products," we should remember both that it was not unusual for evangelical magazines of the period to include advertisements and that a large number of the manufacturers of the advertised goods had a connection with Christian churches. Although monetary idolatry remained a concern, most evangelicals saw little intrinsic conflict between commerce and belief.

19. Anon., *Good Words: The Theology of Its Editor and of Some of Its Contributors,* 5.

evangelicals (sacred) who wrote for the periodical? A sense of the increasing inadequacy of the classifications it was using emerges from the *Record*'s observation that "it is no easy matter to disentangle the finespun web of sophistry, and to lay one's hand on the precise point where deviation from the truth begins."[20] Later on, the *Record* complains of Macleod's theology that "it is very difficult to lay hold of his statements, for they are cleverly and artfully put."[21] At the heart of these concerns about the effect of the intellect and the imagination is a fear that *Good Words* might undermine the evangelical purchase on an easily discerned and incontrovertible truth.

Although we should be cautious about treating the *Record* as representative of the evangelical tradition, there were other evangelicals who also saw the literary imagination as a threat to biblical truth. A decade after the controversy between *Good Words* and the *Record* subsided, George McCrie ruminated:

> Many of our poets and novelists are teaching an erroneous theology with all the earnestness of missionaries. . . . It would be well to remember that heresy is a worse and more insidious evil than licentiousness, and that it cannot assume a more treacherous form than when conveyed in productions which are beyond the ordinary tribunals of theological criticism, and which are recommended to the minds of the young by the irresistible attractions of fancy and genius.[22]

It is easy for us to find fault with the thinking of evangelicals who decry the imagination and claim to know fully what truth is and what it is not. Yet similarly rigid binaries are present in our own discourse. Most problematically, and despite the important interventions of Charles Taylor and others, a great deal of modern scholarship on the Victorian period continues to see the religious and the secular as radically different entities that can be identified with confidence. This is a criticism that one might level against Turner's otherwise helpful analysis of *Good Words*. He perpetuates the idea that the sacred and

---

20. Ibid., 2.
21. Ibid., 18.
22. McCrie, *The Religion of Our Literature* 287. Similar concerns about fancy and imagination were not unknown in the pages of *Good Words*. Arguing that the unreality of fiction threatened readers' zest for life, Isaac Taylor insists that "novel reading is an infatuation which masters souls as surely as dram-drinking does so." He continues: "The alternative for the individual or for the family is this: Novel reading with its consequent *ennui* and utter apathy:—or else genuine feeling, enjoyment, with zest, as to whatever is real in life, in history, in science, in poetry and general literature." Taylor, "The Long Evenings, and Books," *Good Words* (1864), 789.

the secular are discrete and that there was little crossover between religious and nonreligious markets in the mid-nineteenth century: "Strahan came to realize the difficulty in amalgamating two distinct popular audiences. In such a configuration, the tension in attempting to unite two opposites becomes too strong and one of the competing elements must yield."[23] But it is far from clear that the two markets were so distinct.[24] Evangelicalism's penetration into everyday life was extensive by the middle of the nineteenth century, and a number of readers of popular nonevangelical novelists had some allegiance to or sympathy with evangelicalism. The presence of polemical pieces by certain evangelical critics, asking fellow believers to choose more carefully what they read, would seem to confirm that there was considerable overlap between the "religious" and "secular" markets.

Turner is not alone in exaggerating the separation between sacred and secular when reading the literature of the period, and it may well be that our perpetuation of this binary is rooted in nineteenth-century evangelical discourse. The long history of this discourse is such that one struggles to throw it off altogether, and I do not pretend that my own writing is free from misleadingly sharp distinctions. But it is worth considering how positioning the sacred and secular as opposites makes it harder for us to see some areas of nineteenth-century life. Take, for instance, the potential compatibility between religious belief and commercial activity. When Turner constructs a narrative in which the changes to *Good Words* are evidence of the commercial Strahan's increasing domination over the frail and naïve religiosity of Macleod, he ignores the possibility that Strahan's business decisions were also shaped, at least in part, by evangelical belief.[25]

Lorraine Janzen Kooistra tells us, "There can be little doubt of Strahan and Macleod's joint Christian agenda."[26] Tracing precisely the myriad of ways in which someone's religious beliefs shape their actions is difficult, perhaps impossible, but one does not have to isolate every detail to see evidence of

---

23. Turner, *Trollope and the Magazines*, 86.
24. For more on the crossover between religious and secular periodicals, see Knight, "Periodicals and Religion," in King, Easley, and Morton, eds., *The Routledge Handbook to Nineteenth-Century British Periodicals and Newspapers*, 355–64.
25. By contrast, Srebrnik's book on Strahan acknowledges his religious interests and details some of the religious figures (particularly in Scotland) that he knew well. Nevertheless, she still has a tendency to downplay the causal influence of the publisher's evangelical commitment: "Strahan's lifelong interests—in evangelical religion, in democratic political movements, in children's literature—were already apparent in these early lists [of publishing titles]. . . . But he placed his greatest faith in the power of general literature to transform the world socially and morally." Srebrnik, *Alexander Strahan*, 34.
26. Kooistra, "'Making Poetry' in *Good Words*," 127.

Strahan's religious commitment in his publishing decisions. Following the decision to launch *Good Words* with Macleod as editor, Strahan went on to launch the *Sunday Magazine* in October 1864 with another evangelical theologian, Thomas Guthrie, as editor. The *Contemporary Review* began life in January 1866 with Henry Alford (an evangelical Anglican and the Dean of Canterbury) taking the editorial reins, and the editorship of *Good Words for the Young* started with Macleod and then passed to MacDonald (who had a substantial religious following by the 1860s). It is hard to miss the religious dimension of these working relationships, and it is wrong to conclude that Strahan must have been using men like Macleod and MacDonald in a cynical appeal to the religious market. The close friendship that existed between the three men suggests that none of them felt used. In addition, MacDonald published his most overtly religious work with Strahan and Co., including *Unspoken Sermons* (1867) and *The Miracles of Our Lord* (1870), and there was a large number of other religious titles on Strahan's list (some reprinting work first published in *Good Words*), including books by Alford, Guthrie, Macleod, John Henry Newman, Edward Irving, Henry Mansel, and A. K. H. Boyd.

Recognizing the sincerity of Strahan's religious commitment helps us appreciate the extent to which it aligns with Macleod's missionary agenda for *Good Words*. Describing his motivation, Macleod wrote in his personal journal: "Now I have a purpose—a serious, solemn purpose—in *Good Words*. I wish in this peculiar department of ministerial work to which I have been 'called,' and in which I think I have been blessed, 'to become all things to all men, that I might by all means gain some.'"[27] The missionary imperative that led Strahan and Macleod to shape *Good Words* in the way they did was rooted in an evangelical commitment to preach the gospel and convert those who did not know Christ as their personal savior. Corresponding with J. M. Ludlow in August 1861, Macleod explained: "My calling is the gospel, to give myself wholly to it, as I know it and believe it."[28] The pages of *Good Words* were filled with frequent reminders, from Macleod and others, about people's need for salvation. Emphasizing the Great Commission given by Jesus at the end of Matthew's Gospel, evangelicals read their own commitment to the teaching of Jesus in terms of a willingness to make the gospel known and convert others. While the foreign mission field offered a more visible space for fulfilling the Great Commission, evangelicals also recognized the need for the gospel to be preached at home. Admitting that there "may be, in reality, fewer conversions now than in the Church's earlier and brighter days," John Caird nevertheless

---

27. February 22, 1861, entry, cited in D. Macleod, *Memoir of Norman Macleod*, 2:110.
28. Ibid., 2:113.

insisted, in the pages of *Good Words,* that the passing "from nominal to real Christianity" was a "necessity" for individuals in Great Britain.[29] Proselytizing fellow citizens who were already familiar with the Christian faith was less clear-cut than preaching the gospel to those who had no knowledge of Christ, but this did not stop evangelicals from committing themselves to the work of salvation and seeking new evangelistic opportunities.

It was obvious to all but the most theologically conservative evangelicals that proclaiming the gospel would require a significant level of accommodation to the prevailing culture, yet many evangelicals were reluctant to admit the difficulties openly. One regular contributor to *Good Words* acknowledged the problem in the following, grudging manner: "Let us face the fact, that because our nature is not what it ought to be, and what it once was, it is harder to make religious thoughts interesting and real-like than common thoughts."[30] The desire of *Good Words* to attract an audience beyond its core evangelical readership left it with the question of determining how far it might go in adapting the evangelical message to cultural sensitivities. In response to criticisms about the content of *Good Words* articulated by a professor of divinity at the University of Edinburgh, Macleod answered the question about adaptation and defended his "editorial plan": "It is this: that I defy any man to select a number in which there has not been again and again repeated a full statement of Gospel truth."[31] Yet in spite of the forthright tone, the rest of the article indicates an important departure from common evangelical practice regarding the work of proclaiming the gospel. Macleod writes:

> Your third objection is worthy, however, of a more lengthened and serious reply. I quite sympathize with those who urge it:—I mean the fact of writers belonging to different schools in theology, and different departments in literature,—such as Mr. Trollope, Professor Kingsley, and Dr. Stanley,—writing in the same journal with men of acknowledged "Evangelical" sentiments. Now, whether the idea of a religious magazine which shall include among its writers men of all parties and churches be right or wrong, I beg to assure you that I am willing to take on myself all the responsibility for it. Moreover, I can very sincerely say that it was not adopted without most grave, mature, and prayerful consideration. I say *prayerful,* not as a mere phrase, but as expressing a real fact. . . . With these convictions soberly formed, we

---

29. Caird, "Essays for Sunday Reading. I.—Conversion in Primitive and in Modern Times," *Good Words* (1863), 76.

30. Anon. [AKHB], "Concerning the Reasonableness of Certain Words by Christ," *Good Words* (1862), 22.

31. D. Macleod, *Memoir of Norman Macleod,* 2:144.

resolved to make the experiment and to face all its difficulties. I frankly tell you, for I have nothing to conceal, that our purpose was to combine as far as possible in "Good Words" all those elements which have made what are called "secular" periodicals attractive, whether in good fiction, wholesome general literature, or genuine science,—to have these subjects treated in a right and therefore religious spirit, and to add what are called "religious articles," containing a full and uncompromising declaration of the Gospel of Jesus Christ, in every number. I hoped that a journal so conducted would find its ways in sections of society where other periodicals more exclusively "religious" had not penetrated.[32]

Macleod defends the inclusion of different voices on the grounds that they are harmonious with a right religious spirit, but his willingness to distinguish such voices from "a full and uncompromising declaration of the Gospel" and to insist that both elements are necessary if the message is to be made attractive suggests that there is something missing or lacking in the evangelical presentation of the gospel.

Although Macleod's defense of his practice is in keeping with the pragmatism of nineteenth-century evangelicalism, we catch a glimpse of the underlying insecurity that often accompanied evangelical proclamations of the gospel. Evangelicals were frequently reminded that their message was not always perceived to be "good news" by those outside the "religious world." Alarmed that they might not be able to fulfill the Great Commission, evangelicals were forced to admit other nonevangelical voices, to ensure that the gospel was heard widely and had a greater chance of being received enthusiastically. Because Macleod refused to locate any fault in the gospel itself, and because he was only willing to apportion so much blame to the apathy or stubbornness of those he was seeking to reach, his position ends up implying that evangelicals did not have a full and complete purchase on what the gospel was. In looking beyond the confines of their own religious world, and doing so for sound missionary reasons, evangelicals risked compromising or refocusing their message. In this sense, at least, the *Record* was right to complain that "it is no easy matter . . . to lay one's hand on the precise point where deviation from the truth begins."

---

32. Quoted in Strahan, *Norman Macleod*, 14–15. Strahan's extended reprinting (11–21) of the 1863 letter contains a number of textual variations from the version of the letter given in Donald Macleod's *Memoir of Norman Macleod* (2:142–46). The most obvious explanation for the differences is the difficulty of reading Macleod's handwriting.

NOT ALL THAT IT SEEMS: THE STORY OF *OSWALD CRAY*

By turning to *Oswald Cray*, a work first serialized in *Good Words* between January and December 1864, we can see how the evangelical message underwent a shift when expressed through people and forms that were not so closely integrated into the evangelical movement. The shift could also go in the other direction. Commenting on the novel by Ellen Wood, an unnamed reviewer for the *Athenaeum* noted that *Good Words* was a periodical "in which a writer of fiction is placed under some limitations" and inferred that this was why the story was "inferior" to the rest of Wood's novels.[33] The largely negative review included an extensive summary, and as the novel is no longer read widely, if at all, it is worth following the lead of the reviewer and recounting what happens in the tale of domestic drama. When Lady Oswald accidentally dies from a dose of chloroform administered during surgery, the senior attending doctor, Dr. Davenal, takes responsibility for the fatality, even though the death is the fault of his younger colleague and junior partner, Mark Cray. The death creates suspicion about the doctor in some quarters, leading to one of the book's central characters, Oswald Cray, breaking off his provisional engagement to Dr. Davenal's daughter, Sara. Dr. Davenal's other ward, Caroline, is no more successful in love: she marries Oswald's half-brother, Mark Cray, the younger doctor who is actually responsible for Lady Oswald's death. Dr. Davenal's grief at the death of his patient is quickly overtaken when his son, Edward, comes to him to confess involvement with a forgery that now risks being exposed through blackmail. The father agrees to spend his life savings securing his son's reputation, but when Dr. Davenal dies from illness, the job of securing Edward's reputation falls to Sara. Having sacrificed her inheritance, Sara's financial predicament is made more acute when Mark Cray embarks on a financial speculation that fails: he and Caroline end up destitute, and Sara loses the small bit of income that she is due. Just as all hope appears to be lost, Oswald realizes that he has judged Dr. Davenal wrongly and marries Sara in the final stages of the novel. These latter stages also see Caroline dying and Edward returning from military service married to Rose, a young woman who subsequently inherits a fortune that helps facilitate a happy resolution to the story.

The summary helps explain why Turner refers to the novel as the "most sensational novel serialized in the periodical [*Good Words*] in the early 1860s."[34] But while Wood makes deliberate reference in the novel to many

---

33. Anon., Review of *Oswald Cray*, *The Athenaeum* (1864), 859.
34. Turner, *Trollope and the Magazines*, 85.

of the elements associated with the genre of sensation fiction—including bigamy, a contested inheritance, murder, poisoning, and fraud—the events that unfold play down more shocking narrative possibilities. The revelation of Edward's earlier involvement with fraudulent activity is not allowed to become climactic, and the sinister figure of Neal, a servant who spies on the family and breaks into locked desks, turns out to be more of an irritation than a threat. Julie Bizzotto sides with the *Athenaeum* reviewer in suggesting that the editorial style of *Good Words* was responsible for suppressing Wood's sensational tendencies, leaving the author with "little authorial space" to explore the "full potential" of sensation fiction, and she supports her view by comparing *Oswald Cray* with Wood's concurrently serialized novel [published in *Once A Week*], *Lord Oakburn's Daughters*.[35] But it is easy to overplay this line of argument. Emma Liggins, Lyn Pykett, and Jennifer Phegley have claimed elsewhere that that Wood's favored genre was domestic drama, with an infusion of sensation, and despite the fact that some of that drama arises from the criminal and scandalous activity common to sensation fiction, much of what happens in *Oswald Cray* turns out, as in so many other novels by Wood, to be the result of mistrust and misunderstanding.[36] Wood does seem keen though to make her readers think that they are reading a sensation novel of sorts: *Oswald Cray* opens with a decrepit building reminiscent of the opening of *Lady Audley's Secret* (1862); the reference to a Chancery Suit early on recalls the suspense-driven narrative of *Bleak House* (1852–53); the railway is used to symbolize a physical nervousness that, as Nicholas Daly has observed, is endemic to the modern life and reading that preoccupies sensation fiction; and the narrator of Wood's novel refers to one of the character's secrets as a "skeleton [that] would be there to keep."[37]

Sensation fiction is not the only style that Wood seems to feign in *Oswald Cray*. Describing the tone established by Wood during her time as editor of the *Argosy* (1867–87), a periodical that Wood took over from Strahan, Beth Palmer argues that her "overt piety, manifested in her prose as an evangelically

---

35. Bizzotto, "Sensational Sermonizing," 306. Bizzotto argues that the hybridity of *Good Words* also constrained *Oswald Cray*'s religious tone.

36. See Emma Liggins, "Good Housekeeping? Domestic Economy and Suffering Wives in Mrs Henry Wood's Early Fiction," in Liggins and Duffy, eds., *Feminist Readings of Victorian Popular Texts*, 59–60, and Pykett, *The Improper Feminine*, chapter 13. Focusing on Wood's involvement from 1867 with the *Argosy Magazine*, a magazine she bought from Strahan, Phegley argues that the novelist used the editorial power to purvey "a more respectable genre of fiction that I call domesticated sensationalism." Phegley, "Domesticating the Sensation Novelist," 183.

37. Wood, *Oswald Cray* (1864), 201. For an account of the link between railways, sensation, and nerves, see Daly, *Literature, Technology, and Modernity*, chapter 2.

influenced emphasis on the felt nature of belief and the suffering of earthly life, proved more controversial for some critics than her sensationalism."[38] The evangelical influence brought with it certain advantages, as Palmer acknowledges, including a "trustworthy" "house style."[39] It was this sort of house style that some reviewers came to associate with the fiction in *Good Words*, and it was a style that the more theologically aware MacDonald complained about during the period of his own involvement with the magazine. Writing to his wife Louisa in December 1868, MacDonald complains that if "he [Strahan] is going to twin goody with *Good Words*, it has seen the last of me."[40] MacDonald's frustration with Strahan was fleeting but the suspicion of a "goody" style seems to have been present throughout the MacDonald household, with Lily explaining to her mother the surprise discovery of being given a novel by Mary Braddon: "I do not think it will hurt me, it is such slow trash—much more moral than I should have thought, some of it verging on the goody."[41] The objection to a "goody" style was very different from the MacDonald family's concern with narrower elements of evangelical theology, and Lily's comment suggests that Wood was not the only writer in the 1860s to write in this manner, even if she was the best known.[42] Although "goody" writing found a ready audience among some evangelicals, others were more suspicious. Writing in *Good Words*, R. W. Dale warned: "When good men, who have no great religious fervour, use fervent language, which they have caught from others . . . they cannot tell what a disastrous impression they produce upon keen and discriminating minds."[43]

---

38. Palmer, "Dangerous and Foolish Work," 188.
39. Ibid., 190. Bizzotto helpfully points out that Wood's evangelical connections were in evidence before the publication of *Oswald Cray*, with serialized work appearing in the *Quiver* and the *Leisure Hour*. See Bizzotto, "Sensational Sermonizing," 302.
40. George MacDonald to Louisa MacDonald, December 1868, in Beinecke Manuscript Library, Yale, George MacDonald Collection, Gen MSS 103, Box 8, Folder 251. The OED defines "goody" as follows: "*adv.* In accordance with conventional standards of moral conduct or good manners; *esp.* in an affectedly or self-consciously virtuous manner."
41. Lily MacDonald to Louisa MacDonald, June 2, 1869, in Beinecke Manuscript Library, Yale, George MacDonald Collection, Gen MSS 103, Box 8, Folder 255.
42. Charles Wood offered the following assessment of his mother's religious beliefs: "Petty rules and ceremonials formed no part of her creed, but the state of the heart. Into her religion she carried her simple doctrine [enjoy all things in moderation]. . . . In all such things there was the inevitable danger of substituting the ceremonial for the spiritual. Yet she never belonged to the extreme Low Church Party. As a girl she had attended the good old-fashioned High Church Services of the Cathedral. . . . But the services of those days and of these are widely separated. For her religious views Mrs Wood went to the New Testament. . . . Arguments and dogmas she avoided, leading others insensibly by the strongest of all influences—the unerring force of a consistent life." C. Wood, *Memorials of Mrs Henry Wood*, 263–64.
43. Dale, "Unwholesome Words," *Good Words* (1867), 630.

Dale's suspicion becomes more understandable when we consider how a "goody" style pervades the pages of *Oswald Cray*. Toward the close of the novel, Oswald Cray reminds his wife that "it is only through God's mercy that we do repent" and the narrator uses the occasion to conclude with a short homily: "Only though God's mercy! My friends, may it be shed on us all throughout our pilgrimage in this chequered life, and ever abide with us unto the end! Fare you well."[44] Pious though the tone may seem to readers, the evangelical gospel was predicated on a more definite and intentional understanding of salvation. Despite Dr. Davenal reminding his daughter that "we can but cling to Him, and plead our Saviour's sacrifice," most of the sacrifices that take place in the novel do not encourage any sort of analogy with a divine sacrifice.[45] When Oswald's reflection on the sacrifice that he must undertake is used by the narrator to convey a moral lesson to the reader, the philosophy invoked owes more to the golden rule than it does to evangelical theology: "Oswald as a child had learnt the good wholesome doctrine of doing to others as we would be done by: and he *carried it out practically in life*, content to leave the issue with God. How many of us can say as much?"[46] It is hard to identify the theological "doctrine" that the narrator is referring to here. Elsewhere, Wood's house style continually shifts responsibility onto the characters rather than God, to a degree that exceeds the recognition of human free will that exists in some strands of evangelicalism. Take, for instance, the telling use of punctuation in the description of Sara deciding how to pay off the man who has blackmailed her brother: "With God for her guide—and she knew He would be her guide—Sara was not hopeless. She sat down and considered what was to be done."[47] Or the similar parenthetical effect of the punctuation used at the start of the novel to describe a gravestone: "Thoughtful natures would glance at that stone as they passed it, with an inward breath of hope—perhaps of prayer—that the misery experienced by its unhappy tenant in this world, had been exchanged for a life of immortality."[48] In both cases, explicit reference to Christian practice is placed firmly in the margins.

The novel's divergence from orthodox evangelical thought is most apparent when Oswald Cray seeks reconciliation with Sara Davenal. Confessing his "shame and repentance" and seeking "forgiveness," Oswald asks Sara how he might "atone" for what he has done.[49] His language is particularly evoca-

---

44. Wood, *Oswald Cray*, 916.
45. Ibid., 459.
46. Ibid., 689.
47. Ibid., 617.
48. Ibid., 33.
49. Ibid., 909.

tive of evangelical belief, yet his practice differs markedly when he goes on to propose atonement by means of marriage. To appreciate how some of the more conservative evangelicals might have responded to Wood's narrative, it is worth recalling Ryle's account of what evangelical belief is and what it is not:

> The Gospel in fact is a most curiously and delicately compounded medicine and a medicine that is very easily spoiled.
>
> You may spoil the Gospel by *substitution*. You have only to withdraw from the eyes of the sinner the grand object which the Bible proposes to faith,—Jesus Christ; and to substitute another object in His place,—the Church, the Ministry, the Confessional, Baptism, or the Lord's Supper, and the mischief is done. Substitute anything for Christ, and the Gospel is totally spoiled. Do this, either directly or indirectly, and your religion ceases to be Evangelical.[50]

For someone like Ryle, atonement was not an open-ended trope that could be interpreted through the idea of the marriage; on the contrary, it meant substitution and the belief that Jesus' death at Calvary pays off a debt that sinners cannot pay by themselves.[51]

Explaining the techniques by which the Religious Tract Society sought to publish Christian work on more "secular" subjects in the middle of the century, Fyfe tells us that they took inspiration from the work of Thomas Arnold and promoted a "Christian tone," a "literary style intended to create a mood of sound morality and Christian faith."[52] Yet an evangelical commitment to a narrowly demarcated gospel did not always coexist easily with this model of writing in a Christian tone. Evangelicals insisted that there should be adequate reference to humanity's need for salvation. In the case of the Religious Tract Society, Fyfe tells us that its "Christian tone" had "very specific requirements."[53] She elaborates: "The publications had to be read but they also had to convert their readers, and every publication by the Society included a statement of Christ's sacrifice."[54] Although Wood's pious style might seem to be in keeping with the Christian tone expected from an evangelical periodical, the content of her stories can hardly be said to satisfy the evangelical demands for a full expression of the gospel.

---

50. Ryle, "Evangelical Religion: What It Is and What It Is Not," 153–54.
51. See the previous chapter for a more detailed consideration of evangelicalism and the atonement.
52. Fyfe, *Science and Salvation*, 101.
53. Ibid., 105.
54. Ibid., 108.

While it might be argued that the full expression of the gospel was left to some of the other writers of *Good Words*, the problem with including Wood in the periodical was that, like some of the other writers of fiction commissioned to write for *Good Words*, her words lacked the unambiguous commitment of evangelicalism to a clearly delineated version of the gospel message. Yet Macleod was more concerned with making the good news known than he was in securing a narrow definition of evangelical identity. Rather than simply thinking that the inclusion of writers like Wood was a necessary concession if nonevangelical readers were going to be persuaded to read the overt evangelical proclamations of the gospel found elsewhere in the periodical, he thought that Wood and others had a role to play in helping people to understand what the gospel was. The editor's opening "address" in the first issue of *Good Words* made reference to the "literary aid" that had been promised by "writers connected with almost every branch of the Church of Christ" and went on to express Macleod's hope that the words in the periodical would "prove winning words to the young, instructive words to the uninformed, comforting words to the afflicted, and to all words of truth, wisdom, and love, so that after they have been uttered they may leave behind 'endless echoes.'"[55] Although Macleod's providential view of words leaving a legacy of "endless echoes" did not exorcise authorial intention completely, his view that words had a life apart from their human author made him more positively inclined toward fiction and more open to writers who were not demonstrably evangelical in their own religious beliefs. Whatever the failures of Wood's attempt to write *Oswald Cray* for an implied evangelical readership, her lack of success was not a problem for Macleod, who thought of a readership outside the evangelical cohort and believed that Wood's words might help that readership grasp some aspect of the gospel message. As Macleod phrased the hope in a sermon that *Good Words* published when *Oswald Cray* began its serialization: "May the Spirit of God, without whose teaching man's teaching is vain, open the eyes of your understanding, that you may know the truth as it is in Jesus; and open your hearts to receive it in love; that believing in Christ, and receiving his Spirit, you may be saved."[56]

A commitment to the unexpected possibilities of words is a recurring theme in *Oswald Cray*. Words are frequently misheard and misunderstood by characters, registering surprising effects that often prove disturbing. The "eaves-dropping" of Neal, for instance, contributes to the novel's drama, as he hears words out of context and conjectures falsely: "The words which Neal

---

55. Macleod, "Opening Address," *Good Words* (1860).
56. Macleod, "Evenings with Working People in the Barony Church: First Evening—'Not Saved,'" *Good Words* (1864), 29.

heard—and he heard them correctly—would have borne to his mind a very different interpretation had he been enabled to hear the *whole*."[57] In the February issue, the narrator laments more than once the "careless" and secretive words spoken by Lady Oswald.[58] Elsewhere, the text echoes John Milton's motif of poisonous words being poured into unsuspecting ears—Neal is said to have "dropped" a "poisonous hint" to Oswald Cray, even though it is clear that the servant has no real foresight about the harm that will result.[59] Not all of the unexpected consequences of words are bad, however. When, toward the end of the novel, Captain Davenal tells Oswald Cray that it was Mark who administered the chloroform, he has no idea that "the sound of the words [that] fell upon Oswald's ear" will clear up the latter's suspicions and result in a marriage to Sara.[60] Wood uses the ambiguity of language to generate drama rather than make a theological point, but in doing so she unintentionally gives credence to Macleod's belief that the "good words" published in his periodical might aid the cause of the evangelical gospel and be "worth much" more than their authors could have imagined.

GEORGE MACDONALD AND THE THREADS OF A BIGGER GOSPEL

MacDonald shared Macleod's theological commitment to stories with a divine influence extending beyond the conscious imagination of their human authors. Recognizing the importance of human free will and the imagination, both men published stories between 1860 and 1872 embodying a less deterministic version of the Calvinism they had grown up with in Scotland. While some evangelicals criticized the fiction of both men for its "strong revulsion against extreme Calvinism," others praised the way in which their more moderate version of Calvinism lent itself to a broader understanding of the gospel story.[61] In an extended discussion of MacDonald's work, the reviewer for *The British Quarterly Review* observed:

> The practical result is that, in what is generally held to be the most Calvinistic country in Europe [i.e., Scotland], the form of preaching which an

---

57. Wood, *Oswald Cray*, 536, 361.
58. Ibid., 138; see also 141.
59. Ibid., 379.
60. Ibid., 905.
61. Anon., "George MacDonald as a Teacher of Religion," *The London Quarterly Review* (1869), 403.

Englishman commonly understands by Calvinism, that is to say, the express limitation of the Gospel offer[ed] to a few, is all but banished from the pulpit. The Chalmerses, Guthries, Cairds, Macleods, make offer of salvation in the name of Christ as freely, fully, cordially, as ever was done by John Wesley.[62]

When Macleod and MacDonald moved from the pulpit sermon to the periodical story, they sought ways of imagining this freedom without losing sight of what they believed to be God's guiding spirit.[63] In August 1860, *Good Words* serialized Macleod's story for the young, "The Gold Thread," a story in which a young boy, Eric, gets lost in a forest and finds his way out with the aid of a gold thread; in 1867, MacDonald's use of a related motif was signaled by the title of "The Golden Key," the last story in *Dealing with the Fairies*; and three years later, MacDonald developed the trope of a divine guiding thread further in *The Princess and the Goblin* (1870–71), a story that was published initially as a serial in *Good Words for the Young*.

The fact that both Macleod and MacDonald were theologians with a mutual interest in the human imagination was one of the many reasons for the close friendship that flourished between them and also extended to Strahan.[64] These friendships shaped the direction that *Good Words* took in the 1860s. Strahan got to know Macleod when he invited him to become the editor of *Good Words*, and after years of a strong working relationship, Strahan went so far as to call Macleod the father of *The Contemporary Review, The Sunday Magazine, Good Words for the Young*, and *Good Words*. It is less clear when Strahan first met MacDonald, although by the late 1860s Strahan was a regular and welcome guest in the MacDonald household, making jokes with the

---

62. Anon., "George MacDonald," *British Quarterly Review* (1868), 6–7.

63. Reflecting on the impact of evangelicalism on MacDonald, Martin Dubois writes: "The complexity in MacDonald's mature relationship with the religion of his youth . . . is nowhere more evident than in his fictional renderings of its central act of worship: the sermon. Most of MacDonald's realistic novels are heavily autobiographical, and in their portrayal of pulpit religion, draw upon MacDonald's early experience of evangelical revivalism at the Missionar Kirk at Huntly, Aberdeenshire, which he attended in his youth." Dubois, "Sermon and Story," 580.

64. For a more detailed account of MacDonald's theology of the imagination, see his essay "The Imagination: Its Functions and its Culture," first published anonymously in the *British Quarterly Review* (1867). In that essay, MacDonald defends the imagination on the grounds that it is concerned with inquiring "into what God has made." Likening the imagination giving "form to thought" to God's creative activity, MacDonald nevertheless insists that it "is better to keep the word *creation* for that calling out of nothing which is the imagination of God" (46). Further theological discussion of MacDonald's views of the imagination can be found in Dearborn, *Baptized Imagination*, chapters 4 and 5.

family through correspondence and regularly spending time with them.[65] It is similarly difficult to be sure when Macleod and MacDonald first met. MacDonald's son Greville wrote of Macleod's "long affectionate friendship with my father" that was "cemented by a mutual admiration," and in 1865 MacDonald received a warm and jovial endorsement from Macleod in support of his application to become the Chair of Rhetoric at the University of Edinburgh.[66] Following MacDonald's multiple contributions to *Good Words* in the 1860s, the two men worked even more closely on *Good Words for the Young*, with MacDonald taking over as editor in November 1869.

Although MacDonald and Macleod had a similar theological outlook in many respects, the serialization of MacDonald's novel *Guild Court: A London Story* in *Good Words* from January to December 1867 was precipitated by some doctrinal disagreement. Strahan recalled: "When our common friend, Mr George MacDonald, was about to write 'Guild Court,' Dr Macleod was very anxious that no 'heterodox' views on the subject of future punishment should be introduced into it. For hours, the two discussed the matter in the publishing-office with friendliest warmth."[67] In many ways, the novel was an important milestone in the periodical's history, even though the story attracted lukewarm reviews and is typically ignored in MacDonald scholarship. *Guild Court* tells the story of a small group of people in London and focuses on two individuals, Lucy Boxall and Thomas Worboise. Their love for one another undergoes a severe trial when Thomas forsakes a difficult religious upbringing and runs away from home; in the latter stages of the novel, Thomas returns home as a penitent prodigal (albeit one without a welcoming father) and is reunited with Lucy. Reviewing the book for the *Argosy*, Ellen Wood showed little interest in the love story and focused her half-hearted praise on other elements of MacDonald's novel. Expressing pleasure at his choice on this occasion of realism over fantasy, Wood identified what she

---

65. See, for instance, the twenty-seven letters from Strahan to different members of the MacDonald household, in the Beinecke Manuscript Library, Yale, George MacDonald Collection, Gen MSS 103, Box 3, Folder 134.

66. See Greville MacDonald, *George MacDonald and His Wife*, 416. Macleod's accompanying note to his endorsement reads: "My dear MacDonald. I would sooner endow a chair than write a reference for any candidate wishing to fill it. . . . Burn the enclosed if it doesn't suit, but never expect another edition, which w^d bring on a fit of Palsy, what the Scotch old women call a Pop Puff. Wishing you good luck but offering no apologies for having tortured myself by Procrastination . . . I remain, Ever yours." The signature includes a cartoon drawing of a man being hung. See Beinecke Manuscript Library, Yale, George MacDonald Collection, Gen MSS 103, folder 144. The letter is one of two unidentified letters by the same hand in this folder, but the address on one of them (Adelaide Place, Glasgow) is Macleod's.

67. Strahan, *Norman Macleod*, 21.

believed to be the "direct religious lesson" of MacDonald's novel: "Even on a nature with a vast amount of good in it [i.e., Thomas's], the narrowing influence of the strict Evangelical training that would piteously run all characters into one mould, may simply squeeze the sap of religious instinct out of the human being altogether."[68] Wood's reference here is to the evangelical training that Thomas receives at the hands of Mrs. Worboise and a clergyman named Mr. Simon.

The claustrophobic Calvinism of the evangelical Mr. Simon is evident from the start of *Guild Court*: "Your son thinks me too anxious about the fruits of his labour, Mrs. Worboise. But when we think of the briefness of life, and how soon the night comes when no man can work, I do not think we can be too earnest to win souls for our crown of rejoicing when He comes with the holy angels."[69] It would have been difficult for readers of *Good Words* to have missed the allusion of the name that MacDonald chose for his other main evangelical character: Emma Jane Worboise was a well-known evangelical writer who had begun editing *The Christian World Magazine* in 1866. Other elements in *Guild Court* are no less subtle in the way that they invoke elements of evangelicalism only to complain of their violence, narrowness, and blindness. Mr. Simon is said to have "pressed" Thomas "so hard with the stamp of religion that the place was painful" and the former's insistence that one's eternal destination is all that matters renders him incapable of appreciating the latter's livelihood or the "essential sacredness of the work which God would not give a man to do if it were not sacred."[70] Detailing the problem of an evangelical theology that allows the fear of hell to dictate everything else, the narrator writes, this time of (the fictional) Mrs. Worboise: "Her theory of the world was humanity deprived of God. . . . All her anxiety for her son turned upon his final escape from punishment."[71] It is with some justification then that Wood describes the novel's critique of evangelicalism in the way that she does. Yet her limited grasp of evangelical theology leads her to inadvertently misrepresent matters, with Wood erroneously declaring that the main thrust of MacDonald's complaint is directed against the dangers of an evangelical upbringing. This reading sits uneasily alongside the publication of *Guild Court* in a periodical that had a core evangelical readership and a desire to spread the evangelical gospel, and it ignores the fact that the publication of *Guild Court* strengthened the relationship between Macleod and MacDonald rather than rupturing it.

---

68. [Ellen Wood], "Our Log Book," *The Argosy* (1867): 77–78.
69. MacDonald, *Guild Court*, 5.
70. Ibid., 149.
71. Ibid., 217.

What marks out *Guild Court*'s theological critique is the novel's damning account of the narrow vision of the gospel that sometimes circulated within evangelical circles. Thomas complains of his mother that "she and her set use Bible words till they make you hate them," and the failure in the novel of any member of this set to convert others or lead them to what might be described as a closer knowledge of Christ supports Thomas's criticism.[72] By contrast, Lucy, Thomas, and a series of other characters find spiritual sustenance through Mr. Fuller, whose name, like that of Mrs. Worboise, seems deliberately chosen. Asked by his mother to describe Mr. Fuller's theology, Thomas replies: "Mr Fuller, I think, would not feel flattered to be told that he belonged to any party whatever but that of Jesus Christ himself. But I should say, if he belonged to any, it would be the Broad Church."[73] For many commentators, from the nineteenth century to the present, the term "broad church" evokes a theological liberalism at odds with evangelical belief and part of an inevitable transition to secularism. Yet the term "broad church" was used much more variously in the middle of the nineteenth century, and there is not always that much theological coherence between the various figures (F. D. Maurice, Benjamin Jowett, Charles Kingsley, etc.) associated with it. Indeed, the theological position that Mr. Fuller (and, by proxy, MacDonald) occupies is close to the version of evangelicalism advocated by Macleod, indicating considerable overlap between the more orthodox members of the "broad church" and the more moderate expressions of evangelicalism that abounded in the middle part of the century. This overlap can be seen throughout MacDonald's novel but never more so than in the climactic scene, where Mr. Fuller leads the returning Thomas in a prayer of repentance:

> You must give yourself up to the obedience of his Son entirely and utterly, leaving your salvation to him, troubling yourself nothing about that, but ever seeking to see things as he sees them, and to do things as he would have them done. And for this purpose you must study your New Testament in particular, that you may see the glory of God in the face of Christ Jesus; that receiving him as your master, your teacher, your saviour, you may open your heart to the entrance of his spirit, the mind that was in him, that so he may save you.[74]

The gospel outlined here is recognizably evangelical but in a way that avoids the truncated and austere message proclaimed by Mrs. Worboise and Mr. Simon.

---

72. Ibid., 294.
73. Ibid., 762.
74. Ibid., 764.

Rather than seeing the gospel according to Fuller as an alternative to evangelicalism and evidence of a theological liberalism that encouraged the secularization of British religious life, we might read it in the light of MacDonald's friendship with Macleod and conclude that it was consistent with the broad gospel of *Good Words*.[75] In making this suggestion, I am aware that it is not a view that would have been shared by every evangelical during the 1860s. But to presume that the criticism leveled by *The Record* or the clear dividing lines constructed by Ryle constitute the only expressions of authentic evangelicalism is to ignore the internal debates and diversity within this movement during the nineteenth century.[76] Although a figure such as Macleod had his doubts about elements within the evangelical church, his involvement with the creation of the Evangelical Alliance in the 1840s and his commitment in the 1860s to the missionary potential of literary periodicals confirm that he offers as good an example as any of midcentury evangelicalism. MacDonald is less identifiable as an evangelical, for sure, but *Guild Court*'s concern for the gospel is easier to locate within evangelicalism than it is within the more skeptical wing of the broad-church tradition, and there is little doubt that moderate evangelicals found much to admire in MacDonald's writings. To concern oneself with the nature and expression of the Christian "gospel," as in *Guild Court*, or to talk about the meaning of being a follower of Jesus, as MacDonald spoke about repeatedly in his sermons, is to participate in a discussion that, for so much of the nineteenth century, was shaped by a distinctly evangelical discourse.

Throughout *Guild Court*, the narrator sides with Mr. Fuller's understanding of the gospel and articulates a theology that is more wide-ranging, more practical, and more interested in the minutiae of human affairs, than the theology of Mrs. Worboise and Mr. Simon. Describing the influence of Lucy on those in her care, the narrator insists that she "never taught them any religion: she was only, without knowing it, a religion to their eyes," and other less obviously virtuous characters are also said to reveal something of the divine.[77]

---

75. Not every evangelical was convinced that MacDonald had anything to offer evangelicalism, however. In *The Religion of Our Literature*, McCrie insisted that MacDonald's work expressed "intense dislike of evangelical doctrine, as we understand it in Scotland," and McCrie went on to complain about the dissemination of "religious opinions, which are most unsound and dangerous" (295).

76. An interesting case study in this respect is John McLeod Campbell (1800–1872), the nineteenth-century theologian, minister, and cousin of Norman Macleod, who is best known for his work on the atonement. As Peter Kenneth Stevenson observes, Campbell's theological development "should be seen as a theological journey within evangelicalism rather than a way of leaving it behind." See Stevenson, *God in Our Nature*, 221. I am grateful to Andrew Jones for alerting to me this book.

77. MacDonald, *Guild Court*, 220.

Even Thomas points to God when, at the height of his depravity, he rescues a drowning child and elicits the following comment from the narrator: "I think it was the divine, the real self, aroused at the moment by the breath of that wind which bloweth where it listeth, that sprung thus into life and deed, shadowing, I say *shadowing* only, that wonderful saying of our Lord that he that loseth his life shall find it."[78] For MacDonald, the novel's sacramental style, in which all aspects of creation are mined for their ability to convey something of the divine, does not ignore the world's sin and suffering, nor does it contradict evangelical teaching and imply that salvation is possible without the intervention of Christ. What it does instead is to allow the novel to reimagine the gospel in a form that is relevant enough to be grasped and encountered by a multitude of characters in a range of settings. Such imaginative work is in keeping with the missionary ambition of evangelicalism, and presents a significantly different picture from the one offered by Philip Davis when he claims that "already by the mid-1830s Evangelicalism was becoming a victim of its own initial success, a rigidified force whose spiritual dynamic was becoming increasingly absorbed into those worldly practices of frugal economy, paternalistic discipline, and industrious self-help which were to become known as the puritan work ethic."[79]

MacDonald's sacramental style of writing emerged from his reading of pre-Reformation Christian writers and the theology of German Romanticism, and it did not always sit easily with an evangelical tradition that was sometimes skeptical about the ability of the natural world to reveal God. While the use of sacramentalism could support an evangelical desire to make the gospel known through any means possible, its latitude regarding the nature of God's revelation risked destabilizing evangelical ecclesial identity by not describing the gospel within narrow parameters. Unlike the strictly controlled allegory deployed by John Bunyan (in which the literary dimensions of language and the open-ended possibilities of story are played down to ensure that the message remains on point) or the popular evangelical view of language as a means to an end ("now, parables are just stories; they are told for instruction through means of entertainment"), MacDonald insisted on the sacred capacity of words to reveal more than any single part of the church might hold within its grasp.[80] An essay by MacDonald published by *Good Words* in 1865 insisted

---

78. Ibid., 582. I am reminded, here, of the central motif in MacDonald's *At the Back of the North Wind*, serialized in *Good Words for the Young* between November 1868 and October 1870.
79. Davis, *The Oxford English Literary History*, 8:105.
80. Guthrie, "The Parables, Read in the Light of the Present Day," *Good Words* (1863), 1. Commenting on MacDonald's break from a stricter mode of allegory, Stephen Prickett explains: "[He] is not against allegory as such.... What he wants to do is to differentiate

on pursuing the multiple revelatory possibilities of the word "polish," and elsewhere, his fairy stories were committed to exploring new realms of the imagination, even though, as Wood's review of *Guild Court* had reminded readers, this made such work less didactic than many of MacDonald's Scottish realist novels.[81] MacDonald's belief that language could communicate more than we can comprehend was consistent with the evangelical call to make the gospel known in all its fullness, but an enlarged view of the gospel risked extending the story of salvation beyond the limits of a strictly evangelical theology. In the pages of *Guild Court*, a vast array of words, images, and actions are used to invite the reader into the world of the imagination and encourage him or her to see the gospel from different perspectives. Talking to Thomas about the kindness of God, Mr. Fuller explains: "God is all that, and infinitely more! You need not call him by any name till the name bursts from your heart. God our Saviour means all the names in the world and infinitely more."[82] Mr. Fuller's reluctance to prescribe the limits of the gospel is accompanied by a respect for language, as his subsequent comments on the relationship between prayer and an intercessor's love for the person being prayed for, reveal: "I cannot exactly tell how this should be, but if we believe that the figure St Paul uses about our all being members of one body has any true deep meaning in it, we shall have just a glimmering of how it can be so."[83]

The enlarged sense of the gospel in *Guild Court* is made possible by a vocabulary that threads an open-ended alternative to the closed linguistic choices of evangelicals such as Mrs. Worboise. Describing her manipulative reasoning, as she contemplates asking Thomas to use his knowledge of the Greek language to help her read extracts from St. Paul's Epistle to the Romans, the narrator explains: "It was not that she was in the least difficulty about the Apostle's meaning. She knew that as well at least as the Apostle himself; but she would invent an innocent trap to catch a soul with."[84] In contrast to

---

between the mechanical rigidity of 'strict allegory' and what he calls a 'fairy-tale,' which uses allegory as one of a number of modes of symbolic narration." Prickett, *Victorian Fantasy*, 159. The MacDonald family were huge fans of Bunyan's work and staged family performances of *The Pilgrim's Progress*.

81. For some reviewers, the move away from didactic writing was a religious strength. An anonymous reviewer writing in the broadly evangelical *North British Review* commented: "It is not that Mr MacDonald's tales are tagged with a moral. Didactic fiction is bad enough; but didactic fairy tales are the most abominable of literary impositions. Mr MacDonald is not exposed to this censure.... The truth is, that although Mr MacDonald's fairy stories have not, in the technical sense, a moral, they are inspired, like everything else he writes, by a profound religious feeling." Anon., "Mr George MacDonald's Novels," *North British Review* (1866), 4.

82. MacDonald, *Guild Court*, 758.
83. Ibid., 764.
84. Ibid., 433.

Worboise's desire to close in on her prey, the same (July) installment of *Guild Court* finds Lucy contemplating the need for those who have faith in God to outgrow the "swaddling bands of system or dogma" and sees her entering into a conversation with Mattie about the idea that flowers constitute "some of God's Word."[85] The latter image not only embodies the idea of something opening outward but also gestures toward MacDonald's belief that the language of flowers, with its ambiguity of meaning, is integral to divine revelation. Good words are words that live on rather than dying "as soon as they are out of my [Lucy's] mouth," and they are too powerful to be conducted or controlled by any individual.[86] Anticipating the concern of some evangelicals about where this might lead, Mattie complains that the language of flowers gives up its meaning less easily, but Lucy's rejoinder—"you must . . . try to read them and understand them"—offers a different route to comprehending the meaning of the gospel.[87]

While MacDonald was less personally invested in evangelical debates than Macleod or Strahan, the involvement of all three men with *Good Words* and *Good Words for the Young* had a significant effect in the 1860s on evangelical attitudes to the novel. Exploring different ways in which fiction might convey the good news of salvation in Christ was, in so many ways, more evangelical than the "goody" style of a writer like Wood. The fact that Strahan records Macleod's initial reluctance to call the periodical *Good Words*—"His religion was of a robust type, and he thought it sounded too 'goody-good'"—shows the extent to which elements within the evangelical church were worried about losing sight of the missionary orientation of the "good news."[88] In seeking to reappropriate "good words," MacDonald and Macleod urged evangelical literary publishing in the 1860s to be more gospel-centered. *Good Words* may not have been altogether successful in escaping association with "goody" writing, but its content did go some way to proclaiming something other than a moralistic message. The cost, however, was a dissolution of evangelical identity. It was with the Great Commission firmly in mind that Macleod and Strahan commissioned the writers that they did. But by the time *Good Words* had done its missionary work, the gospel was no longer synonymous with the evangelical wing of the church. The story of salvation had become a great "co-mission" rather than the exclusive work of any single Christian movement.

---

85. Ibid., 439.
86. Ibid.
87. Ibid.
88. Strahan, *Norman Macleod*, 10.

CHAPTER 4

Hermeneutics, Evangelical Common Sense, and *The Moonstone*

One does not have to be a great detective like Sergeant Cuff to realize that the "first and greatest of modern detective novels," as T. S. Eliot famously described Wilkie Collins's *The Moonstone* (1868), is concerned with much more than the theft of a diamond.[1] A clue to the novel's lofty preoccupations can be found in the title of the second and longest section: "The Discovery of the Truth." Although the precise nature and identity of that "truth" remains debatable, much of the criticism on the novel written over the last few decades has focused on British Imperialism. Descriptions of Hindu practice open and close the novel, and scholars have written at length about how *The Moonstone* highlights the problems of the British Empire, including the imperial struggle to come to terms with religions other than Christianity.[2] Rather than examining the shadow of religion from the perspective of nineteenth-century imperialism and its critique, this chapter will put the spotlight on Christianity and consider how the novel's "discovery" of the truth relates to the hermeneutical questions faced by evangelicals

---

1. Eliot, "Wilkie Collins and Dickens," in *Selected Essays*, 464.
2. See, for instance: Nayder, *Unequal Partners*, chapter 6; Reitz, *Detecting the Nation*, chapter 3; Free, "Dirty Linen," 340–371; and Arnold, *Victorian Jewelry*, chapter 4. For an excellent survey of older material, from John Reed's seminal 1973 essay on *The Moonstone* to work published in the 1990s, see Nayder, "Recent Wilkie Collins Studies," 257–329 (especially 298–303).

in the 1860s.[3] This line of enquiry may sound a little too convenient, coming as it does in a book that foregrounds the evangelical contribution to the nineteenth-century novel, yet there are good reasons for seeking out connections between the novel that *All the Year Round* serialized from January to August 1868 and the evangelical debates about biblical interpretation that were so prominent throughout the decade.

While *The Moonstone* is frequently read as hostile to evangelicalism, the hermeneutical concerns of this religious movement are integral to the mystery that preoccupies the narrative. Collins may have moved firmly away in adult life from his evangelical upbringing, but this did not stop him from continuing to occupy "common ground" with the religious tradition in which he grew up.[4] Though critical of ideas such as eternal punishment and total depravity, Collins retained an interest in other areas of evangelical belief and practice, and his novels are not averse to locating some of their most "truthful" insights within the discourse of this religious tradition. I am not, then, trying to read Collins as a closet evangelical but seeking, rather, to explore the "subtlety of Collins . . . in his response to evangelicalism."[5] In doing so, I intend to explore the interpretative space opened up by Collins's engagement with evangelicalism, a space that William McKelvy explores in other ways by reading *The Moonstone* as a novel of conversion and tying that idea to the biblical figure of Ezra, nineteenth-century debates about global mission, and the relationship of Christianity to other religious traditions.[6] My chapter not only argues for the importance of biblical hermeneutics to Collins's novel but also for the way in which one aspect of the evangelical contribution to these debates might have ongoing significance for our professional reading in the academy today.

The Moonstone is just one of the novels written by Collins in the 1860s to engage critically and constructively with evangelical theology. We might also consider the recurring arguments about "clap-trap" morality in the introductions to *Armadale* and *No Name*, the Calvinistic overtones in the debates about free will and determinism in *Armadale* (which are linked to the subject of sin through the faintly coded surname of the novel's femme fatale, Lydia Gwilt), the "numerous vague but suggestive mythic and Biblical resonances"

---

3. For a thoughtful exploration of the relationship between religion, empire, and *The Moonstone*, see Gannon, "Hinduism, Spiritual Community and Narrative Form in *The Moonstone*," 297–320.

4. Oulton, *Literature and Religion in Mid-Victorian England*, 195. Oulton explains that "although Collins did not attend a public place of worship as an adult . . . this failure to attend church, unusual though it was, does not necessarily mean that he was not interested in religion" (11–12).

5. Ibid., 197, 198.

6. See McKelvy, "The Importance of Being Ezra."

in *Armadale,* the biblical impulse of the fallen-woman narrative in *No Name,* the prominent placement of Mrs. Catherick's Bible in *The Woman in White,* and the newly (and dubiously) converted Mother Oldershaw at the end of *Armadale.*[7] Collins was evidently conscious of the evangelical community by the time he got to *The Moonstone.* Miss Clack's noisy chatter provides the most explicit evidence of Collins's engagement with evangelical thought, but Godfrey Ablewhite is also conceived of along similar ecclesial lines. Though the references to Godfrey's evangelicalism are less overt than in the case of Collins's tract-wielding spinster, the text is clear about Godfrey's religious orientation. Miss Clack is impressed by "the fascination of his Evangelical voice and manner," and the reader's introduction to Godfrey comes when Gabriel Betteredge describes his experience of hearing the man speak at Exeter Hall, the famous venue in London for evangelical gatherings.[8] Collins's correspondence with his mother suggests that he was conscious of Godfrey's positioning as an evangelical. In a letter to his mother (October 26, 1867), Collins wrote: "You will not be sorry to hear that (on consideration) I have taken the clergyman out of the story—he is Godfrey Ablewhite now, instead of the Reverend. And his line in life is—to manage and advise *Ladies Charities.*"[9]

The Moonstone's engagement with the limitations and insights of evangelical hermeneutics appeared toward the end of a decade in which the question of how the Bible should be read was at the forefront of people's thinking. *Essays and Reviews* (1860) was published at the start of the decade, and by 1869 it had been through thirteen editions and sold 24,250 copies.[10] Its notoriety, however, circulated far more widely. Offering seven critical essays on the Bible, by prominent Anglicans, the book had a seismic effect on those within the established and dissenting church and, by extension, the rest of Victorian society.[11] The impact of the publication was compounded by the subsequent

---

7. Jaffe, *The Victorian Novel Dreams of the Real,* 119. For further discussion about the biblical allusions of *No Name* and the relationship in *The Woman in White* between propriety and the Bible, see Mark Knight, "Sensation Fiction and the Bible" in Lemon et al., eds., *The Blackwell Companion to the Bible in English Literature.*

8. Collins, *The Moonstone,* 280, 89.

9. Baker and Clarke, eds., *The Letters of Wilkie Collins,* 2:297.

10. Shea and Whitla, eds., *Essays and Reviews: The 1860 Text and Its Reading,* 25. This impressive scholarly edition by Shea and Whitla is full of important material regarding the publication history of *Essays and Reviews.*

11. In his influential study of the controversy over *Essays and Reviews,* Josef L. Altholz makes a strong case to support his claim that it "was the religious press that carried the debate" (34). But although he makes reference to the periodicals of evangelical dissent, his emphasis is elsewhere, namely on debates within the Church of England between the evangelicals, the Tractarians, and the "broad church." In this respect, Altholz follows Ieuan Ellis, mistakenly in my view, in seeing *Essays and Reviews* almost exclusively as an internal Anglican affair. See Altholz, *Anatomy of a Controversy*; Ellis, *Seven against Christ.*

appearance of Bishop Colenso's *The Pentateuch and the Book of Joshua Critically Examined* (1862), a skeptical reading of the historical claims in the first few books of the Bible. As Collins remarked in a letter to his mother (November 18, 1862): "Nothing stirs the stagnation of London but Bishop Colenso. A bishop who doesn't believe in Moses and who writes a book to say so, is an Episcopal Portent which makes clergy and laity stare alike."[12]

A brief look at evangelical periodicals of the 1860s makes it clear that the challenge to biblical interpretation was of greater concern than the questions posed by Charles Darwin in *On the Origin of Species* (1859). Throughout publications as varied as the *Christian Observer,* the *Evangelical Magazine,* the *Patriot,* and the *Record,* it is the Bible, not Darwinism, that receives the most attention and is subject to the fiercest debate. When evangelicals did consider scientific challenges to existing bodies of knowledge, their comments were often prompted by figures such as Colenso rather than the work of Darwin, and the emphasis was on insisting that the Word of God remained true: "If what man says is against what God says, it is common sense not to put Scripture aside and to believe what finite man will tell you. . . . I cannot pause to ascertain all that science may say. . . . Thy Word is truth, and whether I understand it or not, I cling to it as such."[13] It would be wrong to imply that evangelical belief in the Bible suddenly collapsed in the 1860s: the German scholarship that informed many of the ideas in *Essays and Reviews* had existed for several decades, and, as their prolific responses demonstrate, evangelicals were used to arguing against such findings and reaffirming the authority of the Bible. Nevertheless, in bringing to the surface long-standing questions about the way in which evangelicals read scripture, *Essays and Reviews* did mark something of a turning point for this religious movement.

The first section of what follows explores the place of evangelicalism within the broader trajectory of Victorian hermeneutics. Locating evangelicalism's attitudes to reading the Bible within the wider interpretive context of the nineteenth century helps us appreciate why *Essays and Reviews* and the publications that followed in its wake were so troubling for evangelicals. It also establishes a context for thinking about some of the ways in which *The Moonstone* critiques the common-sense reading of the Bible promoted by evangelicals. Common sense "affirm[s] that its tenets are immediate deliverances of experience, not deliberated reflections upon it," and in the sphere of textual interpretation, this attitude manifested itself in the claim that the meaning

---

12. Baker and Clarke, *The Letters of Wilkie Collins,* 1:213.
13. Cowan, *Why Is the Bible True?,* 14–15.

of the Bible was plain and self-evident.[14] But this is precisely the claim that is critiqued in *The Moonstone*, as I explore in the second section of this chapter. In the final section, I go on to consider some of the other targets of *The Moonstone*'s hermeneutical critique, especially the professional individual hermeneutic fostered by German Higher Criticism. Ultimately, I suggest, the novel returns to one crucial aspect of a wider evangelical hermeneutic that it otherwise leaves behind: the collective reading of the common-sense tradition.

UNDERSTANDING EVANGELICAL HERMENEUTICS

Given the interests of Samuel Taylor Coleridge, Matthew Arnold, George Eliot, Christina Rossetti, Robert Browning, John Ruskin, and others in the hermeneutical intersections between religion and literature, it is not surprising that literary critics working on the Victorian period have long been interested in biblical hermeneutics. George Landow's *Victorian Types, Victorian Shadows* (1980) and Stephen Prickett's *Words and the Word* (1986), with their respective emphases on typology and the Romantic hermeneutics, made key interventions in the late twentieth century, and work on nineteenth-century biblical hermeneutics has continued to produce important work in the ensuing years.[15] Since the 1990s, however, the attention that Victorian studies as a field has given to questions of evidence and interpretation has, for the most part, shown less interest in the theological roots of hermeneutics and focused more on science and the genre of detective fiction. In *Violent Women and Sensation Fiction: Crime, Medicine and Victorian Popular Culture* (2007), for instance, Andrew Mangham reads the disjunction in Wilkie Collins's fiction between appearance and reality almost entirely in the light of nineteenth-century medical discourse about criminality.[16] Elsewhere, in *Detective Fiction and*

---

14. Geertz, *Local Knowledge*, 75. I quote Geertz in recognition of his influence on subsequent critics in the humanities. It should be noted, however, that his critique of common sense lacks any explicit awareness of the philosophical tradition of Thomas Reid and others.

15. See, for example: Schaffer, *Kubla Khan and the Fall of Jerusalem*; Peterson, "Restoring the Book," *Victorian Poetry* (1994): 209–32; Zemka, *Victorian Testaments*; Styler, *Literary Theology by Women Writers of the Nineteenth Century*; Larsen, *A People of One Book*; LaPorte, *Victorian Poets and the Changing Bible*; and Vance, *Bible and the Novel*. Outside the immediate sphere of Victorian Studies, David Jasper turns his attention to the interpretation of the Bible in the eighteenth and nineteenth centuries in two of the chapters in *A Short History of Hermeneutics*, and there is a wealth of useful material in Hass, et al., eds., *The Oxford Handbook to Theology and English Literature*; Lemon, et al., *The Blackwell Companion to the Bible in English Literature*; Knight, ed., *The Routledge Companion to Literature and Religion*, and the journals *Christianity and Literature*, *Literature and Theology*, and *Religion and Literature*.

16. See Mangham, *Violent Women and Sensation Fiction*.

the Rise of Forensic Science (1999), Ronald Thomas considers how the "detective story often functioned as a kind of lie detector redefining truth for its culture," and he pursues this line of thought without reference to religious epistemology.[17] Sarah Dauncey's contribution to *A Companion to Crime Fiction* (2010) makes the secular implications of this methodological trajectory more explicit when she claims that nineteenth-century views of evidence left theology behind:

> The links between the Sherlock Holmes stories and the reconstructive sciences, such as paleontology, archaeology, and geology, have been well documented by critics.... Over the course of the nineteenth century, traditional religious conceptions of the past were challenged by secular explanations.... This "transition from sacred to secular explanations of the past" gave rise to a new attitude towards the value of material evidence.[18]

Although the reasons for a critical shift away from theological criticism are complex, it is worth noting some of the gaps that the shift creates. The scientific orientation of Lawrence Frank's book *Victorian Detective Fiction and the Nature of Evidence: The Scientific Investigations of Poe, Dickens, and Doyle* (2003) provides a useful starting point, although it would be unfair to imply that the book can serve as a representative of all that has been written recently on the subject of Victorian hermeneutics.[19] In drawing attention to Frank's scientific focus, I do not want to suggest that one must choose between religion and science. There is no reason why a concern with Victorian science must bring with it a neglect of theology, as several recent critics have made clear, and the boundaries between the two disciplines remain highly permeable.[20] Yet Frank follows a number of others in allowing our contemporary sense of a stark choice between religion and science to exaggerate the way we read the Victorian period.[21] Introducing his thesis via an account of John Stuart Mill's

---

17. Thomas, *Detective Fiction and the Rise of Forensic Science*, 6.
18. Dauncey, "Crime, Forensics, and Modern Science," in Rzepka and Horsley, eds., *A Companion to Crime Fiction*, 165–66. Dauncy is quoting here from Rzepka, *Detective Fiction*.
19. Interestingly, Frank deliberately excludes Wilkie Collins from his argument. See Frank, *Victorian Detective Fiction and the Nature of Evidence*, 4.
20. See, for example, Fyfe, *Science and Salvation*, Wheeler-Barclay, *The Science of Religion in Britain, 1860–1915*, and Dixon, Cantor, and Pumfrey, eds., *Science and Religion*, as well as the work of critics such as David N. Livingston, James Moore, Ronald L. Numbers, Jon Topham, and Amy King.
21. I am thinking here of work such as Levine's *Darwin Loves You*. While Levine's reading of Darwin is nuanced and subtle, his provocative, perhaps even antagonistic, choice of title (and approach), parodying the "Jesus loves you" evangelical slogan of the late twentieth and early twenty-first centuries, offers a reading of religion that is heavily marked by contemporary

critique of older, unexamined notions of common sense, Frank writes: "Poe, Dickens and Doyle promoted a *new*, emerging worldview that was secular and naturalistic in opposition to nineteenth-century scriptural literalism, Natural Theology, and the vestiges of an Enlightenment deism that was often conservative in their political perspectives."[22] Frank continues:

> In turning to these disciplines [philology, geology and paleontology, archaeology, and evolutionary biology] and those who wrote about them, Poe, Dickens, and Doyle were to reject the prevailing common sense of the eighteenth and early nineteenth centuries and were to promote a new version of common sense that seemed to defy the everyday experiences of their readers. In this way the detective fiction of Poe, Dickens, and Doyle possess, to this day, a complex intellectual dimension: they promoted a worldview that many modern readers, particularly in the United States, still reject as they introduced a middle-class readership to a universe governed by chance *and* necessity.[23]

The argument that Frank goes on to construct in the book is informative and tells us a great deal about the ways in which detective fiction drew on scientific epistemology when dealing with evidence, but the treatment of philosophy and theology is less convincing. Science's own ongoing debt to the "common-sense" philosophy that Frank wants to question is downplayed, and different approaches to theology (natural theology and what Frank terms "literalism") are misleadingly conflated and reductively described. As a result, the long history of Christian hermeneutics is reduced to the sort of caricatured position that we tend to associate with extreme expressions of Christian fundamentalism in the United States. It is revealing, then, that the one major religious reference in Frank's index consists of "Christianity, rejection of."

One important attempt to restore a theological dimension to our understanding of nineteenth-century hermeneutics is Suzy Anger's *Victorian Interpretation* (2006). Anger takes issue with what she sees as the distorting lack of historical awareness among literary scholars during the 1970s and 1980s, and urges us to see the influence of biblical hermeneutics in the nineteenth

---

American culture wars. Levine's other works are less confrontational but still locate science and religion as polar opposites. For example: "Where scientific discovery constantly puts pressure on religious explanation, the novel's secular epistemology puts pressure on religious interpretations of life and morals. It tests piety's forms and conventions in large part by forcing readers to recognize the full personal engagement of the pious and the moral in the details of ordinary life." Levine, *Realism, Ethics and Secularism*, 223.

22. Frank, *Victorian Detective Fiction and the Nature of Evidence*, 3.
23. Ibid., 4.

century.[24] She argues that with "the spread of theories of biblical exegesis that regarded the Bible as a historical document, scriptural interpretation moved out from the church to become more humanistic" and, consequently, that twentieth-century debates about literary interpretation are firmly rooted in the concerns of Victorian theology.[25] Anger's meticulous work shows how productive it can be to think further about theology, and the roots she uncovers are informative. But while the book's emphatic insistence on the importance of biblical hermeneutics makes it essential reading for anyone interested in the subject of Victorian interpretation, theology receives surprisingly little coverage. After the chapter on "Victorian Scriptural Hermeneutics: History, Intention, and Evolution," theology slips largely into the background as Anger turns to other interpretative discourses (such as science and the law) and sets out her case for the secularization of hermeneutics.

When Anger does consider biblical hermeneutics, she positions two figures against each other. On the one hand, she gives us John Henry Newman, a figure who, for much of his life, argued that biblical texts need to be interpreted with the help of tradition (i.e., the church) and that their meaning changes as interpretative communities read them differently. On the other hand, she gives us Benjamin Jowett, perhaps the most influential of the contributors to *Essays and Reviews*. Jowett was heavily influenced by Friedrich Schleiermacher, the father of modern hermeneutics, and Jowett follows Schleiermacher in arguing for a systematic and rigorous hermeneutical effort centered on the recovery of authorial meaning.[26] Anger's comparative reading of Newman and Jowett is insightful on several levels, although the tendency to try and hide her preference for Jowett can be frustrating. Yet there is a problem with allowing Newman to stand for the conservative wing of the church. As a key figure in the Oxford Movement and, later on, Roman Catholicism, Newman can rightfully be located in a part of the church labeled theologically conservative. Yet other parts of the Christian church, notably evangelicalism,

---

24. One has to look at the endnotes of Anger's work to see where some of her criticism is aimed. Noting the concealed nature of much of Anger's critique and questioning whether the Yale School of Deconstruction were as theologically ignorant as Anger alleges, Linda Peterson points out that J. Hillis Miller (and others) taught at Yale University at the same time as Hans Frei was in Yale Divinity School and exploring the history of hermeneutics. Peterson insists that the literary scholars at Yale were familiar with the work of their theological colleagues. See Peterson, "Review of Suzy Anger, *Victorian Interpretation*," 524–30.

25. Anger, *Victorian Interpretation*, 3.

26. Jowett's debt to Schleiermacher is also noted by Ellis, who points out that "Jowett possessed all the collected works of Schleiermacher." Ellis also informs us that it was noticed in Oxford in the "forties that Jowett was reading Schleiermacher." Ellis, *Seven against Christ*, 305.

also offered a "conservative" hermeneutic, and their reading of scripture was very different from Newman's.

The comparison of Jowett and Newman enables Anger to develop the idea of a nineteenth-century secularized hermeneutic in which, with the help of Schleiermacher, Jowett, and others, the interpretive authority and function of the church was undermined and replaced by a pseudoscientific approach to interpretation. In many ways, Anger's sophisticated interjection into the subject of interpretation theory prepares the way for her own unacknowledged methodology. A long history of interpretative arguments concludes with the adoption of a historical method in which the role of the critic is to try and reconstruct the historical past as objectively as possible and free us from the prejudice of grand theoretical narratives. It is only a short step from this methodological position to Frank's suggestion that the detective novel provides a scientific forum in which the professional expert offers a secularized interpretative solution. The master detective and the learned literary scholar become almost indistinguishable.[27]

Yet the presence of evangelical interpretation complicates the picture: on a more general hermeneutical level, as I will consider in the final section of this chapter, and in terms of my immediate efforts to trace the salient aspects of nineteenth-century religious history. Evangelicalism presents us with the possibility that our secular reading habits are formed by a particular religious tradition, and do not suddenly emerge as that tradition collapses. Although there are differences between the theological reading undertaken by evangelicals and the interpretative methods that dominate contemporary literary scholarship, our modern scholarly emphasis on careful individual interpretation has much in common with conservative expressions of evangelical belief, despite the fact that the different interpretative communities seek contrasting ways of adjudicating between the conflicting interpretations that result from private reading.[28]

A commitment to the Bible is at the core of evangelical identity and central to the movement's epistemology. This can be seen from the two opening articles of faith that the Evangelical Alliance adopted when it was formed in 1846. They insist, firstly, on the Bible's "divine inspiration, authority, and sufficiency,"

---

27. For a stimulating exploration of the relationship between master detective and literary scholar, see Felski, *The Limits of Critique*, chapter 3.

28. For more on the way in which religion shaped nineteenth-century reading habits, see McKelvy, *The English Cult of Literature: Devoted Readers, 1774–1880*. Commenting on the link between Protestant reading and modern literary criticism, Price writes: "From Protestant theology, secular explicators have learned to prize spirit over matter—and, by extension, the inwardness of selves produced by reading over the outward circumstances of bodies handling books." Price, *How to Do Things with Books in Victorian Britain*, 28.

and secondly, on the "right and duty of private judgment" when reading it. Years later, addressing the 1869 Conference of the Evangelical Alliance, the Rev. Marston identified the root of good doctrine in similar fashion: "What, then, were the principles which lay at the foundation of the doctrines of the Protestant Reformation? The most fundamental one of all was the Supremacy of the written Word of God."[29] It was from the Reformation that evangelicalism inherited its belief in *sola scriptura*, the idea that the Bible, rather than the church, is the primary means by which we know God and think theologically. But unlike those ecclesial traditions that came to view the reasoning capacity of the individual as the main hermeneutical legacy of the Reformation, evangelicals continued to insist that their faith was marked by an unadulterated commitment to the Word of God: "The Bible is central to evangelicals as a point of doctrine, as the authority by which they defend all their theological convictions, and as a fundamental component of their Christian practice."[30]

Evangelical readings of the Bible in the nineteenth century varied considerably. At one extreme, *The Moonstone*'s depiction of Betteredge randomly opening "that infallible word" in an attempt to find guidance constitutes the sort of interpretative act that, though widely frowned upon in theory, was common in the practice of many evangelical communities.[31] Evangelical testimonies and memoirs are full of instances where someone declares how a particular verse from the Bible has provided divine guidance, but shows little awareness of the extent to which that guidance is based on a reading that bears no relation to the surrounding text. In large part, such reading results from a view of scripture as a collection of verses, instructions, and promises, not a complex and polyphonic narrative. Other evangelicals were aware of these hermeneutical issues, however, and called for a more structured approach to reading the Bible. Disturbed by the habits he observed among fellow evangelicals, Charles Spurgeon argued for the value of commentaries as a means of regulating evangelical reading: "We cannot expect to deliver much of the teachings of Holy Scripture by picking out verse by verse, and holding these up at random."[32] Elsewhere, evangelical publishers produced large numbers of daily reading guides (individual and family) and other aids to the reading of scripture, such as the short tract by William Dalton, *A Course of Scripture Les-*

---

29. Anon., "Proceedings of the Twenty-Third Annual Conference of the British Organisation," *Evangelical Christendom* (1869), 438.

30. Larsen, "Defining and Locating Evangelicalism," in Larsen and Treier, eds., *The Cambridge Companion to Evangelical Theology*, 7.

31. I explore the complicated relationship between Betteredge and evangelicalism later on in this chapter.

32. Spurgeon, *Commenting and Commentaries*, 22.

sons for Sunday and Daily Schools, and Rev. W. B. MacKenzie's *Bible Studies for Family Reading.*[33] While the serious and orthodox tone adopted throughout these guides implies a plain, homogenous evangelical reading of scripture, the reality was much less uniform. As Daniel Treier observes, "stories of evangelical biblical interpretation range from the awe-inspiring to the absurd."[34]

Despite considerable differences in the way that scripture was read, evangelicals were united in their conviction that the Bible was God's inspired Word and true in all it affirmed. Arguments over plenary and verbal inspiration, and, in North America especially, the suitability of "inerrancy" as a description of scripture, did not get in the way of a common belief that the Bible was the only proper starting point for theology.[35] Although this proclamation can sound simplistic, there was considerable tacit agreement among evangelicals about the multiple layers their commitment to the truth of the Bible involved. The meaning of the Bible was understood in static terms, and there was a widely held view that scripture was doctrinally unambiguous, at least when it came to the major points of the gospel. Evangelicals recognized that the Bible needed to be applied differently, depending on one's personal circumstances, but the assumption was that the message of God's Word was unchanging. Faithfulness to "orthodox" doctrine won out over theological innovation, even though the "evangelical insistence on the conservative view of Scripture" did not become distinctive until the beginning of the nineteenth century, when attacks on the Bible became more widespread.[36]

Another important element in the evangelical understanding of biblical truth was the commitment to a evidential mindset formed by Enlightenment thought.[37] If God's Word was true, reasoned evangelicals, then the

---

33. Dalton, *A Course of Scripture Lessons*; Mackenzie, *Bible Studies for Family Reading.*
34. Treier, "Scripture and Hermeneutics," in Larsen and Treier, eds., *The Cambridge Companion to Evangelical Theology,* 40. For a highly informative account of the diverse ways in which Victorian figures (evangelical and otherwise) read the Bible, see Larsen, *A People of One Book.*
35. On the difference between plenary and verbal inspiration, Birks explains: "A distinction may thus be drawn between plenary inspiration, in the loose sense, which claims the authority of God for every book and passage of Scripture; and verbal inspiration, which extends the principle to every word, and implies that the first autographs were entirely free from verbal oversights, and errors either in numbers or in names." Birks, *Modern Rationalism and the Inspiration of the Scriptures,* 111. For a more technical discussion of verbal and plenary inspiration, see Kenneth J. Stewart, "The Evangelical Doctrine of Scripture. 1650–1850. A Re-examination of David Bebbington's Theory," in Haykin and Stewart, eds., *The Emergence of Evangelicalism: Exploring Historical Continuities.*
36. Stephen R. Holmes, "British (and European) Evangelical Theologies," in Larsen and Treier, eds., *The Cambridge Companion to Evangelical Theology,* 244.
37. For a more detailed discussion of the link between evangelicalism and the Enlightenment, see Bebbington, *Evangelicalism in Modern Britain,* and Harris, *Fundamentalism and*

events it recorded needed to have happened.[38] Although evangelicals from the Reformed theological tradition were typically hostile to Christian apologetics relying on natural theology, such as William Paley's *Natural Theology; or Evidences of the Existence and Attributes of the Deity* (1802), they were just as likely as evangelical supporters of Paley to treat truth and historical fact as near synonyms. In Edward Garbett's *God's Word Written: The Doctrine of the Inspiration of Holy Scripture Explained and Enforced* (1866), for example, chapter 11 addresses the nature of truth and introduces the idea of correspondence: "Truth is the correspondence of a representation with the thing represented."[39] Yet almost immediately "correspondence" is said to "involve the actual existence of the things . . . represented," and the following two chapters of the book are on "Historical Truth" and "The Truth of Scripture Proved by The Testimony of Facts."[40] The evangelical assumption that historicity is the highest form of truth explains the considerable effort that went into resisting the claims of the higher critics that the history of the Bible was suspect and that the supernatural claims recorded in it needed to be ruled out a priori. Time and again, evangelical works on the Bible focused on "proving" the veracity of the Bible's historical claims and demonstrating that apparent inconsistencies could be explained.

Evangelicals frequently explained their emphasis on the historical truth of the Bible by insisting that the Word of God needed to be entirely trustworthy if it was to constitute a reliable and harmonious guide to godly living. J. C. Ryle reasoned:

> If the Bible is anything at all it is the statute-book of God's kingdom,—the code of laws and regulations by which the subjects of that kingdom are to live,—the register-deed of the terms on which they have peace now and shall glory hereafter. Now, why are we to suppose that such a book will be loosely and imperfectly drawn up, any more than legal deeds are drawn up on earth? Every lawyer can tell us that in legal deeds and statutes every word is of importance, and that property, life, or death may often turn on a *single word*.[41]

Evangelicalism. Harris's study is particularly relevant to my own discussion in this chapter as she discusses at length the evangelical debt to Scottish common-sense philosophy.

38. Evangelicals were not alone in conflating truth and history. For a more detailed and seminal account of how the Enlightenment came to place undue emphasis on the Bible's historicity, and thereby separate the reading of scholars from the reading of religious communities, see Frei, *The Eclipse of Biblical Narrative*.

39. Garbett, *God's Word Written*, 145.

40. Ibid,. 146.

41. Ryle, *Bible Inspiration*, 45.

Ryle's use of a legal metaphor when thinking about the Bible offers further evidence for just how indebted evangelicalism was to Enlightenment thought. Crucially, however, evangelicals such as Ryle did not always think about how the discourse they imported had consequences for their approach to interpretation. There is considerable irony in the way that evangelicals commonly attacked Jewish Pharisees for allegedly reading the Bible legalistically, yet replicated such reading themselves, and it is not surprising that some of the best-known novelists of the mid-Victorian period regularly featured evangelical characters that were marked, negatively, by their "pharisaic" legalism and hypocrisy.

The evidential and legal discourse that evangelicals inherited from the Enlightenment was combined with a more personal, devotional hermeneutic, derived from Pietism and Romanticism. This devotional reading was an anathema to German Higher Critics—in some ways, the more obvious descendants of the Enlightenment emphasis on individual rationality.[42] Believing that the gospel was primarily a call to individual conversion and active involvement in the world, evangelicals read scripture with a view to grappling with the personal implications for their lives rather than more technical scholarly debates—whatever their doctrinal differences, evangelicals read "from a common starting point of deep personal investment."[43] In one tract on the inspiration of the Bible, the writer exemplified the frequent transition from apologetics to personal application by following his defense of the Bible's historical authority and internal consistency with a personal challenge: "*What effect has been produced by Scripture truth on your conscience, heart, and life? Great is the difference between the impressions made on the mind and those on the heart.*"[44] Variants of the question "What does it mean to me?" permeate all evangelical writing on the Bible, and the preference for passages where a personal application was more readily apparent meant that certain books of the Bible (e.g., the New Testament letters) tended to be favored over books with less applicable historical details (e.g., 1 Chronicles) or more poetic lan-

---

42. Charles LaPorte does make a convincing case though for the role of myth in the thought of the higher critics. See LaPorte, *Victorian Poets and the Changing Bible*.

43. Mark A. Noll, "The Bible and Scriptural Interpretation," in Larsen and Ledger-Lomas, eds., *The Oxford History of Protestant Dissenting Traditions*, 3:324. Noll is speaking here specifically about dissenters, although it is clear from his essay that his reading of dissent is informed predominantly by the evangelical tradition.

44. Marston, *Inspiration*, 23. The distinction between a head and heart knowledge of the Bible was common to evangelical discourse. Spurgeon, for example, warned that "he who merely comprehends the meaning of the letter without understanding how it bears upon the hearts and consciences of men, is like a man who causes the bellows of an organ to be blown, and then fails to place his fingers on the key." Spurgeon, *Commenting and Commentaries*, 29.

guage (e.g., Song of Songs). Again, as with their evidential discourse, evangelicals were sometimes unaware of the problems raised by their devotional and practical emphasis, failing to see the incompatibility of professing a commitment to the whole of the Bible as the sole source of God's revelation while focusing so heavily on certain parts of it.

Their evangelical commitment to the personal and individual truth of the Bible lies behind their repeated insistence on the meaning of the Bible being plain. This insistence is evident in a range of publications, from the nuanced context of the eight-volume *"Plain Commentary" on the Gospels* (1860) to the choice of title for the small collection of devotional thoughts on biblical texts, *Precious Truths in Plain Words* (1865).[45] As the Rev. Adolph Saphir explained: "We cling to the Bible because it is there that we find Jesus, and because it is through its living pages He gives rest and peace to our labouring minds.... The Romanists put tradition between the people and the Bible.... The Rationalists put their own opinions between the people and the Bible."[46] The preference for plain or common-sense readings of the Bible recurs time and again in evangelical discourse. It has roots in the Scottish common-sense tradition of Thomas Reid, and, before that, the evidential philosophy of John Locke. Evangelical religious leaders such as Thomas Chalmers (1780–1847) and James McCosh (1811–94) saw the philosophy of Reid as a bulwark against modern skepticism and helped fellow evangelicals to translate the findings of philosophy into their everyday practice.[47] Yet when it came to the Bible, evangelicals were not just seeking an alternative to the skepticism of German thought. The idea that the meaning of the Bible needed to be plain was rooted in a major concern of both the Protestant Reformation and the Puritans, an important forerunner of evangelicalism: if the Bible was too complex and obscure, there was every risk of an elite priesthood who would be required to make sense of God's revelation. As with their predecessors, there was a democratizing agenda to the evangelical conviction that the efficacy and universality of God's revelation required simplicity and transparency.

Evangelicalism's insistence that truth was plain and capable of discovery by all was key to their distrust of many in the broad church movement. Complaining about a contribution by Dr. John Caird to the March 1868 edition of *Good Words,* Spurgeon wrote:

---

45. Anon., *A Plain Commentary on the Four Holy Gospels*; Anon., *Precious Truths in Plain Words.*
46. Recorded in Anon., "The British and Foreign Bible Society," *The Revival: An Advocate of Evangelical Truth* (1866), 275.
47. See Hoeveler, *James McCosh and the Scottish Intellectual Tradition.* See also Noll, "Common Sense Traditions and American Evangelical Thought," 216–38.

He sees no need to warn ministers to cultivate fellowship with God, but much more cause to bid them keep abreast of the culture of the age and know something of what its deepest speculators have said and its sweetest poets have sung. . . . He is very severe upon those "who insist upon our identifying divine truth with the historical accidents and archaic forms in which it has been couched, with the literal interpretations of the language of allegory and symbol, with statements, which true and beautiful as poetry, lose their reality and beauty when construed as literal fact." What that fine jargon means, those who are acquainted with Broad School innuendoes very well know.[48]

In his distrust of fine jargon and literary modes of expression that encouraged ambiguous or equivocal interpretations of the Bible, Spurgeon echoes the complaint made by an anonymous reviewer (signed P. B.) in *Evangelical Christendom*, who complained about the "literary" reading of the broad church: "There is not a sentence [in the Bible] requiring or inviting us to observe the beauty of its diction, the aptness of its metaphors. . . . The Bible speaks with authority. Its tone is that of an Imperial decree. It states, as from the Almighty, the terms on which man is offered salvation; it commands him to accept them or to perish."[49] In criticizing the lack of plain sense among broad church readings of the Bible, the evangelical writer here fails to recognize the mixed messages of his own choice of vocabulary: the "Imperial decree" that "offer[s] salvation" but "commands him to accept."

The hermeneutical emphasis of "On the Interpretation of Scripture," Jowett's contribution to *Essays and Reviews*, was especially challenging for evangelicalism. Evangelical periodicals were vociferous in their complaints about all the essayists. But whereas Baden Powell's skepticism about certain miraculous narratives in the Bible or Rowland Williams's questioning of the predictive power of biblical prophecy raised issues for which evangelical apologists had well-rehearsed answers, Jowett's work provided the movement with a subtler and less familiar challenge. Thomas Rawson Birks admitted: "Open blasphemies are more easily repelled. . . . But the sapping and mining process of a covert infidelity, which borrows the very phrases of the gospel, to give them a philosophical meaning, and will own almost every kind of excellency in the Scriptures, except the authority of a Divine message, is far more peril-

---

48. Spurgeon, "Dr John Caird on the Declining Influence of the Pulpit," *The Sword and the Trowel* (1868), 174.

49. Anon. [P. B.], "The Defects of Broad Church Theology," *Evangelical Christendom* (1865), 216.

ous and seductive to thoughtful and serious minds."[50] It was easy for evangelicals to reject Jowett's call for the Bible to be interpreted "like any other book," and argue, in response, that scripture was written primarily by God rather than man.[51] It was much more difficult to dispute his claim that "the book in which we believe all religious truth to be contained, is the most uncertain of all books, because interpreted by arbitrary and uncertain methods," for, at least ostensibly, Jowett's insistence on interpreting God's Word rigorously appeared to be consistent with the priority that evangelicals gave to scripture.[52]

Evangelicals were uneasy about the method of reading that Jowett sought to promote. By advocating a more scholarly and pseudoscientific reading of the Bible, he called into question the evangelical belief that God's revelation was transparent and plain. Evangelicals like Spurgeon were very willing to acknowledge the value of commentaries as supplementary tools that might help read the Bible, and they readily promoted their use. But Jowett placed such tools at the center of the interpretative task. His view seemed to necessitate specialized and professional interpreters who were trained to read between the lines. Complaining about this paradigm shift, an anonymous writer for *The Revival: An Advocate of Evangelical Truth*, protested: "The truth that the Bible is self-interpreting is as precious and all-important as the corresponding truth that it is the inspired Word of God. The message from heaven would, indeed, be of no use to men if it required any interpreter beside itself."[53]

Sue Zemka insists that "the driving force in the Bible Society's narratives was the desire to believe that English Evangelicalism did not insert itself as an interpretative authority between the Bible and its newly extended world readership."[54] In this respect, the Bible Society, like the writer for *The Revival*, was expressing a widely held evangelical view. Back in 1778, John Brown published *The Self-Interpreting Bible*. While it is difficult to imagine how early readers cannot have seen the irony of a work with that title, which ran to well over one thousand pages and contained extensive commentary, evangelical interest in the book encouraged repeated re-publication in the nineteenth cen-

---

50. Birks, *The Bible and Modern Thought*, 3.

51. Jowett, "On the Interpretation of Scripture," Shea and Whitla, eds., *Essays and Reviews: The 1860 Text and Its Reading*, 504. Most evangelicals admitted that the books of the Bible also had human authors, but this human contribution was consistently downplayed. The wording of Birks's observations on the matter—"we cannot get rid of a human element"—is revealing. Birks, *The Bible and Modern Thought*, 249.

52. Jowett, "On the Interpretation of Scripture," Shea and Whitla, eds., *Essays and Reviews: The 1860 Text and Its Reading*, 501.

53. Anon., "Unity of Creed: The Union of the Christian Church," *The Revival: An Advocate of Evangelical Truth* (1866), 71.

54. Zemka, *Victorian Testaments*, 193.

tury. The 1855 edition contained a preface by Rev. Dr. Henry Cooke, who had taken on the role of editor in one of the many re-publications. His explanation of why the Bible was to be seen as self-interpreting is worth quoting at length:

> If God has given a revelation of his nature and will, and intended it not for any particular class or nation, but for all ranks, conditions, and countries, it seems natural to conclude that such revelation should be plain and level to every capacity. But are not the Books called the Holy Scriptures full of difficulties in narrative, doctrine and precept? and is not the existence of these difficulties manifest by the continued efforts, uncertainty, or contrariety of interpretations? True; the Holy Scriptures present many difficulties, and have received various interpretations; but the existence of difficulties, or varieties of opinion, are so far from furnishing any object to their divine origin, that they furnish, on the contrary, one of its internal proofs. For as, in painting, sculpture, and the mechanical arts, men often discover the author of one work by its marks of similarity to some of his acknowledged productions; even so, the visible world, which all except the atheist acknowledge to be the work of God, presents so many difficulties to the eye of science—difficulties which, observation, experiment, and theory, have laboured in vain to overcome—that in any other work professing to come, either directly or mediately, from God, similar difficulties are not only to be expected, but are, in some sense, necessary to prove that the work is his. Yet notwithstanding all their acknowledged difficulties, the works of God are, for every practical purpose of light, and labour, and enjoyment, perfectly level to all capacities; and, in like manner, they who read and search the Holy Scriptures with an humble, sincere, and prayerful desire to discover what is sin, what is duty, and who is the Saviour, will find no difficulties beyond those that arise from the world, the flesh, and the devil, seeking to blind their eyes "lest the light of the glorious gospel of Christ should shine unto them" (2 Cor iv. 4).[55]

Blaming wrong or confused readings of scripture on a lack of personal piety or the distractions of the world offered a convenient way of defending the plain sense of the Bible. But this apologetic strategy had the unintended consequence of refocusing attention on the tension within evangelical hermeneutics I have highlighted here, namely the perceived need to explain and police the interpretation of a work whose meaning was allegedly plain.

---

55. Cooke, "Preface," in Cooke and Brown, *The Self-Interpreting Bible*.

CRITIQUE OF EVANGELICAL INTERPRETATION

As Collins's 1868 preface to *The Moonstone* is quick to point out, characters play a more influential role in this narrative than in Collins's earlier works. It is through the novel's different narrators, each of whom is invited to "write the story of the Moonstone in turn—as far as our own personal experience extends," that we are encouraged to think about the events that take place and engage with the text's interpretative concerns.[56] In the 1871 preface to a revised edition of the novel, Collins made particular reference to Miss Drusilla Clack, explaining how she provided some element of relief during the writing of the novel: "In the intervals of grief, in the occasional remissions of pain, I dictated from my bed that portion of *The Moonstone* which has since proved most successful in amusing the public—the 'Narrative of Miss Clack.' Of the physical sacrifice which the effort cost me I shall say nothing. I only look back now at the blessed relief which my occupation (forced as it was) brought to my mind."[57] While it is easy to dismiss Miss Clack as an amusing sideshow, her presence in *The Moonstone* is one of several clues to the interest in hermeneutics that pervades the novel. It is Miss Clack who begins the section entitled "The Discovery of the Truth," and she begins her narrative by seeking to defend her credentials as a witness and insisting on her "sacred regard for truth."[58] Miss Clack claims that she will simply "state the facts as they were stated," yet the version of the story that she narrates recasts the morally questionable Godfrey as the "Christian Hero [who] never hesitates where good is to be done."[59] Although her own comprehension of how she interprets events proves to be limited, the satiric mode used to describe her interpretative failures alerts us to some of the weaknesses of evangelical hermeneutics.

In light of evangelicalism's professed commitment to the Bible, Miss Clack's reliance on tracts—her "Books" as she calls them on one occasion—is worth closer investigation.[60] Tracts were a popular form of evangelistic activity in the nineteenth century, and Miss Clack's extensive use of them reflects both a tradition of famous evangelical women, such as Sarah Trimmer and Hannah More, and the midcentury publishing efforts of groups such as the Religious Tract Society. Leah Price encourages us to see tracts and their distribution as a mirror of and rival to the novel in the period: "When characters in tracts read novels or characters in novels reject tracts, the stakes are intellectual-

---

56. Collins, *The Moonstone*, 40.
57. Collins, preface to 1871 revised edition of *The Moonstone*.
58. Collins, *The Moonstone*, 235.
59. Ibid., 237, 239.
60. Ibid., 268.

historical (Evangelical fiction opposite the epic of a world without God) as much as formal (both torn between narrative and didactic modes)." Price goes on to think about their affective and economic parallels, the latter described in terms of how: "Both widely distributed, neither much respected, tract and novel achieved their common ubiquity via opposite routes—one anonymously or even surreptitiously bought and rented, the other forced on readers through face-to-face relationships."[61] The potential rivalry between tract and novel is brought out well in Price's suggestive and contextually rich reading of *The Moonstone*, as she details the way in which the genres "fight to occupy the same space."[62] But I am less convinced by the religious-secular binary that underwrites Price's argument, in part because the "secular" novel is not the only rival to the tract in Collins's work. Miss Clack's favored publications also expose an unresolved tension between tracts and the Bible, one that revolves around the question of interpretation even more than it does around matters of textual distribution, handling, and recycling.

For the evangelicals that invested so heavily in them, tracts were seen as an unproblematic partner to the biblical text. Yet Miss Clack's anxious insistence that the tracts in her possession are "all suitable to the present emergency, all calculated to arouse, convince, prepare, enlighten, and fortify my aunt," ends up prompting the question of why it is they, rather than the Bible, that are so described.[63] Price suggests that the preference for tracts has to do with economic value—the cost of paper, and, on other occasions, a desire to price Bibles in a way that would prevent them from being recycling as waste—but this answer only takes us so far. When we search Miss Clack's narrative for references to a physical Bible, which she certainly could have afforded and might be expected to carry with her, we discover that she boasts instead of "having always a few tracts in my bag."[64] There is an implication that scripture is no longer adequate for revealing God's plans to those who seek guidance. This suggestion becomes more overt when Miss Clack alludes to the biblical Parable of the Sower and tells us that she "reflected on the *true* riches which I had scattered with such a lavish hand."[65] Whereas evangelicals typically read the seed in the parable as an allegorical reference to the Word of God, Miss Clack aligns the "*true* riches" with her tracts. Her belief in the divine power of tracts goes further, bordering on the sort of idolatry that evangelicals sometimes located in the Roman Catholic use of relics: "I slipped it under the sofa

---

61. Price, *How to Do Things with Books in Victorian*, 207.
62. Ibid., 209.
63. Collins, *The Moonstone*, 258.
64. Ibid., 236.
65. Ibid, 270. The biblical account can be found in Matthew 13.

cushions, half in, and half out, close by her handkerchief, and her smelling-bottle. Every time her hand searched for either of these, it would touch the book; and, sooner or later (who knows?) the book might touch *her*."[66]

By the middle of the nineteenth century much of the Protestant church had found ways to explain how textual supplements might sit alongside the Bible. Some saw the revelation of scripture as just one mode through which God spoke; others insisted that it made no sense to talk of the Bible apart from the ecclesial tradition through which the sacred text was canonized and interpreted. But evangelicals remained committed to the idea that, in J. C. Ryle's words, the Bible "comes to us with a claim which no other book possesses. It is stamped with Divine authority. In this respect it stands entirely alone. Sermons, and tracts, and theological writings of all kinds, may be sound and edifying, but they are only the handiwork of uninspired man. The Bible alone is the Book of God."[67] At least, evangelicals were committed to this idea in theory. Miss Clack's actions suggest a lack of conviction in the idea that scripture is fully sufficient, and her doubts express themselves in increasingly desperate attempts to repackage the Word of God. Near the beginning of her narrative, Miss Clack gives a tract to Penelope Betteredge entitled "A Word with You on Your Cap-Ribbons"; when it becomes apparent that such tracts have little or no intrinsic interest, Miss Clack attenuates her efforts to increase the appeal of her message. This is done partly through the use of increasingly dramatic titles—culminating in *The Serpent at Home*, a title with chapters such as "Satan in the Hair Brush" and "Satan behind the Looking Glass"—and partly through marketing her gospel message more intensely.[68] Having begun by slipping a "tract into the letterbox," explaining "we must sow the good seed somehow," Miss Clack takes to hiding tracts in the bathroom and beneath the canary cage in an attempt to "surprise" Lady Verinder into reading them.[69] When the strategic placement of tracts proves unsuccessful, Miss Clack changes the form of her message, from "Preparation by Books," to "Preparation by Little Notes."[70] Within a remarkably short space of time, the gospel message has shrunk, physically and metaphorically, from the sixty-six books of the Old and New Testaments to shorter pieces of Christian literature and finally to occasional notes by which "previous passages" might be "rein-

---

66. Collins, *The Moonstone*, 269. This is not the only occasion in the nineteenth century when evangelicals seemed to embrace the language of relics. Deborah Lutz explores the relationship between relics and what she describes as the evangelical "good death" in Lutz, *Relics of Death*, chapter 2.

67. Ryle, *Bible Inspiration*, 9–10.

68. Collins, *The Moonstone*, 268.

69. Ibid., 237, 269.

70. Ibid., 273.

troduced . . . under a form which not even the doctor's watchful materialism could suspect."[71]

The commercial awareness of evangelical publishing was far more pervasive in the nineteenth century than we typically think, as I discussed in the previous chapter, but it still leaves certain questions for us to work through. If the Bible was its own witness, a self-sufficient guide to its own veracity and timeliness, then why did evangelical publishing need to interpret and market what it had to say? The tension would be dramatized in the two decades following the publication of *The Moonstone* through the promotional efforts of the Salvation Army, a working-class mission movement that affirmed the Bible alone as "the Divine Rule of Christian faith and practice" yet continued to tell its ministers that "the work of the F[ield] O[fficer] is to publish Salvation, that is to make it known, and those methods must be preferred that most effectively assist them in doing so."[72] While the mixed message of the Salvation Army illustrated the tension in particularly vivid fashion, the same confused attitude to the Bible was already present in the choices made by evangelical publishing firms operating midcentury, all of whom spoke about the complete sufficiency of God's Word yet still worked at great length to help others grasp the meaning and importance of scripture.[73]

Miss Clack's fascination with the rhetoric and public performances of Godfrey Ablewhite—"his unrivalled eloquence at Exeter Hall" as she describes it on one occasion—is not the only occasion when Collins links evangelical rhetoric to the false appearances of Victorian advertising.[74] Yet in the case of Miss Clack, the focus on the rhetorical power of the preacher has to be read alongside the realization that there is no way of avoiding an interpretative intermediary when it comes to making sense of the Word of God. Some recognition of the necessity of hermeneutics even permeates Miss Clack's gloss on her own tracts and her explanation of how they should be read:

> "You will read, dear, won't you?" I said, in my most winning way. "You will read, if I bring you my own precious books? Turned down at all the right

---

71. Ibid., 73.

72. See the first of The Salvation Army's Articles of War, and Booth, *Order and Regulations for Field Officers of The Salvation Army*, 280. The Salvation Army's extensive use of modern advertising techniques is explored in Walker, *Pulling the Devil's Kingdom Down*.

73. Fyfe's work on the Religious Tract Society is particularly important in this regard, as I explored more fully in the previous chapter. For a different approach to the question of economics in *The Moonstone*, focused on the relationship between sacrifice and gift-exchange, and examining how "contemporary Britons, raised at the crux of the evangelical inheritance and the capitalist ethos, attempt and fail to transcend the marketplace logic of self-interest in their personal relations" (173), see Blumberg, *Victorian Sacrifice*, chapter 5.

74. Collins, *The Moonstone*, 275. See also the account of Mother Oldershaw's performance at the end of Collins's *Armadale*.

places, aunt. And marked in pencil where you are to stop and ask yourself, 'Does this apply to me?'"[75]

Further acknowledgement of the need for interpretative guidance recurs later, when Miss Clack follows up Rachel Verinder's claim to have read the publications left out for her: "Had she chanced to look into them?—I asked. Yes—and they had not interested her. Would she allow me to read a few passages of the deeper interest, which had probably escaped her eye?"[76] For all its apparent simplicity, Miss Clack's guidance on reading the Bible intimates that she no longer thinks of the text as self-interpreting.

Miss Clack is not the only religious character in *The Moonstone* who is blind to her interpretative inconsistencies and limitations. Betteredge, the novel's first living narrator, is probably the novel's foremost champion of the view that the obvious and literal reading is most likely to be correct. Betteredge's ecclesial makeup is complex. On the surface he seems to be a nominal broad-church Anglican; yet his absolute insistence on the supernatural power of a "divine" text to provide wisdom when needed suggests that the lapsed "broad church" tag is a red herring, at least when it comes to identifying the religious roots of his interpretative method.[77] It makes more sense, I think, to think of Betteredge within the broader evangelical tradition described in the previous chapter. The text Betteredge seeks inspiration from is Daniel Defoe's *Robinson Crusoe* (1719). Whenever the house-steward needs encouragement or guidance, he opens *Crusoe* at random and seeks a word of inspiration. Much of the humor of these scenes relies on the reader noting the parody of an absolute commitment to the biblical text.[78] Such commitment was far more likely to be associated with evangelicalism than it was with the broad church. The fact that Betteredge turns to a novel so strikingly concerned with

---

75. Collins, *The Moonstone*, 258–59.
76. Ibid., 293.
77. The text is not explicit about Betteredge's churchmanship, although his service with the Verinders makes it more likely that he would be an Anglican than a dissenter, and his narrative is full of theological vocabulary, general religious references, and vague expressions of his own commitment to faith.
78. The way in which we understand the parody depends heavily on the way we think about Daniel Defoe's novel. While much of the critical tradition has followed Ian Watt in thinking about *Robinson Crusoe* as a secular text, which makes Betteredge's obsession with it seem arbitrary and not especially significant theologically, *Crusoe* does not have to be read in this manner. Acknowledging a religious dimension to Defoe's novel might prompt us to see Betteredge's interpretation as a continuation of debates about how Christian reading should proceed. Rather than getting tied up by the question of whether Defoe's novel is religious or not, Kevin Seidel charts a helpful new course when he "sets out to rediscover irony in *Robinson Crusoe* itself—particularly the irony that gathers in its most religiously charged scenes—rather than looking for it, as most critics do, in the historical gap between our secular age and the late Puritan age of Defoe." See Seidel, "*Robinson Crusoe* as Defoe's Theory of Fiction," 166.

individuality, money, and the personal conscience provides additional support for thinking that evangelicalism is the source of the house-steward's religious hermeneutic. Traces of evangelicalism are also apparent in the way that Betteredge defends his particular textual devotion: "You are not to take it, if you please, as the saying of an ignorant man, when I express my opinion that such a book as *Robinson Crusoe* never was written, and never will be written again. I have tried that book for years—generally in combination with a pipe of tobacco—and I have found it my friend in need in all the necessities of this mortal life. When my spirits are bad—*Robinson Crusoe*. When I want advice—*Robinson Crusoe*."[79]

Distracted by the humor of Betteredge's faith in "the one infallible remedy—that remedy being, as you know, *Robinson Crusoe*," modern secular readers often fail to think about the underlying significance of Betteredge's hermeneutic.[80] Yet Collins's novel repeatedly prompts us to ponder the meaning of this hermeneutic: "Let nobody laugh at the unique anecdote here related. You are welcome to be as merry as you please over everything else I have written. But when I write of *Robinson Crusoe*, by the Lord it's serious—and I request you to take it accordingly."[81] Like Miss Clack, Betteredge's hermeneutic is shown to be flawed. The same can be said of the novel's other major evangelical character, Godfrey Ablewhite, although in his case naïve interpretation is more closely associated with manipulation. Ablewhite exploits the hermeneutical weaknesses of those around him but is undone by his own failure to penetrate the disguise of the mechanic who follows him when he collects the diamond. We have to read carefully to realize that Betteredge's claim to record events as they happen is not as neutral as it initially appears, and that Miss Clack's repressed desire for her Christian hero encourages us to see Rachel Verinder as a potentially calculating suspect. Collectively, the novel's three evangelical characters present an ABC of the problems with the reading habits of this religious movement.

A RETURN TO COMMON SENSE

Evangelical modes of reading are not the only target of Collins's critique in *The Moonstone*. As well as exposing the interpretative naïvety of characters such as Miss Clack, *The Moonstone* critiques the hermeneutic employed by German Higher Critics and the pseudoscientific method promoted by Schleiermacher

---

79. Collins, *The Moonstone*, 41.
80. Ibid., 518.
81. Ibid., 519–20.

and Jowett. There is not a direct exponent of German Higher Criticism in Collins's novel, but the tradition that Jowett and others inherited from the Enlightenment is represented through the figure of Sergeant Cuff. To understand the connection, we need to turn to the work of Jan-Melissa Schramm, in *Testimony and Advocacy in Victorian Law, Literature, and Theology* (2000). Schramm examines a range of legal, literary, and theological writings from the eighteenth and nineteenth centuries, and demonstrates how a variety of discourses came together to register the need for evidence to be interpreted by trained experts.[82] Taking issue with the claim of Alexander Welsh in *Strong Representations: Narrative and Circumstantial Evidence in England* (1992) that the loss of confidence in the ability of facts to speak plainly occurred in the mid-Victorian period, Schramm argues that the epistemological shift was older and rooted in wider philosophical developments. It is a persuasive claim. In addition to saving us from forlornly trying to isolate a moment of transformation in which people suddenly stopped believing that the Bible was its own best witness and interpreter, Schramm's thesis enables us to understand how the hermeneutic concerns of *The Moonstone* go beyond explicitly religious references without ever losing sight of the theological dimension.[83]

Observing how the growing belief that facts needed interpretation encouraged the emergence of defense counsel in the eighteenth and nineteenth centuries, Schramm notes the anxiety caused by the growth of interpretative intermediaries. Retaining a residual allegiance to the idea that evidence must speak plainly, the British public were worried about skilled barristers misrepresenting the truth. Such fears are apparent in the courtroom scenes that feature in several works of nineteenth-century fiction, as Schramm observes; but they can also be found elsewhere, such as the anti-Catholic texts that depict Jesuit priests employing fine-sounding and convoluted arguments to justify their behavior. Schramm points out that authors were anxious about their own complex narrative maneuverings, recognizing that these might leave them open to a similar charge of misrepresenting evidence and falsifying truth. In *The Moonstone*, it is the long-established domestic servant, Betteredge, who registers the implied reader's alarm about the intervention of a professional interpreter. Having complained early on about the wrong-headed sophisti-

---

82. As Schramm readily admits, this aspect of her thesis is rooted in the work of others (particularly Michael McKeon, Barbara Shapiro, and Alexander Welsh), although her attention to legal details is much sharper and her conclusions very different.

83. Although my chapter is predicated on the claim that *Essays and Reviews* had a major impact on evangelical hermeneutics, I think Ellis overstates and oversimplifies his case when he writes: "*Essays and Reviews* was a watershed, a suitable point at which to begin or end the church histories of the period. After *Essays and Reviews* the Church of England was different." Ellis, *Seven against Christ*, 260.

cation of German intellectual developments—he dismisses the continental education of Franklin Blake as "foreign gibberish"—Betteredge is concerned about the decision to hand matters over to a detective, who, as Franklin Blake boasts, has "no equal in England" "when it comes to unravelling a mystery."[84] Although Cuff seeks to reassure Betteredge of the detective's English credentials by talking about his love of gardening, this is not enough to stop Betteredge complaining how "the slyness with which he slipped in that last question put me on my guard. In plain English, I didn't at all relish the notion of helping his inquiries, when those inquiries took him (in the capacity of snake in the grass) among my fellow servants."[85]

Betteredge is not entirely wrong in his suspicion of Cuff's interpretative method, for there are dangers in allowing a new professional elite to possess the sole means for determining textual truth. Critics have commented elsewhere about the way in which the nineteenth-century British tradition of crime fiction came to rely on highly professional figures.[86] Although Sherlock Holmes, to take the most obvious example, is not part of the official detective force, he is the consummate professional. His (published) expertise on a range of topics exposes the lack of professionalism within the actual police force and continually sets him apart from others. Only he possesses the knowledge required to interpret the "truth," and this knowledge grants him a privileged position of power. Sherlock Holmes may constantly invite Watson (and, indirectly, the reader) to imitate his deductive method, but Watson is doomed to fail because he does not know what Holmes knows. For all its pretension of democratizing knowledge, the detective genre in Britain quickly came to rely on a professional interpreter who was needed to make sense of the mysteries that could not be understood by ordinary people.[87] Collins's contribution to the genre echoes the Reformation concern about the power of the priesthood. *The Moonstone*'s first description of Cuff's physical appearance reminds us of the historical antecedent through its allusion to the clergy: "He was dressed all

---

84. Collins, *The Moonstone*, 76, 132.

85. Ibid,. 152. For further discussion of the association between Englishness and plain-sense, see Carruthers, *England's Secular Scripture*.

86. See, for example, the discussion by Thomas throughout *Detective Fiction and the Rise of Forensic Science*.

87. Jowett's essay "On the Interpretation Scripture" acknowledged that "criticism is not for the multitude" (523). Recognizing how this view has come to pervade a long history of modern New Testament criticism, Francis Watson complains about the shift away from ordinary readers: "Allegorical interpretation is intended for a learned, scholarly elite that finds itself dissatisfied with the banal obviousness of the literal sense that suffices for ordinary readers. Yet, like many other scholarly constructs, it is vulnerable to the criticism that it is fundamentally *arbitrary*." See Francis Watson, "Towards a Literal Reading of the Gospels," in Bauckham, ed., *The Gospel for All Christians*, 213.

in decent black, with a white cravat round his neck. His face was as sharp as a hatchet.... His walk was soft; his voice was melancholy; his long lanky fingers were hooked like claws. He might have been a parson, or an undertaker—or anything else you like, except what he really was."[88]

Throughout *The Moonstone*, Betteredge and Cuff epitomize, respectively, the different interpretative methods of the plain sense school favored by evangelicalism and the pseudoscientific hermeneutic employed by German Higher Criticism. Whereas Betteredge's role as house-steward typifies the everyday work of interpretation undertaken by those within the English family of God, Sergeant Cuff, for all his pragmatism and homely wisdom, exemplifies the professional outsider, called in for his greater methodological rigor. The difference between the two approaches is evident in the way that their accounts are written, and it is especially pronounced when Sergeant Cuff gives his initial assessment of the case to Lady Verinder and Betteredge. Describing how the Sergeant speaks with "horrid clearness," Betteredge admits in his narrative:

> I said nothing on my side. *Robinson Crusoe*—God knows how—had got into my muddled old head. If Sergeant Cuff had found himself, at that moment, transported to a desert island, without a man Friday to keep him company, or a ship to take him off—he would have found himself exactly where I wished him to be! (*Nota bene:*—I am an average good Christian, when you don't push my Christianity too far. And all the rest of you—which is a great comfort—are, in this respect, much the same as I am.)[89]

Two points are worth noting here: first, that Betteredge aligns his plain sense with Christianity; second, that Collins has him do so through parenthesis, a formal feature that signals the way in which so many of the novel's hermeneutical threads are left in the background.

In view of *The Moonstone*'s canonical status within a tradition of British detective fiction that relies on the all-knowing detective, it is worth considering the failure of Sergeant Cuff to solve the mystery. His professionalism and insight may eventually attract the grudging admiration of Betteredge, but his interpretative prowess does not enable him to discover the truth, at least not in its entirety. Telling Betteredge that he is in no doubt as to what has happened—"I don't suspect . . . I know"—he wrongly concludes that Rachel Verinder is in "secret possession of the Moonstone from first to last," and he mistakenly thinks that "she has taken Rosanna Spearman into her

---

88. Collins, *The Moonstone*, 133.
89. Ibid., 206, 207.

confidence."[90] Welsh sees Cuff's interpretative failure as a sign of the century's growing doubts about circumstantial evidence, but this is not the only way of reading the textual evidence.[91] Schramm points out that circumstantial evidence is not as easily separated from direct testimony as Welsh's argument suggests, and the broader hermeneutical questions raised by *The Moonstone* invite us to think about more than the minutiae of Cuff's deductive method.[92] Cuff is not just any interpreter; he is the expert outsider, a figure whose very presence is predicated on the ability to reconstruct events fully and ascertain what has taken place. But for all his pseudoscientific reasoning and painstaking efforts to interpret the evidence objectively, he gets the culprit and motive wrong.[93] Ironically, the last thing he does get right (before his return at the end of the novel) involves him turning "prophet" and adopting a recognizably religious rhetoric: "Now I'll tell you, at parting, of three things which will happen in the future, and which, I believe, will force themselves on your attention, whether you like it or not."[94] In contrast to Frank's claim that detective fiction creates space for the application of rational scientific method, *The Moonstone* remains ambivalent about the means by which truth might be found and the nature of that truth.

Cuff's absence from the attempt to reenact the night of the theft serves to highlight the limitation of the hermeneutic method he inherits from Schleiermacher and Jowett. For Schleiermacher, Jowett, and a great deal of modern literary scholarship, interpretation was, or is, primarily about historical reconstruction. As Jowett explains: "The office of the interpreter is not to add another [interpretation], but to recover the original one; the meaning, that is, of the words as they first struck on the ears or flashed before the eyes of those who heard and read them."[95] In *The Moonstone,* the failure and depar-

---

90. Ibid., 173.
91. Welsh, *Strong Representations,* 215–36.
92. Schramm, *Testimony and Advocacy,* 19–21.
93. By questioning the efficacy of a more scientific approach to hermeneutics, *The Moonstone* finds itself in an unlikely alliance with a number of prominent evangelicals, past and present. One relatively recent and highly influential evangelical philosopher who has aligned himself with earlier evangelical rejections of German biblical criticism is Alvin Plantinga. In *Warranted Christian Belief,* Plantinga makes a direct attack on Jowett, the most notorious of the contributors to *Essays and Reviews,* and exposes the presuppositions of "historical biblical scholarship." Plantinga's argument that historical method is not as objective or reliable as its proponents typically claim is astute; however, his plain-sense alternative is less convincing and marks a return to arguments that are no more convincing now than when they were put forward in the middle of the nineteenth century. See Plantinga, *Warranted Christian Belief,* chapter 12.
94. Collins, *The Moonstone,* 220.
95. Jowett, "On the Interpretation of Scripture," 481.

ture of Cuff leads to Ezra Jennings taking on the role of interpretative guide. Jennings is a strange, opium-addicted outsider, whose eccentricity and personal investment undermines any notion of hermeneutics being associated with the consummate, detached professional. The reconstruction of Blake's sleepwalking is only a partial success, and for all Jennings's talk of conducting a scientific experiment that reproduces, "as nearly as we can, 'the domestic circumstances which surrounded you [Blake] last year,'" he is forced to abandon the pretense that the science of hermeneutics can reconstruct human actions in their entirety.[96] In place of Cuff's earlier confidence, Jennings's interpretation is openly subjective and provisional, beginning with his attempts to make sense of Mr. Candy's delirious speech and convey it to Blake: "Don't suppose . . . that I claim to have reproduced the expressions which Mr Candy himself would have used if he had been capable of speaking connectedly. I only say that I have penetrated through the obstacle of the disconnected expression, to the thought which was underlying it connectedly all the time. Judge for yourself."[97] Like all the other characters in the novel, Jennings is an imperfect interpreter. His presence may hint at the potential for psychology to contribute to the work of interpretation, but the limitations stop us from thinking that the new "science" of psychology might provide all the hermeneutic answers. Indeed, as important as Jennings's psychological theories are, the greater part of his interpretative contribution is the way in which he alerts us to the role of the reader.

For those of us schooled in the hermeneutic of suspicion that still governs so much critical work on Victorian literature, it is a short step from acknowledging the interpretative failures of all the individuals in *The Moonstone* to thinking that the detective genre the novel helps inaugurate is one that coerces characters and readers alike, tying them to a system of surveillance that occludes any real insight into what is going on. The critic I have in mind here is D. A. Miller. His book *The Novel and the Police* (1988) continues to offer a compelling reading of Cuff's failure, four decades after its first appearance:

> It is not just Betteredge who contracts "the detective fever." Nor is it merely the obvious detective figures (Blake, Bruff, Ezra Jennings) who together with their helpers (Murthwaite, Gooseberry) prosecute the case to a successful conclusion. . . . In effect, the work of detection is carried forward by the novel's entire cast of characters, shifted not just from professional to amateur, but from an outsider to a whole community. Thus, the move to discard

---

96. Collins, *The Moonstone*, 445.
97. Ibid., 437.

the *role of the detective* is at the same time a move to disperse the *function of detection*.⁹⁸

If Miller is right, then the failure of Sergeant Cuff does not announce *The Moonstone*'s return to plain interpretation so much as it points us to the twofold problem of common-sense reading: its failure to discover what texts really mean and its promotion of a mass ideological reading that blinds the interpretative efforts of the individual.

But this is a big "if." Much though I admire Miller's line of argument, I think it fulfils a function common to the detective genre, providing a glimpse of the truth whilst leading us down the wrong path. Miller's reasoning is overly contaminated by the Foucauldian fear that someone or something is conspiring to erase our individuality. Furthermore, it perpetuates the great hermeneutical myth of thinking that the discovery of meaning consists primarily of an individual trying to understand what has really happened. Miller insists that the apparent agency of those who do the work of detection in the Victorian novel is a sham, yet, as others have noted, his own work serves to reinforce the same idea that he rejects, replacing the naïve reader with a more sophisticated individual critic who can penetrate the ideological masks and determine what is really going on.⁹⁹

A more constructive way of thinking about the communal reading at the heart of *The Moonstone* can be found in the work of Hans-George Gadamer, particularly his seminal account of hermeneutics, *Truth and Method* (1960). For Gadamer, the work of interpretation does not so much discover truth as constitute it: "The real meaning of a text, as it speaks to the interpreter, does not depend on the contingencies of the author and his original audience. It certainly is not identical with them, for it is always co-determined also by the historical situation of the interpreter and hence by the totality of the objective course of history."¹⁰⁰ Gadamer's argument is not that texts mean anything readers want them to but rather that interpretation is a living act, a time-dependent activity in which text and communities of readers come together, repeatedly, to produce new meanings. Rather than following Schleiermacher in thinking that interpretation is about isolating meaning through the work

---

98. Miller, *The Novel and the Police*, 42.
99. I owe a debt here to the work of Anna Maria Jones, who insists on the sensational strategies that underlie the interpretative work of Miller and others: "Miller and [Ann] Cvetkovich write themselves into the role of the detective who has discovered a crime, in this case the invisible disciplinary power of the sensation novel itself. They too will track the novel's secrets, revealing them to their readers clue by significant clue, offering a sensational payoff for those who follow their narratives to conclusion." Jones, *Problem Novels*, 8. For further discussion of the difficulty of overcoming suspicious reading, see my discussion in the next chapter.
100. Gadamer, *Truth and Method*, 296.

of historical recovery, Gadamer argues that "reconstructing the original circumstances, like all restoration, is a futile undertaking in view of the historicity of our being."[101] Interpretation is seen as time-dependent in the sense that we participate in a hermeneutic tradition that shapes our reading of the text and to which our reading itself contributes. The refusal to base interpretation around a "science" of objectivity, replication, and reconstruction is part of *Truth and Method*'s underlying insistence that the human sciences should not ape the methodology of the natural sciences.

Gadamer's approach to hermeneutics has much to offer our study of detective fiction. It identifies a role for the reader and, by extension, helps explain why so many people want to continue reading and discussing a work when they already know whodunit. Like the revelation of the Bible, the revelation of the detective story is full of mystery, even when something tangible is understood. G. K. Chesterton's Father Brown stories offer one striking exemplar of this line of thought, and we might turn to essays by Chesterton, Dorothy Sayers, and W. H. Auden to think further about the relationship between detective fiction and theology. My interests here are more specific, though, and I wish to conclude these reflections on Gadamer's significance for Collins by considering what the former has to say on the subject of common sense. Although Gadamer is aware that the common-sense tradition "acquired a quite central systematic function in *Scottish* philosophy, which was directed polemically against metaphysics and against its dissolution in skepticism," he also sees that there is more to common sense than building a new system of knowledge on the basis of plain judgements.[102] What seems to interest Gadamer about common sense is the direction that it took within Pietism, a theological movement that was a vital forerunner of evangelicalism. Pietist thinkers of the eighteenth century, insists Gadamer, sought to maintain the link between knowledge and the social sphere and did not allow theoretical knowledge to become the isolated concern of the philosophical specialist. Gadamer quotes the Pietist theologian, Friedrich Christoph Oetinger: "The sensus communis is concerned only with things that all men see daily before them, things that hold an entire society together, things that are concerned as much with truths and statements as with the arrangements and patterns comprised in statements."[103] While Gadamer chooses not to pursue this theological contribution to hermeneutics much further, his comments alert us to one important way in which the evangelical tradition has understood interpretation as a communal act.

---

101. Ibid., 159.
102. Ibid., 23.
103. Quoted in Gadamer, *Truth and Method*, 24.

It would be misleading to press the case for evangelicalism's communal understanding of interpretation too strongly. We must remember that the text Betteredge substitutes for the Bible is an extremely individualistic piece of fiction. And we should remember, too, how Clack and Ablewhite exemplify the dangers of evangelical self-interest and individualism. Nevertheless, traces of the religious hermeneutic with which Collins grew up are seen positively in *The Moonstone,* even though Collins is antagonistic to other aspects of his religious upbringing. The evangelical reliance on plain speaking interpretation may be satirized and found wanting in the novel, but the social dimension of the common-sense tradition that evangelicalism shares with Pietism is viewed more sympathetically. Noll writes: "Dissenting attention to Scripture began in private and in church, but did not end there."[104] Through sermons, group bible studies, family prayers, and other day-to-day activities, evangelicalism encouraged a communal tradition of applied interpretation that valued contributions from those who were not educated and encouraged modes of thought that were not purely isolated attempts at theoretical reconstruction. Evangelical hermeneutics could (and can) be naïve, conservative, and unnecessarily resistant to different ways of reading, but the belief that the community discovers truth together is a core practice within evangelicalism. This is the sense that pervades *The Moonstone,* and it is this aspect of the common-sense tradition that is preferred to the detached, professionalized approach to interpretation favored by German Higher Criticism and popularized in *Essays and Reviews.*

Although Miller and others may choose to see common reading as an act of indoctrination, the ongoing interpretative debates among evangelicals and between the different characters in the novel suggests something else. Betteredge's reading of *Crusoe* does not constitute gospel truth, yet his willingness to talk with anyone and everyone during the course of the story plays a major role in ensuring that the discovery of the truth remains a communal act. To the extent that the crime fiction genre continues this communality and infects subsequent generations with the detective fever spoken of by Betteredge, we can see a legacy of evangelical hermeneutics beyond the insistence that the meaning of the Bible is plain and self-evident. Perhaps more important though is the possibility that the evangelical tradition with which Collins's novel engages speaks to our ongoing interpretative practice. It is a possibility that should encourage us to make evangelicalism a more integral part of our conversations about the Victorian novel.

---

104. Noll, "The Bible and Scriptural Interpretation," in Larsen and Ledger-Lomas, eds., *The Oxford History of Protestant Dissenting Traditions,* 3:333.

CHAPTER 5

Samuel Butler's *The Way of All Flesh* and Our Stories of Evangelicalism

For many modern readers, evangelicalism belongs to a distant past. It can seem anachronistic to our current literary scholarship, and its prominent role in the US culture wars and elsewhere appears to underline its otherness from a modern academy that typically locates itself on the side of reason rather than faith.[1] Not everyone who reads this book will share this sense of distance or recognize talk of a "secular" academy that "others" evangelicalism, and I expect that some of my readers will be those who already sympathize at some level with the "religious turn" in the humanities.[2]

---

1. For more on the distinction between faith and reason and their mutual interpenetration, see Jacques Derrida, "Faith and Knowledge: Two Sources of 'Religion' at the Limits of Reason Alone," in *Acts of Religion* and the discussion by Lori Branch of the significance of Derrida's essay for the discipline of literary studies in Branch, "The Rituals of Our Re-Secularization," 9–33.

2. The phrase "the religious turn" relates to the increasing theoretical interest in religion since the 1990s among scholars who work in the humanities. It includes, but is certainly not limited to: Charles Taylor and Talal Asad's work on the secular; Jacques Derrida's interest in religion, and the relationship between deconstruction and negative theology explored by Derrida and others; discussions around Walter Benjamin's concept of the messianic; Giorgio Agamben's interest in St. Paul, and, most recently, Pilate; the renewed interest in political theology; and the connection between religion and phenomenology opened up by Jean-Luc Marion and explored further by Kevin Hart. Critics have sometimes linked the religious turn to Stanley Fish's 2005 prediction in the *Chronicle of Higher Education* that religion would "succeed high theory and the triumvirate of race, gender, and class as the center of intellectual

But even if one agrees that criticism and theory have been more willing to talk about religion in recent years, it is hard to see the contribution of evangelicalism.³ Alain Badiou and Giorgio Agamben's interest in St. Paul offers little engagement with evangelical doctrine, despite the historic importance of Pauline theology to the thought of this movement; Jacques Derrida and Geoffrey Hartman share a concern with scripture, but their primary point of reference is Judaism, and, on their reading, evangelical ideas are often seen as part of the problem; Jean-Luc Marion's attention to what is already given when we read is rooted in Roman Catholicism; and Charles Taylor's reshaping of the secular also looks to the intellectual resources of the Roman Catholic faith more than it does to the thinking of Protestantism.

My own efforts in the preceding chapters to examine the influence of evangelicalism on the Victorian novel has drawn considerable inspiration from sources outside the evangelical movement. Theorizing a tradition from the outside can be helpful, and the elasticity and pragmatism of so much evangelical thought might be said to encourage efforts to read evangelicalism via Taylor and scholars from other Christian traditions. But the apparent absence of a recognizably evangelical voice in the explicit theoretical underpinning of this book is worth reflecting on further because it highlights a common feature in the history of scholarship on Victorian literature. If evangelicalism was a major influence on the Victorian novel, as I have been arguing, then why is it so hard to trace an evangelical afterlife in our critical reading? For some, the simple answer is that the evangelical movement no longer has anything significant or relevant to offer. Yet that conclusion is at odds with the material I have been discussing in the previous chapters, and reaching such a view requires a greater knowledge of evangelicalism than many scholars of Victorian literature possess.

While there are limits to the theoretical contribution provided by evangelicalism, it is also the case that evangelicalism has been written out of the intellectual history of literary studies. Despite the detailed attention historians of religion have paid to evangelicalism in recent years, and the increasingly sophisticated treatments of the wider Christian religion undertaken by literary scholars who specialize in this area, those who do not work on religion specifically often adhere to a secular narrative about the Victorian novel in which any and every expression of doubt is taken as evidence for the inevi-

---

energy in the academy," and most recently, the turn has been tied to and theorized through concepts of the postsecular.

3. One can see a renaissance of evangelical thought elsewhere, in areas of analytic philosophy (through the work of Alvin Plantinga, Nicholas Wolterstorff, and others) for instance, but less so in the humanities.

table decline of religion.[4] Evangelicalism suffers acutely because it is thought to have reached its zenith during the same historical period in which secularism is said to have come to the fore. Whereas many of the historians who do think that secularization has taken place in the West now locate the turning point somewhere in the twentieth century, a majority of the undergraduate courses in Victorian literature perpetuate the idea that evangelicalism receded in the nineteenth century as the modern world emerged.[5] The explanations given in these literary classes for the alleged loss of religious belief still depend heavily on unrevised arguments about urbanization, technology, and the rise of science. If the essays and exam scripts that I have seen in Canada and the UK are anything to go by, students continue to read and be told, implicitly or explicitly, that the publication of Charles Darwin's *The Origin of Species* marks the end of all forms of Christianity, evangelicalism included. We see the resilience of the secularization story in scholarship such as Christopher Lane's *The Age of Doubt: Tracing the Roots of Our Religious Uncertainty* (2011), with its admittedly eloquent account of "what it felt like to lose one's religious faith."[6] But perhaps more significant is the less-pronounced versions of the thesis in the thought of those who do not specialize in religion and encounter it casually through novels such as *The Way of All Flesh* (1903).

Samuel Butler's semiautobiographical book, published posthumously but written mostly in the 1870s and early 1880s, seems to illustrate a basic premise of secularization theory by showing how evangelical theology is too limited and too oppressive to respond to the shifting contours of modern culture. Evangelicalism is not the only religious subject of the book's satire, with Pryer's high churchmanship exposed to reveal a metaphorical devil in human form ("glimpses of a pretty large cloven foot kept peeping out from under the saintly robe of Pryer's conversation").[7] But evangelical thought and practice remain the book's chief target, a point signaled from the start by the ironic choice of epigraph on the title page. Romans 8:28—"We know that all things work together for good to them that love God"—was a popular text in Calvinist evangelical theology during the eighteenth and nineteenth centuries, and the narrative's interest in evangelicalism becomes more explicit as the religious movement's negative influence and terminal decline are traced through three

---

4. For more on the significance of thought about the postsecular for our histories of the British novel, see Branch and Knight, "Why the Postsecular Matters: The Rise of the Novel and Literary Studies."
5. For Callum G. Brown, most famously, secularization happens in the 1960s rather than the nineteenth century. See Brown, *The Death of Christian Britain*.
6. Lane, *The Age of Doubt*, 4.
7. Butler, *The Way of All Flesh*, 287.

generations of the Pontifex family. George Pontifex is a commercially successful evangelical publisher who treats his children harshly. His son, Theobald, is an Anglican clergyman of a slightly more moderate evangelical persuasion but no less deliberate in the harsh treatment of his own offspring: "Theobald had never liked children. . . . If Christina could have given birth to a few fully-grown clergymen in priest's orders—of moderate views, but inclining rather to Evangelicalism . . .—why, there might have been more sense in it."[8] By the time we get to Ernest, the legacy of evangelicalism is present primarily through the crippling effects of a severe religious upbringing, though Ernest does have a brief fling as a "religious enthusiast" at the University of Cambridge when he is influenced by followers of the evangelical clergyman, Charles Simeon.[9]

The methods used in *The Way of All Flesh* to make the case against evangelicalism are sophisticated, and the first section of this chapter examines how the novel constructs its story of religious decline. Ultimately, though, it is impossible to separate the workings of narrative from our reading of that narrative, and in the second section I turn my attention to the complex reception of Butler's novel in the history of literary criticism. Others have already undertaken the groundwork of this reception history, and I make no pretense at offering a more exhaustive account than readers can find in the older scholarship of Lee Elbert Holt or the more recent collection on Butler edited by James Paradis.[10] My goal in this second section is to retell this reception history with particular reference to the relationship between evangelicalism and literary studies. Doing so lays the foundation for an argument I go on to develop in the next section regarding the parallel between Overton's narration and our own modern methods of reading. Overton's critical irony is, I suggest, the default mode of reading practiced by modern literary criticism, and this is the central reason why we struggle to see the limitations in what he says about evangelical religion. In making this claim, I do not want to ignore the power of critical irony or play down its potential benefits. But this mode of reading has an inflated view of its own interpretative prowess and makes the mistake of trying to detach the reader from the material that he or she is seeking to understand. There is a danger here of perpetuating the problem I am addressing by positioning my own perspective as superior to the readings of others, and in the concluding part of the chapter, I seek to address this by acknowledging the ways in which my reading of Butler's novel and the broader literary

---

8. Ibid., 116.
9. Ibid., 250.
10. See Holt, "Samuel Butler and His Victorian Critics," 146–59; Holt, "Samuel Butler's Rise to Fame," 867–78; Paradis, ed., *Samuel Butler, Victorian against the Grain*.

history of evangelicalism provided in this book are historically and personally situated. Before we get to my own story, however, let us begin with Butler's.

BUTLER'S STORY

Explaining the vitriolic history of the evangelical Pontifex family in *The Way of All Flesh*, Malcolm Muggeridge writes:

> When Butler, on Miss Savage's and Darwin's advice, sat down to write a novel, there was only one thing for him to write about—himself. All novelists write about themselves; but in *The Way of All Flesh* Butler wrote about himself more intensively than perhaps anyone else ever has. Overton, who tells the story, is himself, and Ernest Pontifex, its hero, is also himself; Theobald and Christina are images of himself through one end of a telescope, and Aunt Alethea and Towneley images of himself through the other end. The book is adolescent in the passion and naiveté of its introspection.[11]

Muggeridge's frustration with his subject is apparent here and throughout his biography, and one can understand why much subsequent scholarship on Butler has been critical of what Muggeridge has to say. Yet Muggeridge is right to insist that the story of *The Way of All Flesh* is intensely personal for Butler. Like so many other children born in the nineteenth century, Butler grew up in an evangelical household and was shaped by his early experiences of this religious tradition. While the children of evangelical families had very different experiences and a wide range of responses to their upbringing, Butler's lasting impression was an acute sense of the way in which the vocabulary and grammar of evangelical religion had been used to justify an abusive household. In his thinly veiled portrait of the young Butler, Overton introduces the means by which the "thumbscrews" were applied from an early age: "Before Ernest could well crawl he was taught to kneel; before he could well speak he was taught to lisp the Lord's Prayer, and the general confession."[12]

Although the Pontifex household is the immediate context for the narrator's satirical gaze, Overton continually implicates the larger evangelical tradition in his critique. On one occasion, he reminds readers that anyone with a "clerical connection, will probably remember scores and scores of rectors and rectors' wives who differed in no material respect from Theobald and Chris-

---

11. Muggeridge, *The Earnest Atheist: A Study of Samuel Butler*, 227.
12. Butler, *The Way of All Flesh*, 211, 117.

tina," and long before we get to that reminder, the following description of Theobald's difficult childhood implicates other evangelical parents:[13]

> To parents who wish to lead a quiet life I would say: Tell your children that they are very naughty—much naughtier than most children. . . . You carry so many more guns than they do. This is called moral influence, and it will enable you to bounce them as much as you please. . . . Feed them spiritually upon such brimstone and treacle as the late Bishop of Winchester's Sunday Stories. You hold all the trump cards, or if you do not you can filch them; if you play them with anything like judgment you will find yourselves heads of happy, united God-fearing families, even as did my old friend Mr Pontifex.[14]

The claim, albeit satirical, that there is a lesson to be learnt is one of the elements that prevent us from thinking of Theobald's experience as isolated. Others include the talk of families in the plural, the reference to a similar model of teaching in the publications of a senior member of the established Church, and the categorization of the Pontifex experience under the term "moral influence." By the time Overton speaks of "guns" and "bouncing" one's children, the picture is clear: the language of violence is endemic to evangelical family life, not peculiar to successive generations of the Pontifex household. There is no concession anywhere in the novel to the possibility that the parenting practiced by Theobald and Christina might be unusual for evangelicals—we are reminded that "it was the system rather than the people that was at fault"—and Butler's choice of names for his characters continues the allegorical form of Bunyan's *The Pilgrim's Progress* to which I have already made reference in chapter 1, encouraging us to think of types rather than individuals.[15]

Overton's narration can be insightful, alerting us to issues with evangelical theology we may not have considered otherwise. Consider, for example, the recurring criticism of evangelicalism's preoccupation with God's justice and the movement's heavy interest, bordering on obsession, in the penalty for sin. According to Overton, the threat of God's punishment was used to make children do as they were told: "The Day of Judgment, indeed, according to the opinion of those who were most likely to know, would not under any

---

13. Ibid., 102.
14. Ibid., 57–58.
15. Ibid., 298. Although Elisabeth Jay is also critical of the narrowness of Butler's religious portrait, she does find some plurality, noting that, "in a strange way Butler's writing can again be compared to George Eliot's in its desire to do justice to the variety to be found within the Evangelical fold. The enthusiasm displayed by Christina and her literary predecessor, Mrs Owen, in their pietistic devotions . . . indicates a strain of fervor unknown to the Laodicean Theobald." Jay, *The Religion of the Heart*, 269.

circumstances be delayed more than a few years longer . . . and we ourselves [would] be consigned to an eternity of torture unless we mended our ways. . . . All this was so alarming that we fell to screaming."[16] Similar claims about the coercive violence in evangelical theology can be found elsewhere in the novel, most notably in the description of "the daily oft-repeated screams that issue from the study" when Theobald instructs his son during lesson hours.[17] Initially, such critiques seem clumsy and exaggerated, and are easily countered by thinking about the more positive instances of evangelical parenting and education that existed in the nineteenth century.[18] Yet Overton is not the only novelist to identify a potentially violent strand within the evangelical concern for God's judgment, and he may be right to suggest that the plain-sense hermeneutics employed by evangelicalism (and its theological forerunner, Puritanism) prevented adequate reflection on the instances of severe judgments that are especially prominent in the Old Testament and were sometimes used as precedents.[19] Overton complains that a hermeneutics in which "every syllable of the Old Testament was taken down *verbatim* from the mouth of God" was liable to think of everything in the Old Testament as an unproblematic model and forget "that the poor abuses of all times want countenance."[20] Later on in the novel, when Ernest returns to visit his father, Theobald is overwhelmed by a desire for punishment, to the extent that his recollection of the Prodigal Son story is theologically distorted: "He wanted Ernest to return, but he was to return as any respectable, well-regulated prodigal ought to return—abject, broken-hearted, asking forgiveness from the tenderest and most longsuffering father in the whole world."[21]

Despite these moments of insight, the cumulative effect of Butler's novel offers a partial and disingenuous account of evangelicalism. The dramatic descriptions of violence, abuse, and fear can distract us from the less spec-

---

16. Butler, *The Way of All Flesh*, 42.
17. Ibid., 97.
18. Acknowledging the patriarchal authority of many evangelical households, Hannah Barker reminds us that this was allied "with an understanding of 'tender' fatherhood that was both religiously inspired by Evangelicalism's religious and emotional expressiveness (though not necessarily exclusively experienced by adherents to Evangelical groups)." Barker, *Family and Business during the Industrial Revolution*, 127–28.
19. Christopher Herbert writes: "The tyrannical frame of mind was in fact, as we have seen, diagnosed as the cultural axis of the age by one Victorian observer after another and was symbolized, for instance, in the grim, repressive, sadomasochistic Evangelicals who populate the novels of Dickens, Thackeray, the Brontës, George Eliot, Trollope, Samuel Butler, and others." Herbert, *Victorian Relativity*, 159.
20. Butler, *The Way of All Flesh*, 53.
21. Ibid., 390. Evangelicals did not typically read the parable of the prodigal son in this way.

tacular claims about evangelical religion that Overton includes within his narrative. Foremost among these is the implication that evangelicals lack any self-awareness. The charge is not entirely unmerited: as I discussed in the previous chapter, evangelicalism was committed to a hermeneutic that saw truth as self-evident, and its preference for action over theory sometimes came at the cost of sustained reflection on the whole range of its beliefs and actions. The movement did encourage some level of introspection, however, through personal devotions, individual Bible reading, and the emphasis in sermons on rooting out one's sin. Yet this is consistently downplayed in Butler's novel, with the Pontifex family lacking any sort of self-awareness. The failure to come to terms with the true nature of his inner life is identified first in George Pontifex, who "was not the man to trouble himself much about his motives. People were not so introspective then as we are now; they lived more according to a rule of thumb."[22] But it is even more pronounced with Christina and Theobald: at no point does their parenting involve conscious doubts as to the righteousness of their actions, and Overton sees it as his job to reveal the internal motivations that Ernest's parents cannot, or do not, see. Christina's lack of self-awareness gives rise to "flights of religious romanticism" and is identified as the primary reason for her selfishness.[23] When Overton describes her contemplating the prospects of becoming the wife of a clergyman, he informs us that she "wondered at times at the blindness shown by Providence towards its own truest interests in not killing off the rectors who stood between Theobald and his living a little faster."[24] Her failure to think about anyone else stands in sharp contrast to the sympathetic imagination valorized by George Eliot and others in the classic realist tradition, and the comparison highlights Christina's stunted emotional and ethical development.

Butler's account of evangelicalism also smuggles in a series of matter-of-fact comments about evangelical religion being defunct and out-of-place in the modern world. Because the immediate context of the novel is Anglicanism, these comments focus on the terminal state of the evangelical movement within the Church of England. Christina and Theobald "hated change of all sorts," and the inability of their beliefs to accommodate the shifting contours of modern life prepares us for the inevitability of evangelicalism's failure to handle changes in the surrounding culture.[25] The view of evangelicalism presented is at odds with the vitality that William Wilberforce had described as integral to evangelicalism at the start of the nineteenth century, and a ques-

---

22. Butler, *The Way of All Flesh*, 54.
23. Ibid., 83.
24. Ibid., 81.
25. Ibid., 100.

tionable historical account of Anglican evangelicalism is conveyed when Overton tells us that "it was Theobald's duty to see the honour and glory of God through the eyes of a Church which had lived three hundred years without finding reason to change a single one of its opinions."[26] Having established this idea of evangelicalism as unchanging, Overton goes on to describe the movement as "almost a matter of ancient history" by 1858, and when that year sees Ernest coming under the influence of the Simeonites, we are encouraged to see this "one phase of spiritual activity which had any life in it during the time Ernest was at Cambridge" as "the remains of the Evangelical awakening of more than a generation earlier."[27]

Overton's insistence that evangelicalism was no longer a significant force in cultural life by the middle of the nineteenth century is reinforced when the narrator moves the story into the 1860s and narrates what happens when Ernest visits his parents in Battersby: "On Sunday Ernest went to church as a matter of course, and noted that the ever receding tide of Evangelicalism had ebbed many a stage lower."[28] When Overton makes this observation, he does so in the context of telling us about the emergence of ritualism in Theobald's church services. Noting that Butler brings forward a shift in Anglican worship preferences by over a decade, Elisabeth Jay explains that the novel's failure to adhere to the facts of history is motivated partly by the need for Butler to "reassure himself that the Evangelicalism he had, or thought he had, suffered from so greatly was in its death throes," and partly by the contribution that this change makes to "the literary torture and murder of Theobald" in the text.[29] But we might also think about Overton's reading of the tide of evangelicalism alongside other writers and register the overlap with Matthew Arnold's language in "Dover Beach," which, though written earlier, was first published in 1867. Both authors see a loss of confidence in religion as part of the natural rhythm of life: whereas Arnold's poem renders the loss of belief a current event, Overton's narration locates it firmly in the past in an effort to support the claim that secularization had rendered evangelicalism obsolete by the 1860s. Overton's narrative is one in which the intellectual simplicity of religious belief gives way to more sophisticated readings of the world: "In those days people believed with a simple downrightness which I do not observe among educated men and women now. It had never so much as crossed Theo-

---

26. Wilberforce, *A Practical View of the Prevailing Religious System of Professed*; Butler, *The Way of All Flesh*, 137.
27. Butler, *The Way of All Flesh*, 230.
28. Ibid., 402.
29. Jay, *The Religion of the Heart*, 268, 269.

bald's mind to doubt the literal accuracy of any syllable in the Bible."[30] In this reading, evangelicalism is replaced by a secularism marked by skepticism and the ability to think critically.

Perhaps the main reason so many critics see *The Way of All Flesh* as a marker of religious decline is that the narrative renders theology almost completely passive. One needs little understanding of the specificities of theological discourse to understand what is going on in the novel because theological terms are continually emptied of content. Examples include the description of "prayer" as "the art of entertainment" at Mrs. Cowey's parties, the symbolic significance of Theobald's Bible study, in which "he cuts little bits out of the Bible and gums them with exquisite neatness by the side of other little bits," and the scene where Overton likens family prayers to bees going up and down flowered wallpaper "without ever suspecting that so many of the associated ideas could be present, and yet the main idea be wanting hopelessly, and for ever."[31] Theological language is shown to offer nothing of worth, a point reinforced in the closing pages when Theobald's "Harmony of the Old and New Testaments which he had compiled during many years with such exquisite neatness and a huge collection of MS. Sermons" fetch "ninepence a barrow load" at auction.[32]

While there are several occasions in the novel when the value of theological writing is called into question openly, the commitment to theological passivity is largely meant to escape notice. Throughout the extensive accounts of the characters' religious psychology, theology is repeatedly ignored as a likely explanatory force, and the only reasons why Christina and Theobald do what they do are a-theological emotional drives (jealousy, insecurity, and so on) and an array of socioeconomic influences that can be understood without reference to Christian doctrine. The same line of reasoning is applied to the Simeonites, whose religious enthusiasm for the ministry is said to be disguised "ambition" for a vocation that might increase their social standing.[33] If theological discourse has any effect at all, it is to blind characters to their real motivations. Turning once more to the actions of Theobald and Christina, Overton writes: "Poor people! They had tried to keep their ignorance of the world from themselves by calling it the pursuit of heavenly things, and then shutting their eyes to anything that might give them trouble."[34] The cumulative effect of this failure to acknowledge any theological contribution to the

---

30. Butler, *The Way of All Flesh*, 81.
31. Ibid., 69, 97, 127.
32. Ibid., 425.
33. Ibid., 233.
34. Ibid., 298.

religious world of the novel is that readers are led to accept Victorian life as a predominately secular affair.

INHERITING BUTLER'S STORY: A VERY BRIEF HISTORY OF LITERARY CRITICISM

There is a long history of literary critics being well-disposed to Butler's reading of religion. This was certainly evident in my own experience of being taught *The Way of All Flesh* as an undergraduate. Although our professor encouraged the class to recognize the bias of the narrator and consider the significance of the novel's delay in naming him clearly, we were encouraged to think of Overton's account of religious decline as essentially true even though we could see its exaggerated and embittered nature. Seeing the flaw in a perspective yet still being persuaded by that view is not entirely surprising—we frequently enjoy a similar experience when reading fiction—yet the suspension of disbelief is rarely prized in criticism, and the willingness of many readers to accept Overton as a broadly reliable guide to the failure of evangelical religion, despite being aware of the bias of his narration, merits further thought. One explanation is the lack of familiarity with religious vocabulary in much of the modern academy. For those unfamiliar with the intricacies of nineteenth-century evangelical theology and practice, it is difficult to determine which of Butler's religious observations are accurate and which are not. But to rely on this explanation too heavily risks missing something more fundamental. Regardless of whether our knowledge of religion is detailed enough to spot specific historical distortions in a work of fiction, Butler's story embodies a larger suspicion of religion that has been passed down through the critical tradition.

Following an uneven critical reception during his lifetime, Butler's stock rose in the early years of the twentieth century when writers such as Arnold Bennett, D. H. Lawrence, Lytton Strachey, George Bernard Shaw, E. M. Forster, Leonard Woolf, and Virginia Woolf highlighted his importance, read him enthusiastically, and paid homage to his writing in their work.[35] Shaw made his debt to Butler most explicit in the preface to *Major Barbara* (1905), a play centered on the experiences of an officer in the Salvation Army who struggles to reconcile the religious beliefs of the evangelical movement she belongs to with the financial pressures of her work. Recognizing a similar preoccupa-

---

35. On the critical reception of Butler in the early twentieth century, see Holt, "Samuel Butler's Rise to Fame"; Paradis, ed., *Samuel Butler, Victorian against the Grain*; and William Van O'Connor, "Samuel Butler and Bloomsbury," in Rathburn and Steinmann, eds., *From Jane Austen to Joseph Conrad*, 257–73.

tion in Butler's novel with the relationship between money and belief, Shaw admits in his preface to "almost . . . despair[ing] of English literature when one sees so extraordinary a study of English life as Butler's posthumous *Way of All Flesh* making so little impression," and the playwright goes on to credit Butler as a major influence on *Major Barbara*.[36] Shaw is not an entirely reliable chronicler here, for Butler's writing made a sizeable impact on a number of writers in the years immediately after *The Way of All Flesh* was published. Looking back, Forster insisted that "to me, and to many others, he quickly became a commanding figure, and with varying ability we interpreted him and preached his gospel."[37] In another of his essays on Butler, Forster sought to explain the qualities he admired: "He stands for the undogmatic outlook, for tolerance, good humour, good taste, empiricism, and reasonableness. Well aware that reason is fallible, he held that we can be reasonable as long as we can, and should not plunge into mysticism because problems are difficult, or in obedience to the command of a priest or a commissar."[38]

Explaining the positive assessment by Shaw, Forster, and others, James Paradis tells us that Butler's "self-fashioning as outsider and antagonist of his own age played well among writers seeking new departures from the vast and imposing panorama of Victorian culture."[39] This certainly appears to be true in the case of Virginia Woolf, who acknowledged the deficiencies and idiosyncrasies of Butler's writing, yet was still a great admirer of him. According to William O'Connor: "He had helped her generation to believe in the individual's right to pursue his own course un-intimidated by the Victorian era's insistence on propriety, on rules, on duties."[40] It is easy to see how Woolf and others came to appreciate Butler's rebellion against those in the Victorian period who were "staid and prim, of evangelical tendencies, and deeply imbued with a sense of the sinfulness of any act of insubordination to parents."[41] But we might go further and consider too why Woolf came to see Butler as an incisive chronicler of changing attitudes to religion. In her essay "Mr. Bennett and Mrs. Brown," Woolf famously explained that "in or about December 1910, human character changed," and she named "religion" among

---

36. Shaw, *Major Barbara*, 23.
37. E. M. Forster, "The Butler Legacy," in Heath, ed., *The Creator as Critic and Other Writings by E. M. Forster*, 313.
38. Ibid., 316.
39. James Paradis, "Butler after Butler: The Man of Letters as Outsider," in Paradis, ed., *Samuel Butler: Victorian against the Grain*, 365.
40. O'Connor, "Samuel Butler and Bloomsbury," in Rathburn and Steinmann, eds., *From Jane Austen to Joseph Conrad*, 264–65.
41. Butler, *The Way of All Flesh*, 80.

the aspects of society that were now seen differently.[42] What is less well known about Woolf's observation is her claim that the first signs of the change "are recorded in the books of Samuel Butler, in *The Way of All Flesh* in particular."[43] Butler's open criticism of Victorian religion, especially in its evangelical form, was bound to appeal to the atheistic Woolf, who, as Pericles Lewis explains, "expressed passionate hostility towards all forms of traditional Christianity." Lewis continues: "Woolf endows some of her characters with her horror of church going and religious belief . . . [and] directs her strongest sense of disgust . . . at what she calls 'this old savage,' God."[44] Although Butler's criticism of religion was appealing in itself, the reason that Woolf was willing to locate *The Way of All Flesh* as an important milestone in the transformation she describes was Overton's willingness to see beyond, beneath, and behind religious surfaces. Modern novelists, insists Woolf, see more deeply and more profoundly than nineteenth-century religion or its practitioners.

The belief that modern thinkers and writers are able to see more incisively than theologians or those within a religious system is taken up by many of the recent critics who have written about Butler's novel. Even when religion is not the focus of their work, its limitations and problems are assumed and seen as antithetical to clear, independent thought. For Susan Haack, Butler's satire is a model of intellectual integrity and deserves to be seen as "one of the finest epistemological novels ever written: a semi-autobiographical *bildungsroman* that traces not only the moral but also the intellectual growth of its central character, Ernest Pontifex, as he fumbles his way from a fog of self-deceptive pseudo-belief and sham inquiry to an appreciation of what it means really to believe something."[45] Danielle Nielson is similarly suspicious of religion when she reasons that *The Way of All Flesh* "illustrates the power of cultural controls such as the church and the paterfamilias when the novel confronts Britain's hegemonic class, gender, and religious systems; within these systems it is impossible for one to obtain individual fulfillment."[46] And Sally Shuttleworth's article on *The Way of All Flesh*, which explores the novel's interest in spiritual pathology and roots it in the publication of a "confessional manual

---

42. Woolf, *Mr Bennett and Mrs Brown*, 4, 5.
43. Ibid., 4–5. Given my previous citation of Shaw's admiration for Butler, it is also worth noting that Woolf tells us in *Mr Bennett and Mrs Brown* that "the plays of Bernard Shaw continue to record it [the change in character]" (5).
44. Lewis, *Religious Experience and the Modernist Novel*, 142. Lewis does acknowledge, however, how Woolf's work might be read in terms of a more constructive engagement with religious ideas. In addition to the material on Woolf in his book, see the cowritten essay with Elyse Graham, "Private Religion, Public Mourning, and *Mrs. Dalloway*," 88–106.
45. Haack, "The Ideal of Intellectual Integrity," 361.
46. Nielsen, "Samuel Butler's *Life and Habit* and *The Way of All Flesh*," 82.

for clergy, *The Priest in Absolution* (1866, 1872)," proceeds in a similar vein as she declares that the "novel first exposes the self-justifying hypocrisies of Theobald's religion, then attacks a more dangerous enemy—religion dressed as science."[47] Shuttleworth continues: "Butler's whole oeuvre can be seen as an assault on the manipulative power of religion."[48] On one level, these comments are unexceptional: the novel is clearly critical of religion and, as Shuttleworth points out, religion is not the only target of Butler's satire. On another level, however, it is never entirely clear from Shuttleworth's description whether she is just telling us what happens in the text or offering her own view of the dangers to which religion is prone. Throughout her article, we find a number of assumptions that pervade older accounts of secularization, including the inevitable trajectory from religious belief to scientific enlightenment. I do not want to be too critical here: Shuttleworth's investigations into the novel's spiritual pathology are informative; it would be misleading to describe her article as polemical; and I have no problem with the thought of history being prejudicial. But religion fares badly on her reading, and I suggest that what she and others say about religion can be located within a long-standing interpretative arc that includes Overton's narration and the way in which literary criticism frequently tells largely negative stories about the Christian faith.

THE LIMITS OF OUR READING

While we might expect literary critics to be more sensitive to the difference between recording and constructing history, we are all prone to lose sight of this distinction as we read other people's accounts and subconsciously admit only those insights that accord with our own experience of the world. George Pontifex is criticized by Overton for making "up his mind to admire only what he thought it would be creditable in him to admire" when he visits mainland Europe, but Overton admits later on that his dislike of Ellen has shaped the way he "got out [from Ernest] pretty nearly the whole story" of their attempts to set up shop in London.[49] Prejudging what we read is an inevitable and potentially creative part of all interpretation, and Overton's narration should not be dismissed on these grounds. His story, after all, makes for a fascinating work of literature, one that I and many others enjoy reading. The problem lies with a particular aspect of his prejudice: modern interpretative superiority, by which I mean the assumption that modern interpreters are always

---

47. Shuttleworth, "Spiritual Pathology," 625, 647.
48. Ibid., 647.
49. Butler, *The Way of All Flesh*, 45, 339.

more sophisticated than their predecessors and always able to see far more than those from previous generations.[50] Overton continually looks back and seeks to expose the truth behind the naïve religious experiences of Ernest and the Pontifex family. This looking back includes the particularly egregious and unlikely claim that, even toward the end of his third year at the University of Cambridge, Ernest "had never seen anyone who doubted, nor read anything that raised a suspicion in his mind as to the historical character of the miracles recorded in the Old and New Testament."[51] Post university, Ernest's continued slowness "at detecting false analogies and the misuse of metaphor" makes him "a mere child in the hands of his fellow curate."[52] Something similar might be said about his treatment in the writing hands of Overton, whose mature interpretative ability is accentuated through juxtaposition with Ernest's ignorance. Although Overton does not claim perfect knowledge, acknowledging on one occasion "how little do we know our thoughts," his narrative is predicated on the belief that the critic is a superior reader whose elevated vantage point enables them to see what those in the mi(d)st of belief cannot see for themselves.[53]

What interests me most about Overton's reading is its similarity with much of the literary criticism that we practice today. I am aware of the difficulties with trying to link a present moment in criticism, if such a thing can be said to exist at all, back to Overton's narration. Overton is highly dismissive of those who work in the academy ("the worst teachers in the world"); the seismic yet overlapping shifts in twentieth-century and twenty-first-century criticism rupture any straightforward history of influence; and there are noticeable geographic differences between the types of criticism undertaken by scholars of Victorian literature (let alone scholars of other periods).[54] Yet I want to suggest that many of us who teach in Anglo-American departments of literature share his commitment to critical irony, a hermeneutic that privileges detachment and the distance that accompanies it. This hermeneutic is predicated

---

50. For a lucid exploration of the theological stakes at work when one generation reads the work of the critical generation that went before, see Charles LaPorte, "Post-secular English Studies and Romantic Cults of Authorship," in King and Werner, eds., *Constructing Nineteenth-Century Religion* (forthcoming).

51. Butler, *The Way of All Flesh*, 230.

52. Ibid., 259. Overton's willingness to judge Ernest's reading of metaphors a failure and presume that he [Overton] interprets them with greater superiority and clarity misses the "indirectness and elusiveness of metaphor, [which] holding together quite explicitly the affirmation that 'it is' with the vital qualifier that, even so, 'it is not,' grants it an epistemic modesty." See Hart, *Between the Image and the Word*, 26. As Hart acknowledges, he is drawing here on Gunton, *The Actuality of Atonement*.

53. Butler, *The Way of All Flesh*, 53.

54. Ibid., 369.

on the idea that we read between the lines more effectively if we stand apart from what is read; it presumes that the more knowing understanding of language exemplified in irony is the chief means by which one might transcend common-sense knowledge and articulate positions that remain aware of their provisional contributions to what might have been described as truth by earlier generations. Overton reflects that "people almost always want something external to themselves to reveal to them their own likes and dislikes," and the alleged capacity of critical irony to offer this revelation whilst remaining detached is crucial to the style of writing that is pervasive in modern departments of literature.[55] Literary scholars do not claim to know everything about their subject, but we do tend to think that we know much more than anyone else, or, to put the point more precisely, that what we know is more sophisticated, more astute, and more self-aware than the understanding of lay readers. Our claim to special knowledge is not wholly unreasonable, of course, and it would be more than a little depressing if years of training as readers did not enable us to see things that have escaped the attention of others. But what is missing from so much of our modern literary scholarship is recognition of our interpretative limits; an acknowledgement that "the light of a later knowledge," as Overton puts it, is not as revealing as we sometimes think, and that we might have missed important issues seen by lay readers.[56]

My reservations about critical irony are part of a growing body of scholars who want to rethink the way in which we read literature. Stephen Best and Sharon Marcus turn to the concept of "surface reading" in their effort to bring together the eclectic interpretative approaches featured in a special issue of *Representations*; Eve Kosofsky Sedgwick considers whether "reparative reading" might help us avoid an overly paranoid hermeneutic; Michael Warner explores "uncritical reading" as an alternative to the narrow conception of "critical reading" that dominates many departments of literature; and Rita Felski details the limits of critique.[57] The work of Warner and Felski is closest to the line of thought I pursue here, with Warner noting how "various styles of religious reading" are the "most obvious candidates for such a program of 'uncritical' reading."[58] Rather than seeking to replace one type of "critical" reading with another described as "uncritical," or replace secular interpreta-

---

55. Ibid., 303.
56. Ibid., 108. Exploring the way in which talk of affect might help shift us away from too narrow a reliance on critique, Felski notes how it might also make us "less dismissive of lay experiences of reading." Felski, *The Limits of Critique*, 179.
57. Best and Marcus, "Surface Reading: An Introduction"; Sedgwick, *Novel Gazing*; Michael Warner, "Uncritical Reading," in Gallop, ed., *Polemic*, 13–38; Felski, *The Limits of Critique*.
58. Warner, "Uncritical Reading," 16.

tion with a religious hermeneutic, Warner prefers to try and understand the historic workings of our critical practice as professional readers, from the way in which it "is an image of a certain kind of critical reason" to the preoccupation with "critical distance towards" our "interpretive objects."[59] His approach differs from my own in emphasis and where it ends up, but it does provide several useful points of overlap.

There is crossover, too, between what I term critical irony and what Rita Felski names as critique. Felski traces the limits of a mode of reading which, urged on by a *"literary suspicion* [that] presses to the fore" from the late nineteenth century onward, is fundamentally suspicious and always seeking to get beneath/beyond/behind its subject.[60] As Felski makes clear, her work is not an attempt to abandon critique altogether, a move she acknowledges to be impossible and undesirable. Instead, she redescribes the work of critique so that we might see its workings and limits in new ways and make space for other modes of reading alongside it.[61] While critique and critical irony are not synonyms, some of the questions I ask here of contemporary literary criticism echo Felski's recognition of the drawbacks to a mode of thinking that often results in "a regrettable arrogance of intellect, where the smartest thing you can do is to see through the deep-seated convictions and heartfelt attachments of others."[62] If there is a difference in approach—beyond my narrower interest in irony, her more thorough immersion in related theoretical debates, and the distinctively sharp and evocative style of her prose—it lies in my efforts to think about the implications that these discussions have on our reading of religion. It is notable, I think, how Felski frequently plays down the religious ramifications of what she explores, as in the moment when she deploys the rhetoric of faith to clarify what she is *not* doing: "My hope is to steer clear of the hectoring tone of the convert, the sermonizing of the redeemed sinner with a zealous glint in her eye."[63] Felski's argument opens up important questions about religion—consider, for instance the moment when she complains how "critique is often feted in the humanities as a cure-all for dogma and orthodoxy"—but it is a space that she seems reluctant to enter, and her use of religious language is often very guarded.[64]

---

59. Ibid., 24, 17.
60. Felski, *The Limits of Critique*, 41.
61. Felski discusses some of these other modes—recognition, enchantment, knowledge, shock—in *Uses of Literature*.
62. Felski, *The Limits of Critique*, 15–16.
63. Ibid., 9.
64. Ibid., 117. For a stronger critique of Felski's engagement with religion, see Branch, "Postcritical and the Postsecular."

Felski's reluctance to enter the realm of religion is not the same as the hostility to faith one encounters elsewhere in instances of literary criticism where critical irony is dominant. Franco Moretti's *Distant Reading* (2013) initially seems to be working in a different setting than the one I am writing about here: he advocates quantitative analysis as a new way forward that breaks with the model of criticism practiced hitherto. Yet his argument for distant reading continues to make use of the resources of critical irony, deploying them to repurpose a cluster of religious metaphors so that they service his argument:

> The United States is the country of close reading, so I don't expect this idea to be particularly popular. But the trouble with close reading (in all of its incarnations, from the new criticism to deconstruction) is that it necessarily depends on an extremely small canon. This may have become an unconscious and invisible premise by now, but it is an iron one nonetheless: you invest so much in individual texts only if you think that very few of them really matter. Otherwise, it doesn't make sense. And if you want to look beyond the canon (and of course, world literature will do so: it would be absurd if it didn't!), close reading will not do it. It's not designed to do it, it's designed to do the opposite. At bottom, it's a theological exercise—very solemn treatment of very few texts taken very seriously—whereas what we really need is a little pact with the devil: we know how to read texts, now let's learn how not to read them. Distant reading: where distance, let me repeat it, is a condition of knowledge: it allows you to focus on units that are much smaller or much larger than the text.... If we want to understand the system in its entirety, we must accept losing something. We always pay a price for theoretical knowledge.[65]

Moretti's argument is theologically questionable in all sorts of ways: the presumption that theology is only interested in biblical texts; the suggestion that theology has no capacity for understanding complex systems; the implication that theology is an authoritarian alternative to Moretti's more radical pact with the devil; and the underlying idea that theology is a redundant "exercise." But more significant for my argument is the way in which the detached vantage point of irony is mobilized to guard against the proximity favored by religious practice.

The preference for detachment continues an older project. In the context of a chapter on Oscar Wilde's use of irony, Amanda Anderson notes the "predilection among postmodern and literary theorists for the mode of irony, a

---

65. Moretti, *Distant Reading*, 48–49.

form of detachment that can claim the insights of critical distance without carrying the onus of earnest enlightenment."[66] Anderson insists that for Wilde, along with the other nineteenth-century writers she examines in *The Powers of Distance: Cosmopolitanism and the Cultivation of Detachment* (2001), the use of a particular literary form is not so easily separated from other reflections on the moral questions that accompany the pursuit of detached knowledge. Locating irony within a broader tradition of detachment helps Anderson address the complaint that irony sometimes masks a lack of moral commitment, and is part of the wider defense she mounts against charges that detachment is "an illusory ideal" and a "form of power that disavows its own violence and exclusivity."[67] For Anderson, the detached orientation of irony is a good thing: a continuation of Enlightenment values and an important component of cosmopolitan critical thought.

I do not share Anderson's wholehearted enthusiasm for the power of distance, and not just because in so many spheres of life—personal relationships, decisions about where we should live and work, pedagogy in the humanities, the writing of references for students and colleagues, etc.—we value proximity at least as much as we value distance. Although irony appears to leave room for acknowledging the limits of our understanding, especially on Anderson's reading, and is often thought to be on the side of provisional knowledge, its reliance on distance and its belief in the value of standing back imply too clear a distinction in our knowledge between things as they are and things as they appear. Irony leads us to stand back in the belief that doing so will bring clarity to a viewpoint that might otherwise be mistaken. And its use is predicated on the belief that those who get too close to a subject are likely to grow confused by their proximity. Yet the belief that critical irony is a necessary condition of knowledge involves "a withdrawal from our common language and the shared judgments that language makes possible," to appropriate Stanley Hauerwas's reading of Richard Rorty, whereas "it is only through relationships that language makes possible not only our knowledge of others but also knowledge of ourselves."[68] I appreciate that distance can sometimes prove useful but too great a reliance on its epistemic ability results in an interpreta-

---

66. Anderson, *The Powers of Distance*, 152. In her follow-up work, Anderson repeats her insistence on the close relationship between irony and other expressions of detachment, arguing that though "there is a tendency among postmodern critics to valorize detachment only when it is fully ironized or otherwise defined against reflective reason . . . my own position is that the valorized form of ironic detachment in queer and postmodern theory is ultimately a species of—and hence should not be opposed to—the postconventional critical reflection appealed to as the basis for critical social theory." Anderson, *The Way We Argue Now*, 65–66.
67. Anderson, *The Powers of Distance*, 24.
68. Hauerwas, *The Work of Theology*, 159.

tive superiority that fails to see the blindness of its reading.[69] While irony can bring with it a capacity for extensive examination of the self, as in the writing of Søren Kierkegaard, it rarely does so in practice, and one does not have to look far across the academic profession to discover that critical irony rarely leads to as much self-awareness as its proponents claim.[70] More often than not, our reliance on critical irony prevents us from thinking more fully about our participation in the stories we tell about literature.

Warner tells us that "by naturalizing critical reading as mere reflection it obscures from even our own view the rather elaborate forms and disciplines of subjectivity we practice and inculcate."[71] The limited self-awareness that accompanies so much critical irony is certainly evident throughout *The Way of All Flesh*. Overton acknowledges his limits on occasion, but his attempts to turn the ironic gaze inward are frequently disingenuous, leading to evasion rather than any sort of detailed personal examination. At one point, Overton writes: "Every man's work . . . is always a portrait of himself, and the more he tries to conceal himself the more clearly will his character appear in spite of him. I may very likely be condemning myself, all the time I am writing this book."[72] But the attention to self is undone by the casually ironic tone through which it is conveyed, directing us away from the possibility that he is really condemning himself, and the form allows Overton to return to the background and keep the spotlight on others. The technique of separating Butler into Ernest and Overton also helps keep the narrating self out of view. Although Overton is theoretically as representative of Butler as is Ernest, it is Ernest who is put under the critical spotlight, and the mature Butler who narrates the story retains his detached vantage point and struggles to take on board his own finitude and failure.

Critical irony will always struggle to make sense of the Christian religion. The commitment involved in belief seems too strong to stand unquestioned, and although the critic may well be right to say that something else is going

---

69. For further discussion of the way in which critique uses spatial metaphors, see Felski, *The Limits of Critique*, chapter 2.

70. Writing about the contribution of Jonathan Lear's *A Case for Irony*, Hauerwas explains that "Kierkegaard was not suggesting that irony is the same as critical self-consciousness. Rather for Kierkegaard irony has a far more disruptive capacity to unsettle our lives." Hauerwas, *The Work of Theology*, 162. C. Stephen Evans helps explain why irony cannot be equated with self-consciousness in the writing of Kierkegaard: the Danish philosopher sees the self as fundamentally Christian rather than constituted on its own terms—"a conscious relation to God provides the basis for true or genuine selfhood"—and irony is a mode of writing that Kierkegaard uses for decidedly theological ends. C. Stephen Evans, *Kierkegaard on Faith and the Self*, 270.

71. Warner, "Uncritical Reading," in Gallop, ed., *Polemic*, 16.

72. Butler, *The Way of All Flesh*, 91–92.

on when people express faith, we also need to try and understand belief on its own terms, or at least recognize that the terms outsiders use to describe it are not as neutral and capacious as claimed. A commitment to critical irony is one of the reasons why literary critics find it so hard to entertain the idea that belief and emotion might disclose something that we cannot see more clearly through our detached analytical lens: from a critically ironic vantage point, belief and emotion seem too trusting and too caught up in their immediate moment to offer adequate opportunities for thought. In addition, Christianity's insistence on our universal complicity in the sinful state that God's salvific work is said to address makes all attempts at detachment theologically problematic. Rejecting the efforts of the ironist to stand back, Christianity, particularly in its evangelical form, maintains that no one is immune from the sort of judgment that we practice in the name of critique—"for all have sinned, and come short of the glory of God."[73] It is not, then, the specific judgments of critical irony that Christian theology has a problem with, even though religious groups can appear to suggest otherwise when they find the judgments against them uncomfortable, but rather the claim that the critic is too detached to come under scrutiny his or herself.

The conflict between a Christian understanding of universal sin and the neutrality believed to accompany detached reading may help explain the strange account in *The Way of All Flesh* of Mr. Hawke's sermon at Cambridge. The sermon is, in Overton's words, "typical" for evangelicals of the period, with Mr. Hawke beginning with the evidence for the resurrection of Christ and then calling on his audience to heed the fact that one day all will "stand before the Judgment Seat of Christ," turn away from sin, and consider whether they are personally being called, at that moment, to commit their lives to Christ.[74] Assessing the impact of the sermon, Overton writes: "They had heard nothing but what they had been hearing all their lives; how was it, then, that they were so dumbfounded by it?" His explanation is as follows:

> I suppose partly because they had lately begun to think more seriously, and were in a fit state to be impressed, partly from the greater directness with which each felt himself addressed, through the sermon delivered in a room, and partly to the logical consistency, freedom from exaggeration, and profound air of conviction with which Mr Hawke had spoken. His simplicity and obvious earnestness had impressed them even before he had alluded to his special mission, but this clenched everything, and the words "Lord, is

---

73. Romans 3:23.
74. Butler, *The Way of All Flesh*, 248.

it I?" were upon the hearts of each as they walked pensively home through moonlit courts and cloisters.[75]

None of Overton's reasons for the sermon's impact seem especially convincing, and it is odd to describe the content of a sermon as unexceptional yet still repeat that content in full. What is noticeable about Overton's gloss is the way in which he seeks to distance the personal impact that the sermon has on Ernest. The impact is muted first by the prosaic explanations, and then by the way in which the central question of the sermon is transformed into abstract words, existing "upon" (not in) hearts that are themselves a metaphor rather than something more obviously substantive, and eventually dissipating as a moonlit night implicitly gives way to the clear reality of a new day. When that new day comes, the intensity of the sermon's personal import is further undermined by a banal transformation in which Ernest decides to give up tobacco for Christ as a response to what he has heard.

If Overton's attempts to play down Ernest's encounters with the Christian faith are anything to go by, our modern suspicion of religion may be part of a broader intellectual maneuver to extract us from the stories we tell about the world. Not all of these stories involve evangelical belief, but some of the stories are this way inclined, and for anyone interested in the novels of the Victorian period, it is impossible to avoid the Christian faith altogether. I realize that questions need to be asked about the narratives we tell, a work of reflection that theology and critique share in common, but these questions are best asked from the inside, whether that is from a position of faith or a nonbeliever's point of personal contact with some aspect of the Christian story.[76] Trying to stand back can sometimes prove beneficial, but we should not presume that detached readings of faith are inherently preferable, and no reader of this book should think they are entirely detached from the matters at hand. Even if stories of faith are no longer the primary stories with which someone chooses to identify, a view that some of my readers will likely share with Overton, there is still value in trying to think about the story from within: not just because the voice of the other is always worth listening to but because being cognizant of our own experiences with religious people, forms, and ideas is

---

75. Ibid., 248.

76. Consider, for instance, the way in which Michael Warner draws on his religious experiences even though he no longer holds with the Christian beliefs of his youth: "Of course, my life in the bosom of Jesus influenced me; but what interests me more is the way religion supplied me with experiences and ideas that I'm still trying to match." Michael Warner, "Tongues Untied: Memoirs of a Pentecostal Boyhood," in Comstock and Henking, eds., Que(e)rying Religion: A Critical Anthology, 224.

essential if we are to come to terms with our own participation in the religious stories that are told in the Victorian novel.

MY STORY

In the early stages of working on this book, the objective seemed straightforward: I wanted to make a case for the Victorian novel's debt to the beliefs and practices of the evangelical movement. That goal did not disappear as the project matured, but it was joined and complicated by a desire for greater precision in my understanding of evangelicalism and the qualities that distinguish the Victorian novel from other writing of the period. As a result, I have found myself wrestling with the way in which all ideas, religious and otherwise, lose some of their definition amid the ordinary life of fiction. That lack of definition does not mean that the ordinary life of the novel has to be thought of as detrimental to Christianity, as George Levine suggests, for the Christian faith is not fundamentally a religion of purified ideas. Stanley Hauerwas and Romand Coles are right in their response to Taylor's *A Secular Age* to emphasize the importance for Christianity of both an understanding of God grounded in the Incarnation and the role of "a people—call such a people if you will, 'church'—who are able to discern possibilities in the immanent frame that could not be seen if such a people did not exist."[77] Reading evangelicalism in the Victorian novel requires thinking more carefully about the practical claims of the Christian tradition and not always reaching for a vague concept of transcendence as the starting point of faith. My realization of this point is not the only lesson I have learnt over the course of writing this book. Working on the project has encouraged me to attend more closely to several aspects of literary form, history, and methodology. In terms of the latter, I have become aware of how much writing about the literature of an earlier period requires us to pay attention to the way we read now. To mount an argument for the role that evangelicalism played in the development of the Victorian novel means coming to terms with the historic readings of the movement passed down to us. When reading Butler's novel, it means questioning why so many readers are prone to believing what Overton tells them about nineteenth-century evangelical religion.

At the center of the argument in this chapter has been my belief that many scholars side with Overton's view of the evangelical religion because, like them, he insists on reading it at a distance. The preference for detachment is

---

77. Hauerwas and Coles, "'Long Live the Weeds and the Wilderness Yet,'" 350.

always likely to find itself in conflict with a Christian gospel that emphasizes our implication and involvement in the story that it tells. Even if we do not accept the claims of evangelicalism as it narrates an account of the Christian faith, we are likely to have some sort of reaction to what it says, even if that is simply alienation at evangelical modes of thought. It is hard to be neutral about the evangelical gospel. I am not suggesting that one can only understand evangelicalism from the inside, although some level of proximity to the movement is always likely to yield insights that are otherwise harder to attain. But we do need to think carefully about our own relation to evangelicalism and find ways of weaving that relation into the stories we tell about the movement's role in the development of the Victorian novel.

My point, in other words, is that there is always a personal dimension to our reading of evangelical religion. This takes on additional significance because of the attention given to personal experience in the movement's own account of its engagement with the world. I do not think that evangelicalism was finally a religion of the heart, although, to return to the discussion of the introductory chapter, I agree with Elisabeth Jay that personal experience was a key idea for this religious movement. Nor am I suggesting that our personal experience should be the only lens through which we try and comprehend the world: left entirely to its own devices, personal experience can prove epistemologically narrow and may even be delusional. These limits are made apparent throughout Butler's novel. When Christina invites Ernest to join him for a chat on the sofa, she claims to be seeking access to an "inner life" about which "we know nothing beyond such scraps as we can glean in spite of you [Ernest]."[78] Yet the narrative critique of her calculated maneuvering in this scene, however overplayed by Overton, is a reminder that there is no straightforward access to someone's inner life. Christina has an agenda when she asks Ernest what is going on inside his head, and we know, too, that those who volunteer such information about their own state of mind are not necessarily any more innocent or knowing in the stories they tell. Since Sigmund Freud, we have been encouraged to be suspicious about references to the self and individuals' efforts to understand their personhood. Finn Fordham observes how the twenty-first-century iterations of this suspicion share a concern with the self's "dissolution, its illusoriness, its fictionality, its constructedness, especially the latter," and there are good reasons to take these concerns seriously.[79] But while Fordham sides with those who want to "pursue at length and with suspicion . . . discourses of the self" that are not sufficiently

---

78. Butler, *The Way of All Flesh*, 198.
79. Fordham, *I Do I Undo I Redo*, 36.

suspicious, I wonder whether it might be time for a different strategy, one which also seeks ways of registering more constructively the role played by the admittedly fragile, constructed, and narrated self.[80] After all, and despite the multiple and complicating layers at work in his fiction, Butler is writing to some degree about his own experiences. And, as I read him and compose this book, I suppose I am writing about mine.

For a long while now I have identified as a Christian rather than an evangelical. Yet much of my religious life has been spent in and on the margins of the evangelical world. While those experiences have not included the highly politicized conservative expressions of evangelicalism that have been so prominent in the United States since the emergence of the Moral Majority in the 1980s, they have been evangelical nevertheless. As a child, I started attending the Salvation Army church with my mother. The Salvation Army church we went to was part of the Evangelical Alliance, heavily influenced by the evangelical-charismatic renewal led by the house-church movement and marked by a commitment to evangelism, holiness, and social transformation. After a preuniversity gap year spent working for a mission group run by the Salvation Army, and then extensive involvement with the evangelically orientated Christian Union during my time as an undergraduate, my twenties and thirties saw me involved with a new Salvation Army church in southwest London. That church was less clearly evangelical than my earlier experiences: the congregation underwent various journeys in thought during my time there and was theologically eclectic. Some members happily identified as evangelicals, others did not, and although the church remained part of the Evangelical Alliance and was actively involved in evangelically oriented conferences such as Spring Harvest, a good portion of the intellectual energy of the church came from elsewhere. The diversity of thought I experienced during my time in this congregation explains the ease with which I transitioned to a different ecclesial setting when I left the UK in 2012 to spend four years working at the University of Toronto. The Church of the Redeemer in Toronto was predominantly Anglo-Catholic, though it possessed characteristics not always associated with that tradition, including a strong sense of inclusion (e.g., women priests), a commitment to social transformation, and a willingness to embrace informality in its rituals. Since returning to the UK to take up my current

---

80. Ibid., 40. It should be noted that Fordham's comment here is the prelude to his own short "snapshot" (41) of his own personal story and its role in the book that he writes. Furthermore, I remain acutely aware of the difficulty of clarifying what the term personhood means. Christian Smith offers a useful starting point in *What Is a Person?* although literary scholars are likely to share my discomfort with Smith's reliance on a social science methodology and my unease at his preference for a definition of personhood based on what is typical or "normal" rather than a definition that looks to the margins.

post at Lancaster University, I have been going to an evangelical Anglican church, though I admit to feeling more comfortable with the wide-ranging and authentic community of faith I find there than some of the theologically conservative ideas that are voiced from time to time.

My Christian orientation might be described as postevangelical. That term ran out of steam soon after it appeared in the 1990s, partly because of a cultural saturation of words beginning with the prefix "post" and partly because the fervor that proponents of the term brought to discussion seemed too closely tied to the tradition that they were seeking to leave behind. I have no desire to try and resurrect the term postevangelical in the long run, but it does offer a useful piece of shorthand here to connote a theological identity that retains vestiges of evangelicalism while departing from this tradition in other respects. This is the position from which I read evangelicalism in the Victorian novel, now and over the course of writing this book: profoundly aware of some of the limits of evangelical thought and critical of aspects of its theology, but with gratitude for the positive ways in which the movement has shaped and continues to shape my thinking.

I know this potted personal history is subject to the limited, selective, and continually shifting nature of all our private reflections, and I offer it not as a final word on where I am coming from but as a temporal and partial attempt to reckon with the challenge outlined in this chapter—that is, of coming to terms with our own participation in the stories we tell about the Victorian novel.[81] With this in mind, I will finish by pointing to a few of the ways in which my experiences of evangelicalism have helped shape the arguments of the preceding chapters. In doing so, I am still trying to register and understand my participation in the story I tell about evangelicalism and the Victorian novel. But I am also seeking to convey the vitality of evangelical thought and demonstrate how the beliefs and practices of a movement that contributed to the development of the Victorian novel might hold continuing significance for our reading today.

I do not think I would have appreciated Thackeray's concern in *Vanity Fair* for the effect that novels have on those who read them without my evangelical background. The novel's interest in performance is apparent to some readers who have no exposure to evangelicalism, but those familiar with the language of this religious movement are more likely to watch those performances and hear a "call to seriousness" alongside the humor.[82] Insisting that fiction shapes the way we think seems an obvious point, one that I feel foolish repeating so

---

81. For a helpful and carefully delineated account of the value and limits of writing about religious identity, see Kort, *Textual Intimacy*.

82. Bradley, *The Call to Seriousness*.

solemnly, but the impact literature has on us is something that much of the scholarship written in the last few decades has sought to elide, either by ignoring the subject altogether or by talking about affect in a way that keeps literature at arm's length. I do not find most of the assessments of reading offered by nineteenth-century evangelicals convincing, and I do not think that novels harmed readers in the way that evangelicals of the period sometimes claimed. But the Victorian novel did, and does, affect those who read it, and not just because of its power to "transport one . . . allowing us temporarily to feel as though we are someone else."[83] While we sometimes do a reasonable job of acknowledging this affect in the classroom, it is rarely a feature of our written scholarship. As one senior Victorianist confessed to me a few years back, we might cry in private at the death of Jo in Dickens's *Bleak House* (1852–53) but it would not do to admit this in our public scholarship. And we would risk sounding even more gullible and naïve were we to start talking about the difference those tears had made to the way we think about our lives.

I came to see the countercultural significance of the evangelical emphasis on personal response and practical application a few years after completing my PhD, when, having gone to a number of conferences on Victorian literature, I then attended a conference in London on Evangelical Identities. My abiding memory of that conference was the way in which speaker after speaker began his or her talk by declaring that they did not want to get drawn into unnecessarily theoretical discussion. At the time, I was dismissive of this concern, quipping to friends later on that an overly theoretical reading was unlikely to be a characteristic of any of the papers given. Since then, however, I have come to value this call to attend more carefully to the practical and personal implications of our scholarship, and I think I now better understand the reasons for a disquiet about modes of scholarship that seeks to exorcize the personal consequences of reading from our discussion of texts.

My experience at that conference was not the first time I found myself changing my mind about the theological inheritance I had received from the evangelical tradition. One of the challenges for me as a young evangelical going to university and studying English literature was working out how to think about faith with respect to the material I was studying. My initial inclination was to try and read everything in terms of the cross and the story of God's gift of salvation through Christ. The clumsy result did not get me very far in terms of grades or intellectual satisfaction, and, looking back, I am grateful for the patience of those who taught me. Though the theological scope of my writing grew significantly over the course of my undergraduate

---

83. Kate Flint, "Traveling Readers," in Ablow, ed., *The Feeling of Reading*, 27.

studies, it was not until I studied theology during my PhD that I started to appreciate more fully how expansive the set of theoretical resources offered by the Christian tradition really were. In the ensuing years, my reading of literature has sought to draw on those resources in various ways, looking to different areas of theology as a means of imaginatively exploring literature rather than treating the Christian faith as a model of thought that might subsequently be confirmed through literary examples. But in returning to Dickens for this project, I have come to appreciate just how much imaginative potential resides in the evangelical story of conversion. That is not to say that I now want to return to conversion narratives and/or the cross at the expense of other theological resources. But I am struck by how Victorian writers saw the imaginative possibilities of these evangelical ideas, even though many of them had reservations about aspects of the accompanying theology. And I am struck, too, by the way in which some of the problems with nineteenth-century theologies of the cross, namely the way in which certain evangelicals looked to the atonement and used it to try and overwrite other people's narratives, were replicated in Dickens's work as he developed his own quasi-religious vision for the novel.

Seeing evangelicals read the Bible in dramatically different ways was almost certainly the prompt for me to think about the role that the Word of God and its reading plays in the content and structure of *The Moonstone*. I have, over the years, listened to absurd readings of the Bible, such as the time when one preacher interpreted Paul's reference in Titus 2:7 to showing, in doctrine, "uncorruptness, gravity, sincerity" as a prohibition on any sort of humor in church. And it is similarly hard to forget the occasion when one hostile questioner at an evangelical church conference challenged my argument against biblical literalism by suggesting, with reference to the cited example of Jesus as the Lamb of God, that it was not impossible that Christ had been transfigured into an animal when he died at Calvary. These anecdotes are likely to raise a wry smile among some readers, for they appear to confirm popular caricatures of the worst sort of evangelical reading. Yet these experiences should be seen as outliers, and I cite them as evidence of evangelical diversity rather than its norms. Evangelical reading of the Bible is, to my mind, more likely to be unnecessarily conservative, even dull, in its preference for plain-sense interpretation. But I have also heard many moving, imaginative, learned, and astute readings of the Bible by evangelicals. Thus, it was no surprise for me to find that when Collins turns his attention to evangelical hermeneutics, he is able to combine critique with sympathy, lambasting the interpretive naivety of Miss Clack, but recognizing a more positive legacy in the communal reading habits of the evangelicals. I do not wish to minimize the ways in which novel reading and evangelical practice collude in the nineteenth-century promotion of an individual mindset, but we do need to consider, too, the communal dimension of evangelical interpretation—enabled by the imagined spiritual communities of print culture, physical family readings of the Bible, discussions of sermons after church, and group Bible studies where the pursuit of truth is seen as a shared activity rather than one that should be left to the professionals.[84] My own experience of such shared activities leads me to concur with Taylor's claim that, on balance, "evangelicalism was basically an anti-hierarchical force, part of the drive for democracy."[85]

The year I spent working for a Salvation Army mission group before going to university was when I first started giving proper thought to the nature of the evangelical gospel. Those I worked with actively reflected on the nature of the "good news" we proclaimed, and we spent many long journeys across the UK thinking about the sociopolitical implications of our message. Those reflections, ranging from the most effective and faithful ways of incarnating the story we told to knowing how best to assist people in the midst of suffering and wider systems of social injustice, have continued in the ensuing years, with some of those I worked with then and also in the company of others, inside and outside the church. When I began researching the periodical *Good Words*, I found that many scholars outside the evangelical community lacked the nuanced understanding of the gospel that marked the best of my conversations within that community. This is probably inevitable—those who spend most time thinking about something should bring a level of insight to the discussion that others struggle to match—but the dismissive attitude of some literary scholars to the theological concerns of the evangelical community was a point of frustration, and my reading of *Good Words* has been influenced by a desire to convey the complexity of evangelical thought about its message. Complex thinking does not always lead to answers that are convincing or theologically helpful though, and it is the successes and failures of *Good Words* that make the periodical such a fascinating case study for thinking about the wider literary context of the Victorian novel. Clumsy divisions between the secular and the religious do not help us read the journal well. At the same time, different media, messages, and messengers are apparent in the periodical's efforts to communicate the gospel, and they do not always mesh

---

84. On the religious community enabled by print culture, see King, *Imagined Spiritual Communities*. King does not focus on evangelicalism but his line of thought does align with the movement at several points, particularly when he notes the allusion of his book title to the work of Benedict Anderson and insists: "I resist Anderson's implication that imagining national communities is an essentially secular activity" (4).

85. Taylor, *A Secular Age*, 451.

easily. As the periodical's missionary efforts and travails show, the desire to make the gospel known through the novel put the purity of the evangelical message and its accompanying ecclesial identity at risk, not so much because of commercial pressures or sensational strategies, as has been suggested, but because a movement committed to being "all things to all men" was always going to be at risk of losing its distinctiveness.

And finally, back to Butler's novel, where the challenges to evangelicalism are presented as terminal. I do not share Overton's view of the fate of evangelicalism by the middle of the nineteenth century. Yet while it is easy to be critical of Overton's narration and see the downsides of his legacy in the way that evangelicalism is written about in literary scholarship, it is much harder to decide on an alternative. The key to seeking out a more nuanced account is reckoning with our personal participation in the story of evangelicalism, but this is difficult to do in practice. I have an abiding memory from my childhood experiences in church of what was called testimony time, occasions in services where members of the congregation were invited to speak briefly to everyone else about their relationship with God and what had been taking place in their lives. Some of those testimonies seemed predictable, misguided, and self-indulgent; others felt genuinely revelatory in what they had to say about the life of faith. In spite of the mixed success, they were important attempts at a personal reckoning, and my memories of listening to those testimonies are very much with me now as I draw this book to a close and try to conclude my own reckoning. There is no final account of the influence of the evangelical movement on the Victorian novel, just as there was no final word in those testimonies I heard in church. But my experience of evangelicalism leads me to think that its story needs to be heard as it resounds in the pages of the Victorian novel. Ultimately, the problem with Overton's preferred way of reading is not that he is sometimes wrong historically, nor that his criticisms are always without merit; it is that his cynicism toward evangelicalism stops him from listening to what those in the movement have to say.

BIBLIOGRAPHY

Ablow, Rachel, ed. *The Feeling of Reading: Affective Experience and Victorian Literature.* Ann Arbor: The University of Michigan Press, 2010.

Agamben, Giorgio. *The Time That Remains: A Commentary on the Letter to the Romans.* Trans. Patricia Dailey. Stanford, CA: Stanford University Press, 2005.

Alter, Robert. "The Demons of History in Dickens's *Tale.*" *NOVEL: A Forum on Fiction* 2.2 (1969): 135–42.

Altholz, Josef L. *Anatomy of a Controversy: The Debate over Essays and Reviews 1860–1864.* Aldershot, UK: Scolar Press, 1994.

Anderson, Amanda. *The Powers of Distance: Cosmopolitanism and the Cultivation of Detachment.* Princeton, NJ: Princeton University Press, 2001.

———. *The Way We Argue Now: A Study in the Culture of Theory.* Princeton, NJ: Princeton University Press, 2006.

Anderson, Amanda, and Harry E. Shaw, eds. *A Companion to George Eliot.* Chichester, UK: Wiley-Blackwell, 2013.

Anderson, Benedict. *Imagined Communities: Reflections on the Origin and Spread of Nationalism.* London: Verso, 1983.

Anderson, Misty G. *Imagining Methodism in Eighteenth-Century Britain: Enthusiasm, Belief and the Borders of the Self.* Baltimore: The Johns Hopkins University Press, 2012.

Andrews, Malcolm. *Charles Dickens and His Performing Selves: Dickens and the Public Readings.* Oxford: Oxford University Press, 2006.

Anger, Suzy. *Victorian Interpretation.* Ithaca, NY: Cornell University Press, 2006.

Anon. "Brief Notice of Books." *Evangelical Magazine* 6 (1864).

Anon. "The British and Foreign Bible Society." *The Revival: An Advocate of Evangelical Truth* 14 (1866).

Anon. "Character: How It Is Formed and What It Is Worth." *Evangelical Magazine* 8 (1866).

Anon. "Cleaving to the Dust." *Evangelical Magazine* 6 (December 1864).

Anon. [A. K. H. B.] "Concerning the Reasonableness of Certain Words by Christ." *Good Words* 3 (1862).

Anon. [P. B.] "The Defects of Broad Church Theology." *Evangelical Christendom: A Monthly Chronicle of the Churches Conducted by Members of the Evangelical Alliance* 6 (1865).

Anon. "The End of the World." *All the Year Round* (January 13, 1860).

Anon. "George MacDonald." *British Quarterly Review* 47 (January 1868).

Anon. "George MacDonald as a Teacher of Religion." *The London Quarterly Review* 62 (January 1869).

Anon. *Good Words: The Theology of Its Editor and of Some of Its Contributors*. 2nd ed. London: The Record Offices, 1863.

Anon. "The Literature of Our Day." *The Christian Observer* 62 (1862).

Anon. "Mr George MacDonald's Novels." *North British Review* 84 (September 1866).

Anon. [MB.] "The Newspaper." *Good Words* 3 (February 1862).

Anon. *A Plain Commentary on the Four Holy Gospels, Intended Chiefly for Devotional Reading*. London: John Henry and James Parker, 1860.

Anon. "Preaching on the Stage." *Good Words* 1 (1860).

Anon. *Precious Truths in Plain Words*. London: Religious Tract Society, 1865.

Anon. "Proceedings of the Twenty-Third Annual Conference of the British Organisation." *Evangelical Christendom: A Monthly Record of the Protestant Faith* 10 (December 8, 1869).

Anon. "Recent Semi-Religious Works of Fiction." *The Christian Observer* 60 (January 1860).

Anon. "Religious Stories: The Ministry of Life. By Maria Louisa Charlesworth." *The Christian Observer* 59 (1859).

Anon. "Review of *Lady Elinor Mordaunt*." *The Christian Observer* 61 (1861).

Anon. "Review of *Oswald Cray*." *The Athenaeum* (1864).

Anon. "Sensational Literature." *The Christian Observer* 65 (November 1865).

Anon., ed. *Things That Accompany Salvation: In Nineteen Sermons, Preached in St Ann's Church, Manchester, During the Season of the Manchester's Art Treasures' Exhibition, 1857*. London: James Nisbet and Co., 1858.

Anon. "Unity of Creed: The Union of the Christian Church." *The Revival: An Advocate of Evangelical Truth* 15 (1866).

Anon. "Working Christians." *Evangelical Magazine* 8 (1866).

Arnot, W. "At Home in the Scriptures: A Series of Family Readings on the Sunday Evenings of December." *Good Words* 3 (1862).

Arnold, Jean. *Victorian Jewelry, Identity, and the Novel: Prisms of Culture*. Burlington, VT: Ashgate, 2011.

Asad, Talal. *Formations of the Secular: Christianity, Islam, Modernity*. Stanford, CA: Stanford University Press, 2003.

Badiou, Alain. *Saint Paul: The Foundation of Universalism*. Trans. Ray Brassier. Stanford, CA: Stanford University Press, 2003.

Baker, William, and William M. Clarke, eds. *The Letters of Wilkie Collins*. 2 vols. Basingstoke, UK: Macmillan, 1999.

Balthasar, Hans Urs Von. *Theo-Drama*. Trans. Graham Harrison. 5 vols. San Francisco: Ignatius, 1994.

Barker, Hannah. *Family and Business during the Industrial Revolution*. Oxford: Oxford University Press, 2017.

Bauckham, Richard, ed. *The Gospel for All Christians: Rethinking the Gospel Audiences*. Edinburgh, UK: T & T Clark, 1998.

Bebbington, David. *The Dominance of Evangelicalism: The Age of Spurgeon and Moody*. Downers Grove, IL: InterVarsity Press, 2005.

———. *Evangelicalism in Modern Britain: A History from the 1730s to the 1980s*. London: Unwin Hyman, 1989.

Best, Stephen, and Sharon Marcus. "Surface Reading: An Introduction." *Representations* 108.1 (2009): 1–21.

Binney, T. "Our Sunday Evenings in May." *Good Words* 2 (1861).

Birks, T. R. *The Bible and Modern Thought*. London: The Religious Tract Society, 1861.

———. *Modern Rationalism and the Inspiration of the Scriptures: Two Lectures*. London: Seeleys, 1853.

Bizzotto, Julie. "Sensational Sermonizing: Ellen Wood, *Good Words*, and the Conversion of the Popular." *Victorian Literature and Culture* 41.2 (2013): 297–310.

Blumberg, Ilana M. *Victorian Sacrifice: Ethics and Economics in Mid-Century Novels*. Columbus: The Ohio State University Press, 2013.

Booth, William. *Order and Regulations for Field Officers of The Salvation Army*. London: International Headquarters, 1886.

Bradley, Ian. *The Call to Seriousness: The Evangelical Impact on the Victorians*. London: Jonathan Cape, 1976.

Branch, Lori. "Postcritical and the Postsecular: The Horizon of Belief." *Religion and Literature* 48.2 (2016): 160-67.

———. "The Rituals of Our Re-Secularization: Literature Between Faith and Knowledge." *Religion and Literature* 46.2-3 (2014): 9–33.

Branch, Lori, and Mark Knight. "Why the Postsecular Matters: Literary Studies and the Rise of the Novel." *Christianity and Literature* 67.3 (2018): 493-510.

Brantlinger, Patrick. *The Reading Lesson: The Threat of Mass Literacy in the Nineteenth Century British Fiction*. Bloomington: Indiana University Press, 1998.

———. *The Rule of Darkness: British Literature and Imperialism, 1830–1914*. Ithaca, NY: Cornell University Press, 1988.

Brink-Roby, Heather. "Psyche: Mirror and Mind in *Vanity Fair*." *ELH* 80.1 (2013): 125–47.

Brooks, Chris. *Signs for the Times: Symbolic Realism in the Mid-Victorian World*. London: George Allen & Unwin, 1984.

Brown, Callum G. *The Death of Christian Britain: Understanding Secularisation 1800–2000*. New York: Routledge, 2001.

Bunyan, John. *The Pilgrim's Progress*. Ed. Roger Sharrock. Middlesex, UK: Penguin Classics, 1987.

Burstein, Miriam. *Victorian Reformations: Historical Fiction and Religious Controversy*. South Bend, IN: University of Notre Dame Press, 2014.

Butler, Samuel. *The Way of All Flesh*. Ed. James Cochrane. Middlesex, UK: Penguin Classics, 1986.

Caird, John. "Essays for Sunday Reading. I.—Conversion in Primitive and in Modern Times." *Good Words* 4 (1863).

Carpenter, Mary Wilson. *Imperial Bibles, Domestic Bodies: Women, Sexuality and Religion in the Victorian Market*. Athens: Ohio University Press, 2003.

Carruthers, Jo. *England's Secular Scripture: Islamophobia and the Protestant Aesthetic*. London: Continuum, 2011.

Chase, Karen, ed. *Middlemarch in the Twenty-First Century*. Oxford: Oxford University Press, 2006.

Colledge, Gary. *Dickens, Christianity and* The Life of Our Lord: *Humble Veneration, Profound Conviction*. London: Bloomsbury, 2009.

Collins, Wilkie. *The Moonstone*. Ed. J. Stewart. Middlesex, UK: Penguin, 1986.

Colón, Susan. *Victorian Parables*. London: Bloomsbury, 2012.

Comstock, Gary David, and Susan E. Henking, eds. *Que(e)rying Religion: A Critical Anthology*. New York: Continuum, 1997.

Cooke, Henry, and John Brown. *The Self-Interpreting Bible*. Glasgow: Blackie and Son, 1855.

Cowan, C. *Why Is the Bible True?* London: Hamilton, Adams and Co., 1863.

Cox, Jeffrey. *The British Missionary Enterprise since 1700*. Abingdon, UK: Routledge, 2007.

———. "Were Nonconformists the Worst Imperialists of All?" *Victorian Studies* 46.2 (2004): 243–55.

Cumming, John. *The Atonement in Its Twofold Aspects*. London: James Miller, 1861.

———. *The Great Tribulation*. London: Richard Bentley, 1859.

———. *Look to Jesus: Or How We Must Be Saved*. London: James Paul, 1855.

Cunningham, Valentine. *Everywhere Spoken Against: Dissent in the Victorian Novel*. Oxford: Clarendon Press, 1975.

Dale, R. W. "Amusements." *Good Words* 8 (May 1867).

———. "Unwholesome Words." *Good Words* 8 (September 1867).

Dalton, William. *A Course of Scripture Lessons for Sunday and Daily Schools*. 3rd ed. London: Hamilton, Adams and Co., 1853.

Daly, Nicholas. *Literature, Technology, and Modernity, 1860–2000*. Cambridge: Cambridge University Press, 2004.

Dames, Nicholas. *The Physiology of the Novel: Reading, Neural Science, and the Form of Victorian Fiction*. Oxford: Oxford University Press, 2007.

Daniell, Mortlock. *The Christ of Holy Scripture; and the Gospel of Our Salvation*. London: Thickbroom Brothers, 1858.

Davies, Michael. *Graceful Reading: Theology and Narrative in the Works of John Bunyan*. Oxford: Oxford University Press, 2002.

Davis, Philip. *The Oxford English Literary History*. Vol. 8, *1830–1880: The Victorians*. Oxford: Oxford University Press, 2002.

Dawson, Gowan. "Dickens, Dinosaurs, and Design." *Victorian Literature and Culture* 44.4 (2016): 761–78.

Dearborn, Kerry. *Baptized Imagination: The Theology of George MacDonald*. Aldershot, UK: Ashgate, 2006.

Dentith, Simon. *Nineteenth-Century British Literature Then and Now: Reading with Hindsight*. Farnham, UK: Ashgate, 2014.

Derrida, Jacques. *Acts of Religion*. Ed. Gil Anidjar. New York: Routledge, 2002.

Dickens, Charles. *A Tale of Two Cities*. Oxford: Oxford Illustrated Dickens, 1987.

Dixon, Thomas, Geoffrey Cantor, and Stephen Pumfrey, eds. *Science and Religion: New Historical Perspectives*. Cambridge: Cambridge University Press, 2010.

Dubois, Martin. "Sermon and Story in George MacDonald." *Victorian Literature and Culture* 43.3 (2015): 577–87.

Duncan-Page, Anna. *The Cambridge Companion to Bunyan*. Cambridge: Cambridge University Press, 2010.

Ehnes, Caley. "Religion, Readership and the Periodical Press: The Place of Poetry in *Good Words*." *Victorian Periodicals Review* 45.4 (2012): 466–87.

Eliot, George. "Evangelical Teaching: Dr Cumming." *Westminster Review* 16 (October 1855).

———. *Middlemarch*. Ed. Gregory Maertz. Peterborough, ON: Broadview Press, 2004.

Eliot, T. S. *Selected Essays*. London: Faber and Faber, 1951.

Ellis, Ieuan. *Seven against Christ*. Leiden: E. J. Brill, 1980.

Evans, C. Stephen. *Kierkegaard on Faith and the Self: Collected Essays*. Waco, TX: Baylor University Press, 2006.

Felski, Rita. *The Limits of Critique*. Chicago: The University of Chicago Press, 2015.

———. *Uses of Literature*. Oxford: Blackwell, 2008.

Fish, Stanley. *Is There a Text in This Class?: The Authority of Interpretive Communities*. Cambridge, MA: Harvard University Press, 1982.

———. "One Nation under God?" *The Chronicle of Higher Education*. January 7, 2005.

———. "Progress in *The Pilgrim's Progress*." *English Literary Renaissance* 1.3 (1971): 261–93.

Fisher, Judith. *Thackeray's Skeptical Narrative and the "Perilous Trade" of Authorship*. Burlington, VT: Ashgate, 2002.

Ford, David E. "Conversion, as a Matter of Experience." *The Christian Guest* 43 (December 1859).

Fordham, Finn. *I Do I Undo I Redo: The Textual Genesis of Modernist Selves in Hopkins, Yeats, Conrad, Forster, Joyce and Woolf*. Oxford: Oxford University Press, 2010.

Frank, Lawrence. *Victorian Detective Fiction and the Nature of Evidence: The Scientific Investigations of Poe, Dickens, and Doyle*. Basingstoke, UK: Palgrave Macmillan, 2003.

Free, Melissa. "Dirty Linen: Legacies of Empire in Wilkie Collins's *The Moonstone*." *Texas Studies in Literature and Language* 48.4 (2006): 340–71.

Frei, Hans. *The Eclipse of Biblical Narrative: A Study in Eighteenth- and Nineteenth-Century Hermeneutics*. New Haven, CT: Yale University Press, 1974.

Fyfe, Aileen. *Science and Salvation: Evangelical Popular Science Publishing in Victorian Britain*. Chicago: The University of Chicago Press, 2004.

Gadamer, Hans-Georg. *Truth and Method*. 2nd rev. ed. Trans. Joel Weinsheimer and Donald G. Marshall. London: Continuum, 2004.

Gallop, Jane, ed. *Polemic: Critical or Uncritical*. New York: Routledge, 2004.

Gannon, Christiane. "Hinduism, Spiritual Community and Narrative Form in *The Moonstone*." *Dickens Studies Annual* 46.1 (2015): 297–320.

Garbett, Edward, ed. *Evangelical Principles: Doctrinal Papers Explanatory of the Positive Principles of Evangelical Churchmanship*. London: William Hunt and Company, 1875.

———. *God's Word Written: The Doctrine of The Inspiration of the Holy Scripture, Explained and Enforced*. London: The Religious Tract Society, 1866.

Geertz, Clifford. *Local Knowledge: Further Essays in Interpretive Anthropology*. New York: Basic Books, 1983.

Gilley, Sheridan, and Brian Stanley, eds. *The Cambridge History of Christianity*. Vol. 8, *World Christianities c. 1815–c. 1914*. Cambridge: Cambridge University Press, 2005.

Graham, Elyse. "Private Religion, Public Mourning, and *Mrs. Dalloway*." *Modern Philology* 111.1 (2013): 88–106.

Griffin, Cristina Richieri. "George Eliot's Feuerbach: Senses, Sympathy, Omniscience, and Secularism." *ELH* 84.2 (2017): 475–502.

Gunton, Colin E. *The Actuality of Atonement*. Edinburgh, UK: T & T Clark, 1988.

Guthrie, Thomas. "The Parables, Read in the Light of the Present Day." *Good Words* 4 (January 1863).

Haack, Susan. "The Ideal of Intellectual Integrity, in Life and Literature." *New Literary History* 36.3 (2005): 359–73.

Hall, Catherine. *Civilising Subjects: Metropole and Colony in the English Imagination, 1830–1867*. Chicago: The University of Chicago Press, 2002.

Harris, Harriet A. *Fundamentalism and Evangelicalism*. Oxford: Oxford University Press, 1998.

Hart, Trevor. *Between the Image and the Word: Theological Engagements with Imagination, Language and Literature*. Aldershot, UK: Ashgate, 2013.

Hartley, Jenny. *Charles Dickens and the House of Fallen Women*. London: Methuen, 2008.

Hass, Andrew, David Jasper and Elisabeth Jay, eds. *The Oxford Handbook to Theology and English Literature*. Oxford: Oxford University Press, 2007.

Hauerwas, Stanley. *The Work of Theology*. Grand Rapids, MI: Eerdmans, 2015.

Hauerwas, Stanley, and Romand Coles. "'Long Live the Weeds and the Wilderness Yet': Reflections on *A Secular Age*." *Modern Theology* 26.3 (2010): 349–62.

Haykin, Michael A. G., and Kenneth J. Stewart, eds. *The Emergence of Evangelicalism: Exploring Historical Continuities*. Nottingham, UK: Apollos, 2008.

Heady, Emily Walker. *Victorian Conversion Narratives and Reading Communities*. Farnham, UK: Ashgate, 2013.

Heath, Jeffrey M., ed. *The Creator as Critic and Other Writings by E. M. Forster*. Toronto: Dundurn Press, 2008.

Herbert, Christopher. *Victorian Relativity: Radical Thought and Scientific Discovery*. Chicago: The University of Chicago Press, 2001.

Hervieu-Léger, Danièle. *Religion as a Chain of Memory*. New Brunswick, NJ: Rutgers University Press, 2000.

Hilton, Boyd. *The Age of Atonement: The Influence of Evangelicalism on Social and Economic Thought 1795–1865*. Oxford: Clarendon Press, 1988.

Hindmarsh, D. Bruce. *The Evangelical Conversion Narrative: Spiritual Autobiography in Early Modern England*. Oxford: Oxford University Press, 2005.

Hoeveler, J. David, Jr. *James McCosh and the Scottish Intellectual Tradition: From Glasgow to Princeton*. Princeton, NJ: Princeton University Press, 1981.

Hofmeyr, Isabel. *The Portable Bunyan: A Transnational History of* The Pilgrim's Progress. Princeton, NJ: Princeton University Press, 2004.

Holt, Lee Elbert. "Samuel Butler and His Victorian Critics." *ELH* 8.2 (1941): 146–59.

———. "Samuel Butler's Rise to Fame." *PMLA* 57.3 (1942): 867–78.

Iser, Wolfgang. *The Implied Reader: Patterns of Communication in Prose Fiction from Bunyan to Beckett*. Baltimore: The Johns Hopkins University Press, 1974.

Jackson, Gregory S. *The Word and Its Witness: The Spiritualization of American Realism*. Chicago: The University of Chicago Press, 2009.

Jaffe, Audrey. *Vanishing Points: Dickens, Narrative, and the Subject of Omniscience*. Berkeley: University of California Press, 1991.

———. *The Victorian Novel Dreams of the Real: Conventions and Ideology*. Oxford: Oxford University Press, 2016.

Jasper, David. *A Short History of Hermeneutics*. Louisville, KY: Westminster John Knox Press, 2004.

Jay, Elisabeth. *The Religion of the Heart: Anglican Evangelicalism and the Nineteenth Century Novel*. Oxford: Clarendon Press, 1979.

Jeffrey, David Lyle. *People of the Book: Christian Identity and Literary Culture*. Grand Rapids, MI: Eerdmans, 1996.

Johnston, Anna. *Missionary Writing and Empire, 1800–1860*. Cambridge: Cambridge University Press, 2003.

Jones, Anna Maria. *Problem Novels: Victorian Fiction Theorizes the Sensational Self*. Columbus: The Ohio State University Press, 2007.

Jones, Colin, Josephine McDonagh, and Jon Mee, eds. *Charles Dickens,* A Tale of Two Cities *and the French Revolution*. Basingstoke, UK: Palgrave Macmillan, 2009.

Keeble, N. H., ed. *John Bunyan: Conventicle and Parnassus: Tercentenary Essays*. Oxford: Clarendon Press, 1988.

King, Andrew, Alexis Easley, and John Morton, eds. *The Routledge Handbook to Nineteenth-Century British Periodicals and Newspapers*. Abingdon, UK: Routledge, 2016.

King, Joshua. *Imagined Spiritual Communities in Britain's Age of Print*. Columbus: The Ohio State University Press, 2015.

King, Joshua, and Winter Jade Werner, eds. *Constructing Nineteenth-Century Religion: Literary, Historical and Religious Studies in Dialogue*. Columbus: The Ohio State University Press, forthcoming.

Knight, Mark, ed. *The Routledge Companion to Literature and Religion*. Abingdon, UK: Routledge, 2016.

Knight, Mark, and Emma Mason. *Nineteenth-Century Religion and Literature: An Introduction*. Oxford: Oxford University Press, 2006.

Kooistra, Lorraine Janzen. "'Making Poetry' in *Good Words*: Why Illustration Matters to Periodical Poetry Studies." *Victorian Poetry* 52.1 (2014): 111–39.

Kort, Wesley. *Textual Intimacy: Autobiography and Religious Identities*. Charlottesville: University of Virginia Press, 2012.

Kucich, John, and Jenny Bourne Taylor, eds. *The Oxford History of the Novel in English*. Vol 3, *The Nineteenth-Century Novel: 1820–1880*. Oxford: Oxford University Press, 2012.

Kurnick, David. "An Erotics of Detachment: *Middlemarch* and Novel-Reading as Critical Practice." *ELH* 74.3 (2007): 583–84.

Landow, George P. *Victorian Types, Victorian Shadows: Biblical Typology in Victorian Literature, Art, and Thought*. London: Routledge, 1980.

Lane, Christopher. *The Age of Doubt: Tracing the Roots of Our Religious Uncertainty*. New Haven, CT: Yale University Press, 2011.

———. *The Burdens of Intimacy: Psychoanalysis and Victorian Masculinity*. Chicago: The University of Chicago Press, 1999.

LaPorte, Charles. *Victorian Poets and the Changing Bible*. Charlottesville: University of Virginia Press, 2011.

Larsen, Timothy. *Contested Christianity: The Political and Social Contexts of Victorian Theology*. Waco: Baylor University Press, 2004.

———. *Crisis of Doubt: Honest Faith in Nineteenth-Century England*. New York: Oxford University Press, 2006.

———. *A People of One Book: The Bible and the Victorians*. Oxford: Oxford University Press, 2011.

Larsen, Timothy, and Michael Ledger-Lomas, eds. *The Oxford History of Protestant Dissenting Traditions*. Vol. 3, *The Nineteenth Century*. Oxford: Oxford University Press, 2017.

Larsen, Timothy, and Daniel J. Treier, eds. *The Cambridge Companion to Evangelical Theology*. Cambridge: Cambridge University Press, 2007.

Larson, Janet L. *Dickens and the Broken Scripture*. Athens: University of Georgia Press, 1985.

Law, Graham. *Serializing Fiction in the Victorian Press*. London: Palgrave, 2000.

Lear, Jonathan. *A Case for Irony*. Cambridge, MA: Harvard University Press, 2011.

Lecourt, Sebastian. *Cultivating Belief: Victorian Anthropology, Liberal Aesthetics, and the Secular Imagination*. Oxford: Oxford University Press, 2018.

Lemon, Rebecca, Emma Mason, Jonathan Roberts, and Christopher Rowland, eds. *The Blackwell Companion to the Bible in English Literature*. Oxford: Wiley-Blackwell, 2009.

Levine, Caroline. *Forms: Whole, Rhythm, Hierarchy, Network*. Princeton, NJ: Princeton University Press, 2015.

Levine, George, ed. *The Cambridge Companion to George Eliot*. Cambridge: Cambridge University Press, 2001.

———. *Darwin Loves You: Natural Selection and the Re-enchantment of the World*. Princeton, NJ: Princeton University Press, 2006.

———. *Dying to Know: Scientific Epistemology and Narrative in Victorian England*. Chicago: The University of Chicago Press, 2002.

———. *Realism, Ethics and Secularism: Essays on Victorian Literature and Science*. Cambridge: Cambridge University Press, 2008.

Lewis, Pericles. *Religious Experience and the Modernist Novel*. Cambridge: Cambridge University Press, 2010.

Liggins, Emma, and Daniel D. Duffy, eds. *Feminist Readings of Victorian Popular Texts*. Aldershot, UK: Ashgate, 2001.

Lloyd, Vincent W., and Elliot A. Ratzman, eds. *Secular Faith*. Eugene, OR: Cascade Books, 2011.

Lukács, Georg. *The Theory of the Novel: A Historico-Philosophical Essay on the Forms of Great Epic Literature*. Trans. Anna Bostock. London: Merlin, 1978.

Lutz, Deborah. *Relics of Death in Victorian Literature and Culture.* Cambridge: Cambridge University Press, 2015.

Lynch, Beth. *John Bunyan and the Language of Conviction.* Suffolk: D. S. Brewer, 2004.

Lynch, Deidre. *Loving Literature: A Cultural History.* Chicago: The University of Chicago Press, 2015.

MacDonald, George. *Guild Court: A London Story.* Serialized in *Good Words* (1867).

———. "The Imagination: Its Function and Its Culture." *British Quarterly Review* 46 (July 1867): 45–70.

MacDonald Collection, George. Beinecke Rare Book and Manuscript Library.

MacDonald, Greville. *George MacDonald and His Wife.* London: George Allen & Unwin Ltd, 1924.

Mackenzie, W. B. *Bible Studies for Family Reading.* London: The Religious Tract Society, n.d. [1868].

Macleod, Donald. *Memoir of Norman Macleod.* 2 vols. London: Daldy, Isbister & Co, 1876.

Macleod, Norman. "Evenings with Working People in the Barony Church: First Evening—'Not Saved.'" *Good Words* 5 (January 1864).

———. "Missions in the Nineteenth Century." *Good Words* 3 (1862).

———. "Opening Address." *Good Words* 1 (January 1860).

———. "What If Christianity Is Not True?" *Good Words* 3 (1862).

Mangham, Andrew. *Violent Women and Sensation Fiction: Crime, Medicine and Victorian Popular Culture.* Basingstoke, UK: Palgrave Macmillan, 2007.

Marion, Jean-Luc. *The Essential Writings.* Ed. Kevin Hart. New York: Fordham University Press, 2013.

Marston, C. D. *A Manual on the Inspiration of Scripture.* London: Wertheim, Macintosh, and Hunt, 1859.

McCrie, George. *The Religion of Our Literature.* London: Hodder and Stoughton, 1875.

McDermott, Gerald R., ed. *The Oxford Handbook to Evangelical Theology.* Oxford: Oxford University Press, 2010.

McDonagh, Josephine. *George Eliot.* Tavistock: Northcote House, 1997.

McKelvy, William. *The English Cult of Literature: Devoted Readers, 1774–1880.* Charlottesville: The University of Virginia Press, 2007.

———. "The Importance of Being Ezra: Canons and Conversions in *The Moonstone.*" *ELH*, forthcoming.

Meckier, Jerome. *Hidden Rivalries in Victorian Fiction: Dickens, Realism and Revaluation.* Lexington: The University Press of Kentucky, 1987.

Menke, Richard. *Telegraphic Realism: Victorian Fiction and Other Information Systems.* Stanford, CA: Stanford University Press, 2008.

Miller, Andrew H. *The Burdens of Perfection: On Ethics and Reading in Nineteenth-Century British Literature.* Ithaca, NY: Cornell University Press, 2008.

Miller, D. A. *The Novel and the Police.* Berkeley: University of California Press, 1988.

Moretti, Franco. *Distant Reading.* London: Verso, 2013.

Moretti, Franco, ed. *The Novel, Vol. 2.* Princeton, NJ: Princeton University Press, 2006.

Muggeridge, Malcolm. *The Earnest Atheist: A Study of Samuel Butler*. New York: Haskell House Publishers Ltd., 1971.

Nash, Andrew. *Kailyard and Scottish Literature*. Amsterdam: Rodopi, 2007.

Nayder, Lillian. "Recent Wilkie Collins Studies." *Dickens Studies Annual* 28 (1999): 257–329.

———. *Unequal Partners: Charles Dickens, Wilkie Collins, and Victorian Authorship*. Ithaca, NY: Cornell University Press, 2002.

Nielsen, Danielle. "Samuel Butler's Life and Habit and *The Way of All Flesh*: Traumatic Evolution." *English Literature in Transition, 1880–1920* 54.1 (2011): 79–100.

Noll, Mark A. "Common Sense Traditions and American Evangelical Thought." *American Quarterly* 37.2 (1985): 216–38.

———. *The Rise of Evangelicalism: The Age of Edwards, Whitefield and the Wesleys*. Leicester, UK: Apollos, 2004.

O'Malley, Patrick R. *Catholicism, Sexual Deviance, and Victorian Gothic Culture*. Cambridge: Cambridge University Press, 2006.

Orwell, George. *Inside the Whale and Other Essays*. London: Victor Gollancz, 1940.

Otter, Chris. *The Victorian Eye: A Political History of Light and Vision in Britain, 1800–1910*. Chicago: The University of Chicago Press, 2008.

Oulton, Carolyn W. de la L. *Literature and Religion in Mid-Victorian England: From Dickens to Eliot*. Basingstoke, UK: Palgrave Macmillan, 2003.

Owens, W. R., and Stuart Sim, eds. *Reception, Appropriation, Recollection: Bunyan's* Pilgrim's Progress. Bern, Switzerland: Peter Lang, 2007.

Palmer, Beth. "'Dangerous and Foolish Work': Evangelicalism and Sensationalism in Ellen Wood's *Argosy* Magazine." *Women's Writing* 15.2 (2008): 187–98.

Paradis, James, ed. *Samuel Butler, Victorian against the Grain: A Critical Overview*. Toronto: University of Toronto Press, 2007.

Paroissien, David, ed. *A Companion to Charles Dickens*. Oxford: Blackwell, 2008.

Parrinder, Patrick. *Nation and Novel: The English Novel from Its Origins to the Present Day*. Oxford: Oxford University Press, 2006.

Perkin, J. Russell. *Theology and the Victorian Novel*. Montreal: McGill-Queen's University Press, 2009.

Peterson, Linda H. "Restoring the Book: The Typological Hermeneutics of Christina Rossetti and the PRB." *Victorian Poetry* 32.3–4 (1994): 209–32.

———. "Review of Suzy Anger, *Victorian Interpretation*." *Nineteenth-Century Literature* 61.4 (2007): 524–30.

Phegley, Jennifer. "Domesticating the Sensation Novelist: Ellen Price Wood as Author and Editor of the *Argosy Magazine*." *Victorian Periodicals Review* 38.2 (2005): 180–98.

Plantinga, Alvin. *Warranted Christian Belief*. New York: Oxford University Press, 2000.

Pope, Norris. *Dickens and Charity*. London: Macmillan, 1978.

Porter, Andrew. *Religion versus Empire?: British Protestant Missionaries and Overseas Expansion 1700–1914*. Manchester: Manchester University Press, 2004.

Price, Leah. *The Anthology and the Rise of the Novel: From Richardson to George Eliot*. Cambridge: Cambridge University Press, 2000.

———. *How to Do Things with Books in Victorian Britain.* Princeton, NJ: Princeton University Press, 2012.

Prickett, Stephen. *Victorian Fantasy.* 2nd ed. Waco, TX: Baylor University Press, 2005.

Pykett, Lyn. *The Improper Feminine: The Women's Sensation Novel and the New Woman Writing.* London: Routledge, 1992.

Qualls, Barry V. *The Secular Pilgrims of Victorian Fiction: The Novel as Book of Life.* Cambridge: Cambridge University Press, 1982.

Rainof, Rebecca. *The Victorian Novel of Adulthood: Plot and Purgatory in Fictions of Maturity.* Athens: Ohio University Press, 2015.

Randall, Ian, and David Hilborn. *One Body in Christ: The History and Significance of the Evangelical Alliance.* Carlisle, UK: Paternoster Press, 2001.

Rasmussen, Bryan B. "From God's Work to Fieldwork: Charlotte Tonna's Evangelical Autoethnography." *ELH* 77.1 (2010): 159–94.

Rathburn, Robert C., and Martin Steinmann, eds. *From Jane Austen to Joseph Conrad: Essays Collected in Memory of James T. Hillhouse.* Minneapolis: University of Minnesota Press, 1958.

Raven, James, Helen Small, and Naomi Tadmor, eds. *The Practice and Representation of Reading in England.* Cambridge: Cambridge University Press, 1996.

Ray, Gordon. "Vanity Fair: One Version of the Novelist's Responsibility." *Essays by Diverse Hands* New Series 25 (1950): 87–101.

Reitz, Caroline. *Detecting the Nation: Fiction of Detection and the Imperial Venture.* Columbus: The Ohio State University Press, 2004.

Ricoeur, Paul. *Freud and Philosophy: An Essay on Interpretation.* New Haven, CT: Yale University Press, 1970.

Rivers, Isabel. *Vanity Fair and the Celestial City: Dissenting, Methodist, and Evangelical Literary Culture in England, 1720–1800.* Oxford: Oxford University Press, 2018.

Russett, Margaret. "Recent Studies in the Nineteenth Century." *SEL* 47.4 (2007): 943–82.

Ryle, J. C. *Bible Inspiration: Its Reality and Nature.* London: William Hunt and Company, 1877.

———. "Evangelical Religion: What It Is, and What It Is not." Launceston, UK: J. Stephenson, 1867.

Rzepka, Charles J. *Detective Fiction.* Cambridge: Polity Press, 2005.

Rzepka, Charles J., and Lee Horsley, eds. *A Companion to Crime Fiction.* Oxford: Wiley-Blackwell, 2010.

Sanders, Andrew. *Charles Dickens: Resurrectionist.* Basingstoke: Macmillan, 1982.

Schad, John. "Reading the Long Way Round: Thackeray's *Vanity Fair.*" *The Yearbook of English Studies* 26 (1996): 25–34.

Schaffer, E. S. *Kubla Khan and the Fall of Jerusalem: The Mythological School in Biblical Criticism and Secular Literature, 1770–1880.* Cambridge: Cambridge University Press, 1975.

Schramm, Jan-Melissa. *Atonement and Self-Sacrifice in Nineteenth-Century Narrative.* Cambridge: Cambridge University Press, 2012.

———. *Testimony and Advocacy in Victorian Law, Literature, and Theology.* Cambridge: Cambridge University Press, 2000.

Schwartz, Regina, ed. *Transcendence: Philosophy, Literature, and Theology Approach the Beyond.* New York: Routledge, 2004.

Sedgwick, Eve Kosofsky. *Novel Gazing: Queer Readings in Fiction*. Durham, NC: Duke University Press, 1997.

Seidel, Kevin. "Pilgrim's Progress and the Book." *ELH* 77.2 (2010): 509–34.

———. "*Robinson Crusoe* as Defoe's Theory of Fiction." *NOVEL: A Forum on Fiction* 44.2 (2011): 165–85.

Shaw, George Bernard. *Major Barbara*. Ed. Dan Laurence and Margery Morgan. London: Penguin, 2000.

Shea, Victor, and William Whitla, eds. *Essays and Reviews: The 1860 Text and Its Reading*. Charlottesville: University Press of Virginia, 2000.

Shuttleworth, Sally. "Spiritual Pathology: Priests, Physicians, and *The Way of All Flesh*." *Victorian Studies* 54.4 (2012): 625–53.

Singleton, Jon. "Malignant Faith and Cognitive Restructuring: Realism in *Adam Bede*." *Victorian Literature and Culture* 39.1 (2011): 239–60.

Slater, Michael, and John Drew, eds. *The Dent Uniform Edition of Dickens' Journalism*. Vol. 4, *The Uncommercial Traveller and Other Papers, 1859–70*. London: J. M. Dent, 2000.

Smith, Alexander. "Literary Work." *Good Words* 4 (1863).

Smith, Christian. *What Is a Person? Rethinking Humanity, Social Life, and the Moral Good from the Person Up*. Chicago: The University of Chicago Press, 2010.

Spurgeon, Charles H. "The Anxious Inquirer." *The Christian Guest* 7 (1859).

———. *Commenting and Commentaries: Two Lectures*. London: Passmore and Alabaster, 1876.

———. "Dr John Caird on the Declining Influence of the Pulpit." *The Sword and the Trowel* (1868).

Srebrnik, Patricia Thomas. *Alexander Strahan: Victorian Publisher*. Ann Arbor: The University of Michigan Press, 1986.

Stevenson, Peter Kenneth. *God in Our Nature: The Incarnational Theology of John McLeod Campbell*. Milton Keynes, UK: Paternoster, 2004.

Storey, Graham, ed. *The Letters of Charles Dickens*. Vol. 9, *1859–1861*. Oxford: Clarendon Press, 1997.

Strahan, Alexander. *Norman Macleod, DD: A Slight Contribution Towards His Biography*. London: Henry S. King and Co, 1872.

Stubenrauch, Joseph. *The Evangelical Age of Ingenuity in Industrial Britain*. Oxford: Oxford University Press, 2016.

Styler, Rebecca. *Literary Theology by Women Writers of the Nineteenth Century*. Aldershot, UK: Ashgate, 2010.

Taylor, Charles. *A Secular Age*. Cambridge, MA: Harvard University Press, 2007.

Taylor, Isaac. "The Long Evenings, and Books." *Good Words* 5 (October 1864).

Thackeray, William Makepeace. *Vanity Fair*. Oxford: Oxford World's Classics, 1983.

Thomas, Ronald R. *Detective Fiction and the Rise of Forensic Science*. Cambridge: Cambridge University Press, 1999.

Tucker, Trisha. "Gendering the Evangelical Novel." *Rocky Mountain Review of Language and Literature* 66.1 (2012): 83–89.

Turner, Mark. *Trollope and the Magazines: Gendered Issues in Mid-Victorian Britain*. Basingstoke, UK: Macmillan, 2000.

Valman, Nadia. *The Jewess in Nineteenth-Century British Literary Culture*. Cambridge: Cambridge University Press, 2007.

Van Dyke, Carolynn. *The Fiction of Truth: Structures of Meaning in Narrative and Dramatic Allegory*. Ithaca, NY: Cornell University Press, 1985.

Vance, Norman. *Bible and the Novel: Narrative Authority and the Death of God*. Oxford: Oxford University Press, 2013.

Vanhoozer, Kevin. *The Drama of Doctrine: A Canonical-Linguistic Approach to Christian Theology*. Louisville, KY: Westminster John Knox Press, 2005.

Vargish, Thomas. *The Providential Aesthetic in Victorian Fiction*. Charlottesville: University Press of Virginia, 1985.

Walder, Dennis. *Dickens and Religion*. London: George Allen & Unwin, 1981.

Walker, Pamela J. *Pulling the Devil's Kingdom Down: The Salvation Army in Victorian Britain*. Los Angeles: University of California Press, 2001.

Watt, Ian. *The Rise of the Novel: Studies in Defoe, Richardson and Fielding*. Berkeley: University of California Press, 1957.

Welsh, Alexander. *Strong Representations: Narrative and Circumstantial Evidence in England*. Baltimore: The Johns Hopkins University Press, 1992.

Werner, Winter Jade. *Missionary Cosmopolitanism in the British Nineteenth Century: Literary Experiments in Global Thought*. Columbus: The Ohio State University Press, forthcoming.

Wheeler-Barclay, Marjorie. *The Science of Religion in Britain, 1860–1915*. Charlottesville: University of Virginia Press, 2010.

Wilberforce, William. *A Practical View of the Prevailing Religious System of Professed Christians, in the Higher and Middle Classes in this Country, Contrasted with Real Christianity*. London: T. Cadell, Jun. and W. Davies, 1797.

Winter, Sarah. "Curiosity as Didacticism in *The Old Curiosity Shop*." *NOVEL: A Forum on Fiction* 34.1 (2000): 28–55.

———. *The Pleasures of Memory: Learning to Read with Charles Dickens*. New York: Fordham University Press, 2011.

Wolffe, John. *The Expansion of Evangelicalism: The Age of Wilberforce, More, Chalmers and Finney*. Downers Grove, IL: InterVarsity Press, 2007.

Wood, Charles. *Memorials of Mrs Henry Wood*. London: Richard Bentley & Son, 1894.

Wood, Ellen. *Oswald Cray*. Serialized in *Good Words* (1864).

———. "Our Log Book." *The Argosy* (December 1, 1867).

Woolf, Virginia. *Mr Bennett and Mrs Brown*. London: Hogarth Press, 1924.

Wynne, Deborah. *The Sensation Novel and the Victorian Family Magazine*. Basingstoke, UK: Palgrave, 2001.

Zemka, Sue. *Victorian Testaments: The Bible and Literary Authority in Early-Nineteenth-Century Britain*. Stanford, CA: Stanford University Press, 1997.

INDEX

Ablow, Rachel, 37n38
advertising, 13n42, 83, 125
affect, 6, 21, 23, 37–41, 55–56, 152n56, 163
Agamben, Giorgio, 137n2, 138
Alford, Henry, 81, 86
All the Year Round, 21–22, 55, 64n43, 67n54, 70–74, 106
allegory, 30, 44–45, 101n80, 119, 123, 129n87, 142
Alter, Robert, 54
Altholz, Josef L., 107n11
Anderson, Amanda, 154–55
Anderson, Misty G., 8
Andrews, Malcolm, 71, 73–74
Anger, Suzy, 111–13
Anglican Church. *See* Church of England
Anglo-Catholic, 8n24, 161. *See also* Oxford Movement
apocalyptic, 53, 61, 67–68
Argosy, 90–91, 97–98
Armadale (Collins), 106–7, 125n74
Arminianism, 2
Arminius, Jacobus, 57
Arnold, Matthew, 60, 82, 109, 145
Arnold, Thomas, 93
Arnot, W., 72n76
Asad, Talal, 2–3, 20, 137n2
At the Back of the North Wind (MacDonald), 101n78

Athenaeum, 89–90
atonement, 1, 10, 54, 59–60, 62, 92–93, 100n76, 164. *See also* the cross

Balthasar, Hans Urs von, 50
Barker, Hannah, 143n18
Bebbington, David, 3–5, 12, 58–59
Bible, 1, 3–4, 12, 26–28, 53, 55, 59, 65–66, 68–70, 75–76, 78, 83–84, 93, 99, 107–35, 146, 154, 164–65. *See also* books of Bible; bible study; definition of evangelicalism; hermeneutics; plenary and verbal inspiration
Bible, books of: 1 Chronicles, 117; 1 Corinthians, 80n; 2 Corinthians, 121; Ecclesiastes, 33; Ezra, 106; Hebrews, 27; John, 64, 75; Luke, 75; Matthew, 48, 75, 86, 123n65; Revelation, 53–54, 64, 67–69; Romans, 72n76, 102, 139, 157; Song of Songs, 118; Titus, 164
Bible Society, 120
bible study, 15, 99, 144, 146
bildungsroman, 21, 29, 39, 149
Binney, Thomas, 77
Birks, T. R., 115n35, 119–20
Bizzotto, Julie, 90, 91n39
Bleak House (Dickens), 62, 68, 90, 163
Blumberg, Ilana, 55, 60, 125
Book of Common Prayer, 64–65
Booth, William, 57, 125n
Bowen, John, 64n43

Braddon, Mary, 90–91
Bradley, Ian, 5, 77, 80
Branch, Lori, 9n31, 137n1, 139n4, 153n64
Brantlinger, Patrick, 16, 27n4, 46
Brink-Roby, Heather, 30n1
British Quarterly Review, 95–96
broad church, 33, 83, 99, 107n11, 118–19, 126; crossover with evangelicalism, 80, 99–100
Brooks, Chris, 67n57
Brown, Callum G., 139n5
Bulwer-Lytton, Edward, 71
Burstein, Miriam, 1–2, 10, 13
Butler, Samuel, 141, 147–48, 150, 161. See also *The Way of All Flesh*

Caird, John, 86–87, 96, 118
Calvin, John, 40–41, 57
Calvinism, 2, 34, 46, 63, 95–96, 106, 139
Campbell, John McLeod, 100n76
Carlyle, Thomas, 57–58, 67n57
Carruthers, Jo, 129n85
Chalmers, Thomas, 57, 96, 118
Charles, Elizabeth Rundle, 13
Charlesworth, Maria Louisa, 13
Chase, Karen, 18
Chesterton, G. K., 134
Christian Guest, 60n29, 61, 80
Christian Observer, 12, 13n41, 17, 28, 40n53, 41n55, 108
Christian tone, 90–93. See also Thomas Arnold; goody style
Church of England, 2, 7, 9, 11–12, 28, 60, 83, 107n11, 126, 144–45, 162
Colenso, Bishop, 108
Coleridge, Samuel Taylor, 34–35, 109
Colledge, Gary, 58n18
Collins, Wilkie, 56–58, 71–72, 106–10, 164. See also *Armadale*; *The Moonstone*; *The Woman in White*
common sense, 108–9, 111, 115n37, 118–19, 127–35, 152
Contemporary Review, 86, 96
conversion, 3, 10, 19, 20n66, 58–59, 61–62, 66, 73, 76, 86, 93, 106–7, 117, 164. See also conversion narratives; evangelism

conversion narratives, 55–56, 58, 63, 66–70. See also conversion
Cooke, Henry, 121
Cooper, Thomas, 66
Cornhill, 81–82
Cowan, C., 108
Cox, Jeffrey, 15n50, 16n52
critical irony, 23, 140, 151–57. See also critique; irony
critique, 16, 20, 99, 152–53, 156n69, 157–58, 164. See also critical irony; Rita Felski
cross, the, 3, 22, 55, 58–60, 63, 69–70, 77, 93, 163–64. See also atonement
crucicentrism, 3, 59. See also the cross
Cumming, John, 59, 63, 64n43, 67–68
Cunningham, Valentine, 9–10, 17, 73, 76

Dale, R. W., 11, 91–92
Dalton, W., 73, 114–15
Daly, Nicholas, 90
Dames, Nicholas, 37n38
Daniell, Mortlock, 59
Darwinism, 108, 139
Dauncey, Sarah, 110
Davies, Michael, 34–36, 44
Davis, Paul, 54
Davis, Philip, 101
Dawson, Gowan, 55n9
Dearborn, Kerry, 96n64
Dentith, Simon, 56n10
Derrida, Jacques, 137n1, 138
detached interpretation, 18, 20, 23, 39, 135, 140, 151–59. See also Amanda Anderson; critical irony; interpretative proximity
detective fiction, 105, 109–11, 113, 129–35
dialogism, 33, 78n4
Dickens, Charles, 17, 21, 54–58, 60–62, 65–66, 70–76, 111, 163; public readings, 73–74. See also *All the Year Round*; *Bleak House*; *Great Expectations*; *Household Words*; *A Tale of Two Cities*
didacticism, 28, 35, 42, 102, 123
discernment, 44, 45n67, 159
dissenting Christianity. See nonconformism
domestic sphere, 15, 28–29, 68, 90
drama, theological understanding of, 49–50
Dubois, Martin, 96n63

During, Simon, 18

Ehnes, Caley, 81n11
Eliot, George, 4–5, 16–21, 59, 144
Eliot, T. S., 8n24, 105
Ellis, Ieuan, 107n11, 112n26, 128n83
empire, 2, 14–16, 27n6, 35, 105–6
empiricism, 8, 19–20, 46–47
Ermath, Elizabeth Deeds, 18
eschatology, 53. *See also* apocalyptic
Essays and Reviews, 107–8, 112, 119–20, 128n83, 131n93, 135. *See also* Benjamin Jowett; Baden Powell; Rowland Williams
Evangelical Alliance, 2, 100, 113–14, 161
Evangelical Christendom, 114n29, 119
Evangelical Magazine, 11–12, 25, 27, 40, 79, 108
evangelical: activism, 3, 9, 15, 21, 40, 59, 117; anti-Catholicism, 128; attitude to commerce, 83n18, 85, 125; biblical interpretation (*see* Bible; hermeneutics); definition of, 2–4; ethical vision, 42–47; etymological relation to evangelism, 22, 77n2; gospel, 22, 27, 43, 59–61, 63, 73, 77–80, 86–88, 92–96, 99–103, 117, 165; parenting, 142–44; pragmatism, 4, 25, 66, 138; publishing, 28, 78–88, 100, 103, 122–23, 125; "sound" theology, 2, 26, 93, 100n75, 124; violence, 98, 142–43. *See also* conversion; the cross; evangelism
evangelism, 14–15, 25, 51, 78–80, 86–88, 100, 103, 122, 124, 161, 166. *See also* evangelical gospel; missionaries
Evans, C. Stephen, 156n70
Exeter Hall, 2, 15, 45, 107, 125

faith, 7–8, 15, 19–20, 32, 35–36, 44, 80, 103, 137–38, 153–54, 156–58, 163–66
Felski, Rita, 113n27, 152–54, 156n69
Fish, Stanley, 36–38, 137n2
Fisher, Judith, 46–47
Flint, Kate, 38, 163
Ford, David, 61
Fordham, Finn, 160–61
Forster, E. M., 148
Foster, John, 72
Frank, Lawrence, 110–11, 113, 131
Free, Melissa, 105n2
free will, 57, 92, 95, 106. *See also* Arminianism

Freedgood, Elaine, 15
Frei, Hans, 112n24, 116n38
French Revolution, 55, 57–58, 61, 66–68
fundamentalism, 6, 111
Fyfe, Aileen, 28, 79, 93, 110n20, 125n73

Gadamer, Hans-Georg, 38, 133–34
Gannon, Christiane, 106n3
Garbett, Edward, 59n27, 116
Gaskell, Elizabeth, 16, 71
Geertz, Clifford, 109
German Higher Criticism, 116–17, 127–28, 130, 135. *See also* hermeneutics
Good Words, 15, 80–103, 118, 165–66
Good Words for the Young, 82, 86, 96–97, 103
goody style, 91–92, 103
gospel. *See* evangelical gospel
Great Expectations (Dickens), 72
Guild Court (MacDonald), 97–103
Gunton, Colin, 151n52
Guthrie, Thomas, 81, 86, 96, 101

Haack, Susan, 149
Hall, Catherine, 16
Hammond, Mary, 28–29
Harris, Harriet A., 115n37
Hart, Kevin, 137n2
Hart, Trevor, 151n52
Hatchard, John, 13n41
Hauerwas, Stanley, 155, 156n70, 159
Heady, Emily Walker, 55n8
hell, 98
Herbert, Christopher, 143n19
Herbert, George, 80
hermeneutics, 9, 18–19, 34, 36–39, 44–45, 105–35, 143–44, 151–53. *See also* Bible; Hans-Georg Gadamer; German Higher Criticism; Friedrich Schleiermacher
Hervieu-Léger, Danièle, 6, 33
Hilborn, David, 2n4
Hilton, Boyd, 5, 57n15
Hindmarsh, Bruce, 58
Hofmeyr, Isabel, 27n6, 28–29, 34–35
Holmes, Stephen, 115
Holt, Emily Sarah, 13
Holt, Lee Elbert, 140, 147n35

Household Words, 70, 72, 81n12

immanence, 32, 49, 159. *See also* transcendence
imperialism. *See* empire
Incarnation, 32, 159
inspiration, plenary and verbal, 115
instrumentality, 72–73
irony, 41, 74, 117, 120, 126n78, 139, 152, 156. *See also* critical irony
Irving, Edward, 57, 86
Iser, Wolfgang, 30

Jackson, Gregory, 62n36
Jaffe, Audrey, 57, 106–7
Jager, Colin, 9
Jameson, Frederic, 8–9, 18
Jasper, David, 109n15
Jay, Elisabeth, 1, 6–9, 11, 16–17, 142n15, 145, 160
Jeffrey, David Lyle, 45
Johnston, Anna, 14
Jones, Andrew, 100n76
Jones, Anna Maria, 133n99
Jowett, Benjamin, 99, 112–13, 119–20, 128, 129n87, 131
Judaism, 20n66, 138

Kailyard School of Fiction, 12
Kierkegaard, Søren, 156
King, Joshua, 10, 48n78, 165n84
Kingsley, Charles, 87, 99
Kooistra, Lorraine Janzen, 81n11, 85
Kort, Wesley, 162n81

Landow, George, 59n24, 109
Lane, Christopher, 38n42, 139
LaPorte, Charles, 10, 109n15, 117n42, 151n50
Larsen, Timothy, 3n8, 5, 15, 66n51, 109n15, 114, 115n34
Larson, Janet, 54, 65–66
Law, Graham, 78–79
Lear, Jonathan, 156n70
Lecourt, Sebastian, 20n66
legalism, religious, 42, 117
Leisure Hour, 12, 79n9, 91n39
Lever, Charles, 72

Levine, Caroline, 7
Levine, George, 1, 9, 18–19, 31–32, 46–49, 110n21, 159
Lewis, Pericles, 8n24, 149
Liggins, Emma, 90
liturgical, 71
London Missionary Society, 14
Ludlow, J. M., 81n14, 86
Lukács, Georg, 8, 31
Lutz, Deborah, 124n66
Lynch, Beth, 35
Lynch, Deidre, 23n68, 37, 48

Macrae, David, 62
MacDonald, George, 22, 80–82, 86, 91, 95–103. *See also At the Back of the North Wind; Guild Court*
Macleod, Norman, 78–88, 94–100, 103
Mangham, Andrew, 109
Marston, C. D., 114, 117
Mason, Emma, 5n13, 10, 29, 50n84
May Meetings, the, 15
Maurice, F. D., 99
McCosh, James, 118
McCrie, George, 26, 84, 100n75
McDonagh, Josephine, 18
McKelvy, William, 10, 16n52, 20n66, 37n38, 48, 106, 113n28
McKeon, Michael, 31, 128n82
Meckier, Jerome, 57–58
Menke, Richard, 65
Methodism, 5, 8, 57
Miller, Andrew H., 6, 38, 42n57
Miller, D. A., 132–33, 135
Miller, J. Hillis, 112n24
Milton, John, 95
missionaries, 14–16, 35, 78–79, 84, 101–3, 166. *See also* evangelism
Moonstone, The (Collins), 22, 105–9, 114, 122–35, 164
Moral Majority, the, 161
morality, 6, 17, 21, 26–27, 30, 40–44, 62, 78, 80, 85n25, 91–93, 102n81, 142, 155 . *See also* evangelical ethical vision; sin
Moretti, Franco, 154
Mudie, Charles, 13n41
Muggeridge, Malcolm, 141

Index

Mulock, Dinah Maria, 12, 81–82

Nash, Andrew, 12n40
natural theology, 56–57, 61, 111, 116
Nayder, Lillian, 72, 105n2
Newey, Vincent, 34
Newman, John Henry, 86, 112–13
Nielson, Danielle, 149
Noll, Mark A., 77n2, 117, 118n47, 135
noncomformism, 7, 10, 15n50, 28, 35, 46, 107, 135
North British Review, 102n81
novel, rise of, 8–9, 25, 139n4

O'Malley, Patrick R., 10
Orwell, George, 55, 61
Oswald Cray (Wood), 89–95
Otter, Chris, 47
Oulton, Carolyn W. de la L., 56, 60n30, 106
Oxford Movement, the, 48, 112

Paley, William, 116
Palmer, Beth, 90–91
parables, 12, 28, 33, 97, 101, 123, 143
Paradis, James, 140, 147n35, 148
Parrinder, Patrick, 41
Patriot, 108
periodicals, 22, 78, 85n24, 108. See also *All the Year Round*; *Argosy*; *British Quarterly Review*; *Christian Guest*; *Christian Observer*; *Contemporary Review*; *Cornhill*; *Evangelical Christendom*; *Evangelical Magazine*; *Good Words*; *Good Words for the Young*; *Household Words*; *Leisure Hour*; *North British Review*; *Patriot*; *The Quiver*; *Record*
Perkin, J. Russell, 10, 33
personhood, 39, 160–61
Peterson, Linda, 109n15, 112n24
Pharisees, 117
Phegley, Jennifer, 90
Pietism, 58, 117, 134–35
The Pilgrim's Progress (Bunyan), 21, 26, 28–51, 101–2, 142
Plantinga, Alvin, 131n93, 138n3
Pollock, William, 59–60
Pooley, Roger, 45n67

Pope, Norris, 54
Porter, Andrew, 16n52
postevangelical, 162
postsecular, 137–39. See also sacred/secular binary; secularism
Powell, Baden, 119
prayer, 19, 47–48, 53, 57, 92, 99, 102, 135, 146
preaching, 15, 26, 27n6, 32–33, 43–44, 50–51, 61, 71, 73–76, 87, 125, 164. See also sermon
Price, Leah, 13n42, 37–38, 113n28, 122–23
Prickett, Stephen, 10, 101n80, 109
providence, 49, 55n9, 56–58, 68, 72–73, 94, 144
proximity, interpretative, 39, 154–61
Puritanism, 16, 35, 41–42, 49, 58, 118, 143
Pykett, Lyn, 90

Qualls, Barry, 16–17, 31–32, 49
Quiver, The, 12, 79n9, 91n39

Rainoff, Rebecca, 20n66
Randall, Ian, 2n4
Rasmussen, Bryan B., 14n45
Ray, Gordon, 33, 40
Reade, Charles, 72
reader response, 34–51, 133–34. See also Hans-Georg Gadamer; hermeneutics
realism, 8–10, 16–19, 31, 48, 97–98, 144
Record, 83–84, 88, 100, 108
Reformation, the, 27n6, 57, 114, 118, 129
Reid, Thomas, 109n14, 118
Reitz, Caroline, 105n2
Religious Tract Society, 12, 13n42, 78–79, 93
"religious turn," the, 137–38
reparative reading, 152
resurrection, 53, 64, 75–76, 157
Ricoeur, Paul, 9n30, 38
Rivers, Isabel, 5n14
Robinson Crusoe (Defoe), 126–27, 130, 135
Roman Catholicism, 112, 123, 138. See also evangelical anti-Catholicism
Romanticism, 101, 109, 117
Rorty, Richard, 155
Russett, Margaret, 50n84
Ryle, J. C., 2, 59–61, 93, 100, 116–17, 124
Rzepka, Charles, 110n18

INDEX

sacramental, 27n6, 101
sacred/secular binary, 1, 20n66, 21, 28, 34, 79, 82–85, 110, 123, 165. See also postsecular; secularism
sacrifice, 3, 53–54, 55n6, 59–60, 62n40, 63, 69–70, 72, 92, 93, 125n73. See also the cross
salvation, 1, 22, 34–35, 41, 53, 58–64, 67–70, 73, 75, 77, 80, 86–87, 92–93, 99, 101–3, 119, 163. See also atonement; the cross; evangelical gospel
Salvation Army, the, 125, 147, 161, 165
Schad, John, 46
Schaffer, E. S., 109n15
Schleiermacher, Friedrich, 112–13, 127, 131, 133–34
Schramm, Jan-Melissa, 1, 10, 55, 60, 62n40, 71n71, 128, 131
Schwartz, Regina, 9n29
science and religion, relationship between, 28, 79, 108, 110–11, 139, 150
Scott, Caroline Lucy, 13
secularism, 7–10, 19–22, 32, 46–47, 49, 65, 81, 99, 110–13, 137n2, 139, 145–46, 150. See also Talal Asad; postsecular; sacred/secular binary; Charles Taylor
Sedgwick, Eve Kosofsky, 152
Seidel, Kevin, 38, 126n78
Self-Interpreting Bible, The (Cooke and Brown), 120–21
sensation fiction, 12, 89–91, 133n99
serialization, 55n9, 70–74, 81
sermon, 27–28, 32, 50–51, 73–74, 76, 82, 86, 94, 96, 100, 124, 135, 144, 157–58, 165. See also preaching
Shakespeare, William, 71
Shaw, George Bernard, 147–48, 149n43
Sheldon, Charles, 62
Sherlock Holmes, 110, 129
Sherwood, Mary Martha, 13, 28
Shuttleworth, Sally, 149–50
Simeon, Charles, 140, 145–46
sin, 27, 40–41, 43–44, 46, 59–61, 63, 77, 101, 106, 142, 144, 148, 157. See also atonement
Singleton, Jon, 19–20
Smith, Alexander, 72n75
Smith, Christian, 161n80
Smith, George, 82

Smith, Mark, 5
Southcott, Joanna, 73
Spurgeon, Charles H., 60, 114, 117n44, 118–20
Srebrnik, Patricia, 81, 85n25
Stevenson, Peter Kenneth, 100n76
Stewart, Kenneth J., 115n35
Strahan, Alexander, 79–81, 85–86, 88n32, 90–91, 96–97, 103
Stubenrauch, Joseph, 3n8, 4–5, 25
Styler, Rebecca, 109n15
"surface reading," 152
Sutherland, John, 42n59

Tale of Two Cities, A (Dickens), 53–55, 60–70, 73
Taylor, Charles, 32, 84, 137n2, 138, 159, 165
Taylor, Isaac, 84n22
testimony, religious, 166
Thackeray, William Makepeace, 33, 40–43. See also *Vanity Fair*
theater, 15, 74–75
Thomas, Ronald R., 110, 129n86
Tonna, Charlotte Elizabeth, 13–14
tracts, 28, 37n41, 38, 51, 78, 107, 114, 117, 122–26
transcendence, 9, 32, 159. See also immanence
Treier, Daniel, 115
Trollope, Anthony, 81, 83, 87, 143n19
Tucker, Trisha, 13
Turner, Mark, 81n12, 82–85, 89
typology, 59, 109

Valman, Nadia, 20n66
Van Dyke, Carolynn, 44
Van O'Connor, William, 147n35, 148
Vance, Norman, 10, 16, 29, 109n15
Vanhoozer, Kevin, 50
Vanity Fair (Thackeray), 26, 29–34, 38–51, 162
Vargish, Thomas, 54, 56–57
Vaughan, C. J., 81
Venn, John, 59, 73

Walder, Dennis, 54, 56n10, 61n32
Walker, Pamela J., 125n72
Warner, Michael, 23, 152–53, 156, 158n76
Watson, Francis, 129n87
Watt, Ian, 8, 126n78

Way of All Flesh, The (Butler), 139–52, 156–61, 166
Welsh, Alexander, 128, 131
Werner, Jade Winter, 16n52
Wesley, John, 2, 3n8, 96
Wheeler-Barclay, Marjorie, 110n20
Whitfield, George, 2
Wilberforce, William, 4, 57, 144
Wilde, Oscar, 10, 154–55
Williams, Rowland, 119

Winter, Sarah, 55n9, 56n10, 65
Wolffe, John, 4, 5
Woman in White, The (Collins), 70, 107
Wood, Ellen, 81, 89–91, 94, 97–98, 102–3. See also *Oswald Cray*
Woolf, Virginia, 8n24, 147–49
Worboise, Emma, 13, 98
Wynne, Deborah, 71n68, 78n4

Zemka, Sue, 109n15, 120

LITERATURE, RELIGION, AND POSTSECULAR STUDIES
Lori Branch, Series Editor

Literature, Religion, and Postsecular Studies publishes scholarship on the influence of religion on literature and of literature on religion from the sixteenth century onward. Books in the series include studies of religious rhetoric or allegory; of the secularization of religion, ritual, and religious life; and of the emerging identity of postsecular studies and literary criticism.

Good Words: Evangelicalism and the Victorian Novel
MARK KNIGHT

Enlightened Individualism: Buddhism and Hinduism in American Literature from the Beats to the Present
KYLE GARTON-GUNDLING

A Theology of Sense: John Updike, Embodiment, and Late Twentieth-Century American Literature
SCOTT DILL

Walker Percy, Fyodor Dostoevsky, and the Search for Influence
JESSICA HOOTEN WILSON

The Religion of Empire: Political Theology in Blake's Prophetic Symbolism
G. A. ROSSO

Clashing Convictions: Science and Religion in American Fiction
ALBERT H. TRICOMI

Female Piety and the Invention of American Puritanism
BRYCE TRAISTER

Secular Scriptures: Modern Theological Poetics in the Wake of Dante
WILLIAM FRANKE

Imagined Spiritual Communities in Britain's Age of Print
JOSHUA KING

Conspicuous Bodies: Provincial Belief and the Making of Joyce and Rushdie
JEAN KANE

Victorian Sacrifice: Ethics and Economics in Mid-Century Novels
ILANA M. BLUMBERG

Lake Methodism: Polite Literature and Popular Religion in England, 1780–1830
JASPER CRAGWALL

Hard Sayings: The Rhetoric of Christian Orthodoxy in Late Modern Fiction
THOMAS F. HADDOX

Preaching and the Rise of the American Novel
DAWN COLEMAN

Victorian Women Writers, Radical Grandmothers, and the Gendering of God
GAIL TURLEY HOUSTON

Apocalypse South: Judgment, Cataclysm, and Resistance in the Regional Imaginary
ANTHONY DYER HOEFER

www.ingramcontent.com/pod-product-compliance
Lightning Source LLC
Chambersburg PA
CBHW020738230426
43665CB00009B/476